Principle (Buffer Flexibility): *Flexibility rec*
required in a production or supply chain s

Principle (Buffer Position): *For a flow with a fixed arrival rate, identical nonbottleneck processes, and equal-sized WIP buffers in front of all processes:*

- *The maximum decrease in WIP and cycle time from a unit increase in nonbottleneck capacity will come from adding capacity to the process directly before or after the bottleneck.*
- *The maximum decrease in WIP and cycle time from a unit increase in WIP buffer space will come from adding buffer space to the process directly before or after the bottleneck.*

Principle (Pull Efficiency): *A pull system achieves higher throughput for the same average WIP level than an equivalent push system.*

Principle (Pull Robustness): *A pull system is less sensitive to errors in WIP level than a push system is to errors in release rate.*

Principle (Safety Stock): *In a base stock system, safety stock increases in both the target fill rate and (for a sufficiently high target fill rate) the standard deviation of demand during replenishment lead time.*

Principle (Variability Pooling): *Combining sources of variability so that they can share a common buffer reduces the total amount of buffering required to achieve a given level of performance.*

Principle (Multi-Echelon Inventory Location): *In a multi-product, multi-echelon supply chain with an objective to achieve high customer service with minimal inventory investment, a low volume, high demand variability, and/or high cost part should be stocked at a central (high) level, while a low volume, low demand variability and/or low cost part should be stocked at a local (low) level.*

Principle (Inventory/Order Interface Position): *Long production leadtimes require the I/O interface to be located close to the customer for responsiveness, while high product proliferation requires it to be located close to raw materials for pooling efficiency.*

Principle (Bullwhip Effect): *Demand at the top (manufacturing) level of a supply chain tends to exhibit more variability than demand at the bottom (retail) level due to batch ordering, forecasting errors, promotional pricing and gaming behavior by customers.*

Principle (Risk Sharing Contracts): *In inter-firm supply chains, individual decision makers optimizing their local objectives generally suboptimize the overall system because risk falls disproportionally on one party. Contracts that share risk can incentivize decision makers to make globally optimal choices.*

Supply Chain Science

Supply Chain Science

Wallace J. Hopp
University of Michigan

WAVELAND
PRESS, INC.
Long Grove, Illinois

To Melanie, Elliott, and Clara

Acknowledgment

This book would not exist if not for my dear friend and longtime collaborator, Mark Spearman. While Mark did not directly participate in the writing, most of the ideas presented here were developed jointly over the many years we have worked together. I am deeply grateful for the ideas and for the good times we had coming up with them.

For information about this book, contact:
Waveland Press, Inc.
4180 IL Route 83, Suite 101
Long Grove, IL 60047-9580
(847) 634-0081
info@waveland.com
www.waveland.com

Printed in the United States of America

7 6 5 4

This is a management book. As such, it has only one purpose—to help managers do their jobs better.

Why then does it have the word *science* in the title? Isn't science the arcane pursuit of nerdy guys in lab coats? Aren't scientists about as far removed from management as any group of people we can think of (other than artists maybe)?

It is certainly true that managers are *not* generally interested in science for its own sake. But many professionals with no intrinsic interest in science nonetheless rely on it heavily. A civil engineer uses the science of mechanics to design a bridge. A physician uses the science of physiology to diagnose an illness. Even a lawyer (to stretch a point) uses the science of formal logic to argue a case. The main premise of this book is that managers need science too.

But what kind of science? By its very nature, management is interdisciplinary. Managers deal regularly with issues that involve questions of finance, marketing, accounting, organizational behavior, operations, and many other disciplines. Hence, a comprehensive science of management is probably a pipe dream. But the fact that there is no unified science of medicine does not stop physicians from relying on several different scientific frameworks. So why should it stop managers from looking to science for help?

In this book we focus specifically on the *science of supply chains*. This "science" addresses the collection of people, resources, and activities involved in bringing materials and information together to produce and deliver goods and services to customers. Our goal is to provide a framework for understanding how complex production and supply chain systems behave and thereby provide a basis for better decision making in situations such as these:

- You have read the literature on JIT and lean and are up to your eyeballs in stories about Toyota. But your business is very different from the automotive industry. Which elements of the Toyota Production System are relevant and which are not?
- You have implemented some lean manufacturing practices and have reduced in-process inventories. What should be your next step? How do you identify the places in your system that offer the greatest leverage?
- You are managing a service operation and (because services cannot be inventoried) are wondering whether any of the underlying ideas of lean manufacturing apply to you. How can you decide what can be adapted?
- You are managing a multiproduct manufacturing system. Which of your products should be made-to-order and which should be made-to-stock? What should you consider in controlling stock levels of both components and finished goods?
- You have problems getting on-time deliveries from your suppliers. How much of an impact does this have on your bottom line? What are your best options for improving the situation?
- You are considering entering into some kind of collaborative relationship with your suppliers. What factors should you consider in deciding on an appropriate structure for the partnership?
- You feel that better supply chain management could be a source of competitive advantage. How do you identify the improvements that would make the most difference? Once you identify them, how do you justify them to upper management?

Of course, these questions are only the tip of the iceberg. Because each system is unique, the range of problems faced by managers dealing with supply chains is almost infinite. This is precisely the reason that a scientific approach is needed. A book that tells you *how* to solve problems can only provide answers for a limited set of situations. But a book such as this one that tells you *why* systems behave as they do can give you the tools and insights to deal effectively with almost any scenario.

Our goal is to provide the *why* of supply chains.

C O N T E N T S

0   STRATEGIC FOUNDATIONS

A supply chain is a goal-oriented network of processes and stock points used to deliver goods and services to customers.

0.1   Starting with Strategy

All organizations have a basis for making decisions. When this basis is actively planned, rather than passively evolved, we call it a **strategy**. An organization's strategy dictates its policies, activities, and priorities. For example, in the 1990s IBM, under Lou Gerstner, shifted its strategy from an emphasis on computer hardware to a focus on information services. This shift led to outsourcing most manufacturing functions and eventually spinning off the PC division.

The link between strategy and operations lies in an organization's value proposition. Firms that offer products or services to customers compete on the basis of some combination of

- Cost
- Quality
- Speed
- Service
- Variety

Consumers and competing firms attach different weights to these metrics. The following examples illustrate how firms make various trade-offs based on their business strategies.

- *Quality vs. Cost.* Few people would regard the Kia Rio as competition for the Rolls-Royce Phantom. The reason is that,

1

although all of the above dimensions matter to customers for both cars, buyers of the Kia are concerned primarily with cost, while buyers of the Rolls are concerned primarily with quality (as they perceive it). Therefore, the logistics systems to support the two cars should be designed with different priorities in mind. For instance, while the Rolls-Royce system may be able to afford the extra time and technicians necessary to "inspect in" quality, single-pass "quality at the source" methods are almost mandatory for the Kia to compete in its price range.

• *Speed vs. Cost.* W.W. Grainger is in the MRO (maintenance, repair, and operating) supplies business. Through catalog and on-line sales, Grainger offers hundreds of thousands of products, ranging from cleaning supplies to power tools to safety equipment. But all of these products are made by suppliers; Grainger doesn't manufacture anything. So, a customer could choose to purchase any of Grainger's products directly from a supplier at a lower unit cost. Given this, why would a customer choose Grainger? The reason is that Grainger can ship small orders with short lead times, while the suppliers require longer lead times and bulk purchases. Grainger's business strategy is to offer speed and responsiveness in exchange for price premiums. It supports this strategy with a logistics system that inventories products in warehouses and focuses on efficient order fulfillment. In contrast, the logistics systems of the suppliers concentrate on production efficiency and therefore tend to make and ship products in large batches.

• *Service vs. Cost.* Peapod.com advertises itself as an "on-line grocery store." When it was founded, Peapod functioned by "picking" orders from local grocery stores and delivering them to customers' homes. More recently Peapod has developed its own system of warehouses from which deliveries are made. By offering customers the opportunity to shop online and forego visiting the supermarket, Peapod's business strategy is based primarily on service. Customers willing to shop for bargains and transport their own groceries can almost certainly achieve lower costs. To achieve a service advantage over traditional grocery stores, Peapod requires an entirely different logistics system.

• *Variety vs. Cost.* IBM used to manufacture printed circuit boards (PCBs) in Austin, Texas. Although IBM made thousands of different PCBs, a high fraction of its sales dollars came from a small fraction of the end items. (This type of demand distribution is called a **Pareto distribution** and is very common in industry.) Because all of the products required similar processes, it was feasible to manufacture all of the PCBs in a single plant; however, IBM divided the facility into two entirely separate operations. One operation produced low-volume, prototype boards, and one produced

FIGURE 0.1 Strategic trade-offs and efficient frontiers

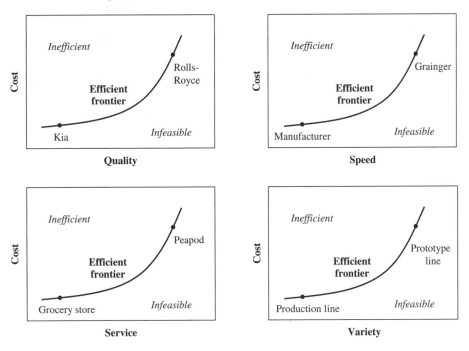

high-volume boards. The high-volume plant utilized specialized equipment to achieve cost efficiency, while the low-volume plant employed flexible equipment subject to frequent changeovers. Because the two environments were so different, it made sense to keep them physically separate. This sort of **focused factory** strategy is well suited to a wide range of production environments with widely varying products.

We can depict the trade-offs inherent in each of the above examples via the curves in Figure 0.1. These **efficient frontiers** represent the most efficient (lowest cost) system for achieving a given performance level. Points below these curves are infeasible given current technology. Points above them are inefficient.

Thinking of supply chain design in terms of these kinds of trade-offs presents two levels of decision making:

1. *Strategic Problem.* Determine where on the efficient frontier to locate.

2. *Operational Problem.* Design a system that achieves performance on the efficient frontier.

Detailed discussion of the strategic problem is beyond the scope of this book. We are neutral on questions such as whether it is better to be Rolls-Royce or Kia. Firms can make money by providing a low-cost/low-quality offering or a high-cost/high-quality offering. Deciding how to position themselves in the competitive landscape is a decision individual firms must make as part of their strategic planning process.

However, we are not neutral on the operational question. Firms cannot make money by providing a high-cost/low-quality offering. In general, firms whose performance is not on the efficient frontier are not competitive and hence they are vulnerable to the competition. We focus on how to achieve world-class levels of efficiency on the chosen metrics.

A common way firms seek this kind of efficiency is by **benchmarking**, which amounts to copying best practices of other firms. But this approach can only partially ensure that a system achieves its strategic goals (i.e., because the benchmarked system can only approximate the system under consideration). Furthermore, benchmarking cannot provide a way to move efficiency beyond historical levels, because it is by nature imitative. Efficient frontiers are not static, so achieving world-class efficiency requires something beyond benchmarking.

0.2   Setting Our Goals

Some firms have been lucky enough to find their special "something" in the form of bursts of genius, such as those achieved by Taiichi Ohno and his colleagues at Toyota in the 1970s. Through a host of clever techniques that were extremely well adapted to its business situation, Toyota was able to translate world-class operations into impressive long-term growth and profitability. But geniuses are scarce, so effective supply chain management must generally be based on something more accessible to the rest of us.

The premise of this book is that the only reliable foundation for designing operations systems that fit strategic goals and push out the boundaries of efficiency is *science*. By describing how a system works, a supply chain science offers the potential to

- Identify the areas of greatest leverage.
- Determine which policies are likely to be effective in a given system.
- Enable practices and insights developed for one type of environment to be generalized to another environment.

- Make quantitative trade-offs between the costs and benefits of a particular action.
- Synthesize the various perspectives of a manufacturing or service system, including those of logistics, product design, human resources, accounting, and management strategy.

Surprisingly, many basic principles of supply chain science are not well known among professional managers. The field of supply chain management is instead plagued by an overabundance of gurus and buzzwords—much style, little substance. This book introduces the major concepts underlying the supply chain science in a structured, although only partially mathematical, format.

0.3   Defining Our Terms

All real-world systems, including supply chains, are too complex to study in their totality. The scientific method for analyzing and understanding complex systems is to reduce them to a manageable size by restricting their scope and by making simplifying assumptions. For example, all introductory physics students begin their study of mechanics by learning about objects moving in frictionless environments. Although almost all practical mechanical systems violate this assumption, the insights gained from the stylized systems of classical mechanics are vital to the understanding of more realistic systems. Hence, the friction-free model of moving bodies satisfies the fundamental criterion of any scientific model—it captures an essential aspect of a real system in a form that is simple enough to be tractable and understandable.

To get anywhere with a science of supply chains we must first reduce the complex arrays of suppliers, plants, warehouses, customers, transportation networks, and information systems that make up actual supply chains to structures that are simple enough to study rigorously. To do this, we must choose a level at which to model a supply chain. Clearly the level of the entire business is too high; the resulting models would be hopelessly complex and the details would obscure important commonalities among supply chains. Similarly, the level of an individual operation is too low; while modeling a specific process (e.g., metal cutting) in detail may be tractable, it will give us little insight into what drives the performance metrics (e.g., profit) a manager cares about. What we need is an intermediate view.

Definition (Supply Chain).   *A supply chain is a goal-oriented network of processes and stock points used to deliver goods and services to customers.*

FIGURE 0.2

Supply chains as flow networks

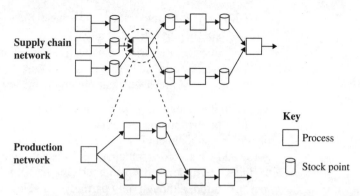

In this definition, **processes** represent the individual activities involved in producing and distributing goods and services. They could be manufacturing operations, service operations, engineering design functions, or even legal proceedings. But, because our focus is on the overall performance of the supply chain, we will concentrate primarily on the flow of goods and services. We will usually view the processes in generic terms, with only as much specification as necessary to describe their effect on these flows. This perspective will enable us to apply our models across a broad range of industrial settings and adapt insights from one industry to another.

In addition to processes, our definition involves **stock points**, which represent locations in the supply chain where inventories are held. These inventories may be the result of deliberate policy decisions (e.g., retail stocks) or the consequence of problems in the system (e.g., a backlog of defective items awaiting repair). Because managing inventories is a key component of effective supply chain management, it is vital to include stock points in the definition of a supply chain.

Processes and stock points are connected by a **network** that describes the various paths by which goods and services can flow through a supply chain. Figure 0.2 represents an example of such a network. In the spirit of scientific reductionism, we will often find it useful to break down complex networks into simpler pieces. A feature of our definition that helps facilitate this is that, at this level of generality, supply chains and production operations are structurally similar. As illustrated in Figure 0.2, if we probe into the details of a specific production system within a supply chain, it will also consist of a network of processes and stock points.[1]

---

[1]Throughout this book we use the term ***production system*** to refer to any system that produces a good or service. Hence, in our terminology, production systems include both manufacturing and service systems.

Although, as we will see in Part III of this book, the size and complexity of supply chain systems does introduce some interesting management challenges, we can make use of the same framework to gain a basic understanding of both individual production systems and aggregations of these in supply chains.

Finally, note that our definition of a supply chain specifies that it is **goal oriented**. Supply chains are not features of nature that we study for their own sake. They exist only to support business activities and therefore must be evaluated in business terms. Specifically, the fundamental objective of a supply chain is to support the strategy of an organization. Usually this means contributing to long-term profitability. We say "usually" here because military and other public-sector supply chains are not tied to profits, but instead have cost effectiveness at the core of their strategic goal.

0.4   Structuring Our Study

Defining a supply chain as a network suggests a natural way to organize the principles that govern its behavior. The basic elements of any network are processes and stock points, which can be configured into systems of varying size and complexity. Our approach is to first understand the behavior of small, simple (low-level) systems and then to use the resulting insights as building blocks for understanding large, complex (high-level) systems.

At the lowest level, we define a single process fed by a single stock point as a **station**, which consists of one or more **servers**. For example, a milling machine that processes castings is a server with the station made up of one or more of these machines working in parallel. Similarly, a bank teller is a server, with the station consisting of a set of tellers fed by a single line of customers. Finally, a CPU (central processing unit) of a computer is a server, with the station made up of one or more CPUs working in parallel (i.e., using parallel processing).

The next level in size and complexity is the **line** (or **routing** or **flow**), which is a sequence of stations used to generate a product or service. A manufacturing line, such as a moving assembly line used to produce automobiles, is the prototypical example of a routing. But a sequence of clerks required to process a loan application and a series of steps involved in developing a new product are also examples of routings. At a high level, the flow of products from one plant to another can also be viewed as a routing. For example, a printed circuit board (PCB) moves from the panel plant that makes the unpopulated board, to the "stuffing" plant that inserts components on to the board, to the assembly plant that assembles

FIGURE 0.3

Example schematics of stations, routings, and networks

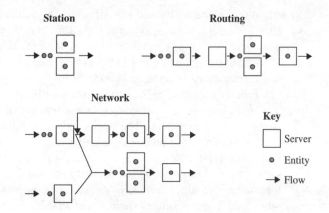

the "stuffed" board into a final product, such as a computer or cell phone.

Finally, the highest-level and most complex type of production or service system is a **network**, which involves multiple lines producing multiple products and/or services. Figure 0.3 illustrates the three levels that make up supply chains.

The remainder of the book is organized into three parts, corresponding to the three levels of a production system. Part I, Station Science, considers the operational behavior of an individual process and the stock point from which it receives material. Our emphasis is on the factors that serve to delay the flow of entities (i.e., goods, services, information, or money) and hence cause a buildup of inventory in the inbound stock point. Part II, Line Science, considers the operational behavior of process flows consisting of logically connected processes separated by stock points. We focus in particular on the issues that arise from the coupling effects between processes in a flow. Finally, Part III, Network Science, considers operational issues that cut across supply chains consisting of multiple products, lines, and levels. Of particular interest is the coordination of supply chains that are controlled by multiple parties.

We realize that some readers may regard the study of stations and lines as belonging in a book on manufacturing engineering, rather than one on supply chain management. But no one would undertake the study of medicine without a preparation in elementary biology. No one would think of trying to learn the science of bridge building without first mastering basic mechanics. Even the most brilliant among us could not begin to comprehend international finance without a background in the basic economic concepts of supply and demand.

Because the behavior of the even most sophisticated supply chain network is ultimately premised on the behavior of its constituent stations, understanding these low-level elements is absolutely fundamental to the science of supply chains. Hence, it is with the lowly station that we begin our journey in Part I.

Questions for Thought

1. How do the strategic priorities differ between the following pairs of firms and what implications do the differences have for desired supply chain capabilities?
   a. Intel (maker of branded microprocessor chips) and Samsung (maker of commodity DRAM chips).
   b. Federal Express and the U.S. Postal Service.
   c. Wal-Mart and Tiffany & Co.
2. Over the past 30 years we have observed a string of "revolutions" in industry. In the 1970s the most prominent movement was material requirements planning (MRP). In the 1980s we saw total quality management (TQM) and just-in-time (JIT). The 1990s brought us business process reengineering (BPR) and supply chain management (SCM). Since 2000, with three-letter acronymns evidently having gone out of fashion, the two most prominent movements are lean production and Six Sigma. Does this progression of "revolutions" represent progress toward a supply chain science? Why or why not?

I   STATION SCIENCE

1 CAPACITY

Over the long run, average throughput of a process is always strictly less than capacity.

1.1 Introduction

The fundamental activity of any operations system centers around the **flow** of **entities** through **processes** made up of **servers**. The entities can be parts in a manufacturing system, people in a service system, jobs in a computer system, or transactions in a financial system. The servers, and hence processes, can consist of machining centers, bank tellers, computer CPUs, or manual workstations. The flows typically follow **routings** that define the sequences of processes visited by the entities. Clearly, the range of systems that exhibit this type of generic behavior is very broad.

In almost all operations systems, the following performance measures are key:

Throughput (TH): Rate at which entities are processed by the system.

Work in process (WIP): Number of entities in the system, which can be measured in physical units (e.g., parts, people, jobs) or financial units (e.g., dollar value of entities in system).

Cycle time (CT): Time it takes an entity to traverse the system, including any rework, restarts because of yield loss, or other disruptions.

Typically, the objective is to have throughput high but WIP and cycle time low. The extent to which a given system achieves this is a function of the system's overall efficiency. One useful measure of efficiency is **inventory turns**, defined as

$$\text{inventory turns} = \frac{\text{TH}}{\text{WIP}}$$

where TH is measured as the cost of goods sold in a year and WIP is the dollar value of the average amount of inventory held in the system. This measure of how efficiently an operation converts inventory into output is the operational analogy of the return-on-investment (ROI) measure of how efficiently an investment converts capital into revenue. As with ROI, higher turns are better.

1.2   Measuring Capacity

A major determinant of throughput, WIP, and cycle time, as well as inventory turns, is the system's **capacity**.

Definition (Capacity). *The capacity of a system is the maximum average rate at which entities can flow through the system.*

Capacity can be defined for a single station, a routing, or a network. For an individual station, we can think of capacity as

$$\text{capacity} = \text{base capacity} - \text{detractors}$$

where base capacity refers to the rate of the process under ideal conditions and detractors represent anything that slows the output of the process.

For example, consider a punch press that can stamp out metal parts at a rate of 2 per hour. The press is subject to mechanical failures that cause its availability (fraction of uptime) to be only 90 percent. Hence, 1 hour in 10, on average, is lost to downtime. This means that over the long term, $(0.1)(2) = 0.2$ parts per hour are lost because of the failures. Hence, the capacity of the process can be computed as either 90 percent of the base rate $(0.9 \times 2 \text{ per hour} = 1.8 \text{ per hour})$ or as the base rate minus the lost production (2 per hour $- 0.2$ per hour $= 1.8$ per hour). Similar calculations can be done for other types of detractors, such as setups, rework, operator unavailability, and so on.

For routings and networks, capacity is constrained by the constituent stations. The process that constrains the capacity of a system is called the system **bottleneck**. Often, this is the slowest process. However, in systems where different types of entities follow different paths (routings) through the system, where yield

FIGURE 1.1

A system with
yield loss

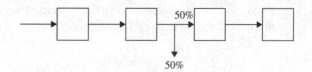

loss causes fallout, or the routings require some entities to visit
some stations more than once (either for rework or because of the
nature of the processing requirements), then the slowest process
may not be the system bottleneck. The reason is that the amount
of work arriving at each station may not be the same. For instance,
consider the system shown in Figure 1.1, in which 50 percent of
the entities drop out (e.g., due to quality problems) after the second
station. This means that the third and fourth stations have only half
as much work to handle as do the first and second.

The station that will limit flow through a line like that in Figure 1.1 is the one that is busiest. We measure this through the
utilization level, which is the fraction of time a station is not idle,
and is computed as

$$\text{utilization} = \frac{\text{rate into station}}{\text{capacity of station}}$$

With this, we can give a general definition of a system bottleneck.

Definition (Bottleneck).   *The bottleneck of a system is the process
with the highest utilization.*

To illustrate the procedure for identifying the bottleneck of a
routing, let us return to the example of Figure 1.1 and assume that
jobs enter the system at a rate of 1 per minute and the processing
times (including all relevant detractors) at stations 1–4 are 0.7, 0.8,
1, and 0.9 minutes, respectively. Because the arrival rate to stations
1 and 2 is 1 per minute, while the arrival rate to stations 3 and 4 is
only 0.5 per minute (due to yield loss), the utilizations of the four
stations are

$$\text{utilization of station 1} = \frac{1}{1/0.7} = 0.7$$

$$\text{utilization of station 2} = \frac{1}{1/0.8} = 0.8$$

$$\text{utilization of station 3} = \frac{0.5}{1/1} = 0.5$$

$$\text{utilization of station 4} = \frac{0.5}{1/0.9} = 0.45$$

Notice that while station 3 is the slowest, it is station 2 that is the bottleneck, because it has the highest utilization level. Given this yield loss profile it is station 2 that will define the maximum rate of this line. Hence, the capacity of the line is the input rate that makes utilization of station 2 reach 100 percent. This is $1/0.8 =$ 1.25 jobs per minute, because this is the maximum rate at which station 2 can work. For any input rate above 1.25 jobs per minute, utilization of station 2 will be above 100 percent and so it will not be able to keep up.

Of course, if the yield loss fraction is reduced, then stations 3 and 4 will become busier. If yield is improved enough, station 3 will become the bottleneck. In systems where conditions (e.g., yield rate, product mix, etc.) vary over time, the bottleneck may "float" between different stations. When this is the case, more than one station is important from a system capacity standpoint.

1.3   Limits on Capacity

We now state the first fundamental principle of capacity as:

Principle (Capacity).   *The output of a system cannot equal or exceed its capacity.*

While this law may appear to be a statement of the obvious (aren't we all prone to saying there are only 24 hours in a day?), it is commonly neglected in practice. For instance, we frequently hear about production facilities that are running at 120 percent of capacity. What this really means, of course, is that the system is running at 120 percent of an arbitrarily defined "capacity," representing one shift with no overtime, normal staffing levels, a historical average rate, or whatever. But it does not represent the true limiting rate of the system, or we could not be exceeding it.

More subtly in error are claims that the system is running *at* 100 percent of capacity. While it may seem intuitively possible for a workstation to be completely utilized, it actually never happens over the long term in the real world. This is due to the fact that all real systems contain *variability*. We will discuss this important issue in more detail in the next chapter. For now, we consider some simple examples to illustrate the point.

First, suppose that in the previously mentioned punch press example the detractors (downtime, setups, breaks/lunches, etc.) reduce the base rate of 2 parts per hour to an effective rate of 1.43 parts per hour. If we were to ignore the detractors and release parts into the station at a rate of 2 per hour, what would happen? Clearly,

FIGURE 1.2

WIP versus time
in a system with
insufficient
capacity

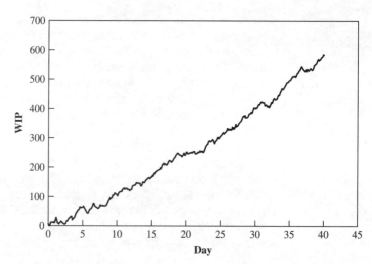

the press would not be able to keep up with the release rate, and
so work in process (WIP) would build up over time, as shown in
Figure 1.2. The short-term fluctuations are due to variability, but
the trend is clearly toward station overload.

Second, suppose that we release parts to the station at exactly
the true capacity of the system (1.43 parts per hour). Now performance is no longer predictable. Sometimes the WIP level will
remain low for a period of time; other times (e.g., when an equipment failure occurs) WIP will build rapidly. Figure 1.3 shows two
possible outcomes of the punch press example when releases are
equal to capacity. The results are very different due to the unpredictable effects of variability in the processing rates. In the left plot,
which did not experience any long equipment outages, the station is
keeping up with releases. However, in the right plot, a long outage

FIGURE 1.3 Two outcomes of WIP versus time with releases at 100 percent capacity

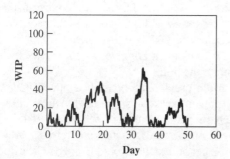
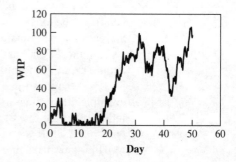

FIGURE 1.4 Two outcomes from releasing at 82 percent of capacity

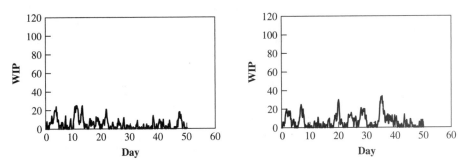

occurred after about 20 days and caused a large increase in WIP. After a period of recovery, another disruption occurred at about the 40-day mark, and WIP built up again.

Unfortunately, over the long run, we *will* eventually be unlucky. (This is what casinos and states with lotteries count on to make money!) When we are, WIP will go up. When release rate is the same as the production rate, the WIP level will stay high for a long time because there is no slack capacity to enable the system to catch up. Theoretically, if we were to run for an infinite amount of time, WIP would go to infinity even though we were running exactly at capacity.

In contrast, if we set the release rate below capacity, the system stabilizes. For example, Figure 1.4 shows two possible outcomes of the punch press example with a release rate of 1.167 parts per hour (28 parts per day), which represents a utilization of $1.167/1.43 = 82$ percent. Although variability causes short-term fluctuations, both instances show WIP remaining consistently low.

1.4   Impact of Utilization

The behavior illustrated in the above examples underlies the second key principle of capacity:

Principle (Utilization). *Cycle time increases with utilization and does so sharply as utilization approaches 100%.*

As we have seen, when utilization is low, the system can easily keep up with the arrival of work (e.g., Figure 1.4) but when utilization becomes high the system will fall behind anytime there is any kind of temporary slowdown in production (e.g., Figure 1.3). You might think that the "law of averages" will make things work out. But because a process cannot "save up" production when it is ready but there is no WIP, the times the process is starved do not make up for the times it is swamped.

To understand the relationship between WIP and cycle time, it is useful to think of WIP as acting as a buffer between the arrival process and the production process. To do this, we think of WIP in units of time. That is, each entity that arrives to the process carries with it a certain amount of processing time. Hence, we can measure the amount of WIP waiting at the production process in terms of the total amount of processing time it represents.

First suppose that there is no WIP in the system other than the entity on which the production process is working. Then, if the production process finishes before the next arrival occurs, the process will starve and utilization will suffer. To bring utilization closer to 100 percent, we can increase the amount of WIP available to protect the production process by increasing the arrival rate. This will put more work in the system, which increases utilization, but will also result in more entities having to wait, which increases the WIP level (and cycle time).

Now suppose that the current arrival rate results in 10 minutes of WIP in the system. Then, for the production process to starve, production will have to outstrip arrivals by 10 minutes (i.e., we will have to complete 10 minutes more work than arrives during some fixed interval). Any sequence of events (e.g., several quick process times coupled with a long interarrival time) that causes this to occur will result in a starvation. Such starvations are what prevent the production process from being 100 percent utilized.

Suppose we increase the arrival rate so that there are 11 minutes of WIP in the system. Now production will have to outstrip arrivals by 11 minutes for a starvation to occur. Hence, all sequences of events that lead to production getting ahead of arrivals by more than 10 minutes but less than 11 minutes will no longer cause starvation. The result will be increased utilization of the production process.

But sequences of events that lead to production outstripping arrivals by 11 minutes are rarer than those that lead to production outstripping arrivals by 10 minutes (because the former include the latter). Events that lead to production outstripping arrivals by 13 minutes are even rarer. This means that each additional minute of WIP results in a smaller and smaller increase in utilization. Therefore, the amount of WIP (and cycle time) will increase faster than the utilization level, as shown in Figure 1.5. Since we know from the capacity principle that we can never actually reach 100 percent utilization, WIP and cycle time go to infinity as the release rate approaches capacity.

FIGURE 1.5

Nonlinear
relationship of
cycle time to
utilization

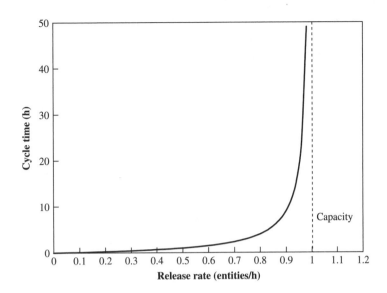

Insight by Analogy

A Highway

On a highway, any empty spot of pavement (i.e., a gap between vehicles) represents underutilized capacity. Hence, the theoretical capacity of a highway is the volume it would handle with bumper-to-bumper traffic traveling at the speed limit.

But, of course, we all know this is impossible. Experience shows us that heavier traffic results in longer travel times. The only time the highway is fully utilized (i.e., completely bumper-to-bumper) is when traffic is stopped (and travel times are hence infinite).

The reasons for this are exactly the same as those responsible for the capacity and utilization principles. The only way for vehicles to travel bumper-to-bumper is for them to move at precisely the same speed. Any variation, whether the result of braking to change lanes, inability of drivers to maintain a constant speed, and so forth will result in gaps and hence less than 100 percent utilization.

Because no highway is completely variability-free, all highways operate at significantly less than full capacity. Likewise, no production system or supply chain is without variability and hence operates at less than full capacity. Furthermore, just as travel times increase with utilization of a highway, cycle times increase with utilization in a production system.

FIGURE 1.6

Mechanics
underlying
overtime vicious
cycle

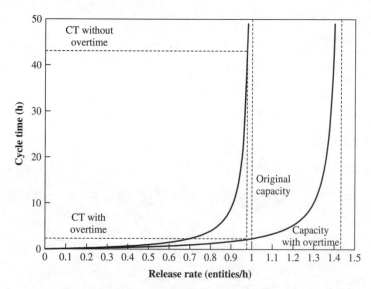

The science behind the above law and Figure 1.5 drives a common type of behavior in industry, which we term the **overtime vicious cycle**. This plays out as follows: Because maximizing throughput is desirable and estimating true theoretical capacity is difficult, managers tend to set releases into their system close to or even above theoretical capacity (see Figure 1.6). This causes cycle times to increase, which in turn causes late orders and excessive WIP. When the situation becomes bad enough, management authorizes overtime, which changes the capacity of the system (Figure 1.6) and causes cycle times to come back down. But as soon as the system recovers, overtime is discontinued, and management vows "not to let *that* happen again," releases are aimed right back at theoretical capacity and the whole cycle begins again. Depending on how much variability is in the system and how close management tries to load to capacity, this cycle can be swift and devastating.

Principles in Practice

Motorola

Prior to being spun off, Motorola's Semiconductor Products Sector produced integrated circuits for use in both Motorola products (e.g., cell phones) and for other OEMs (original equipment manufacturers). They did this in vastly complex wafer fabs that cost $2 billion or more to construct. Not surprisingly, efficient utilization of these enormously expensive resources is a key concern in the semiconductor industry. Despite this, Motorola deliberately sized capacity of each process in a wafer fab so that utilization is no higher than a specified limit, typically in the range of 75 to 85 percent.

Clearly the cost of this excess capacity is very expensive. But Motorola is well aware of the utilization principle. In a system as complex as a wafer fab, the dynamics of Figure 1.5 are dramatic and severe. Operating close to full utilization would require vast amounts of inventory and hence would result in extremely long cycle times. Excessive inventory would inflate costs, while long cycle times would hardly suit the needs of customers who are under their own cost and time pressures. Limiting utilization is expensive, but being uncompetitive is fatal. So Motorola wisely planned to run at less than full utilization.

Questions for Thought

1. If you ask a professional (doctor, lawyer, engineer, etc.) to estimate his personal utilization level, he will frequently claim it to be 100 percent (i.e., always busy with a backlog of work to do). Does this violate the capacity principle? (Hint: Think about whether every scrap of work that could be done by these professionals actually gets done.)

2. During the lunch-hour rush, the arrival rate may well exceed the service rate in a fast-food restaurant. But waiting times never approach infinity. Why not? (Hint: Think about the logic underlying the overtime viscious cycle in Figure 1.6.)

3. In *The Goal* (Goldratt and Cox 2004), the authors use a Boy Scout example to illustrate the concept of a bottleneck. Specifically, they name Herbie (the "fat kid") as the bottleneck, because he is the slowest hiker and therefore determines when the troup will reach its destination. Would Herbie still be the bottleneck if the scouts in the troup took different routes to the destination? Describe how this Boy Scout example could be modified to correspond with the correct definition of the bottleneck as the resource with the highest utilization.

2   VARIABILITY

Increasing variability always degrades the performance of a production system.

2.1   Introduction

Chapter 1 focused on the performance of a single process in terms of throughput and examined the roles of utilization and capacity. We now add two other key performance measures, WIP (work in process) and cycle time.

2.2   Little's Law

The first observation we can make is that throughput, WIP, and cycle time are intimately related via one of the most fundamental principles of operations management:

Principle (Little's law). *Over the long-term, average work-in-process (*WIP*), throughput (*TH*), and cycle time (*CT*) for any stable process are related as follows:*

$$WIP = TH \times CT$$

Little's law is extremely general. The only two restrictions are (1) it refers to long-term averages and (2) the process must be stable. Restriction (1) simply means that Little's law need not necessarily hold for daily WIP, throughput, and cycle time, but for averages taken over a period of weeks or months it *will* hold. Restriction (2) means that the process cannot be exhibiting a systematic trend during the interval over which data are collected (e.g., steadily building up WIP, increasing the throughput rate, or anything else that makes the process substantially different at the end of the data collection interval than it was at the beginning). However, this stability restriction does not preclude cyclic behavior (e.g., WIP rising and falling), bulk arrivals, batch processing, multiple entity types with different characteristics, or a wide range of other complex behavior. Indeed, Little's law is not even restricted to a single process. As long as WIP, TH, and CT are measured in consistent units, it can be applied to an entire line, a plant, a warehouse, or any other operation through which entities flow.

One way to think of Little's law, which offers a sense of why it is so general, is as a simple conversion of units. We can speak of WIP in terms of number of entities or in terms of the work content represented by the entities. For example, a bank teller may look at a queue of customers and see either 12 people or 60 minutes of work (assuming each customer requires an average of 5 minutes of service).

Little's law simply converts WIP from entities to time via the following units conversion:

$$\text{entities} = \text{entities/day} \times \text{days}$$

But entities need not be counted one at a time in Little's law. We could use dollars to measure inventory and output, so that Little's law would have units of

$$\text{dollars} = \text{dollars/day} \times \text{days}$$

This would make it possible for us to aggregate many different types of entities into a single relationship. Note, however, that if we want to, we can also apply Little's law separately to each entity type.

Although Little's law is very simple it is extremely useful. Some common applications include:

1. *Basic calculations.* If we know any two of the quantities, WIP, CT, and TH, we can calculate the third. For example, consider a firm's accounts receivable. Suppose that the firm bills an average of $10,000 per day and that customers take 45 days on average to pay. Then, working in units of dollars, TH is $10,000 per day and CT is 45 days, so WIP (i.e., the total amount of outstanding accounts receivable on average) will be $450,000.

2. *Measure of cycle time.* Measuring cycle time directly can be tedious. We must time stamp each entity as it enters the system, record its completion time, and maintain a running average. While many manufacturing execution systems are capable of tracking such data, it is often simpler to keep track of WIP and throughput than cycle time (i.e., everyone tracks throughput because it is directly related to revenue and tracking WIP involves only a periodic systemwide count, while cycle time requires detailed data on every entity). Notice that we can rearrange Little's law as

$$CT = \frac{WIP}{TH}$$

Therefore, if we have averages for WIP and TH, their ratio defines a perfectly consistent measure of cycle time. Notice that this definition remains consistent even for assembly systems. For instance, the manufacturing cycle time of a personal computer is very difficult to define in terms of tracking entities, because it is made up of many subcomponents, some of which are processed in parallel. However, if we can measure total WIP in dollars and TH in terms of cost of goods sold, then the ratio still defines a measure of cycle time.[1]

3. *Cycle time reduction.* The literature on lean production extols the virtues of WIP reduction, while the literature on time-based competition calls for cycle time reduction. However, because

$$CT = \frac{WIP}{TH}$$

Little's law indicates that WIP and cycle time reduction are really two sides of the same coin. As long as TH remains constant, any reduction in WIP must be accompanied by a reduction in CT and vice versa. This implies that separate programs are not needed to reduce WIP and cycle time. It also implies that "where there is WIP there is cycle time," so the places to look for improvements in cycle time are the locations in the production process where WIP is piling up.

---

[1] Of course, when thinking about cycle time from a customer standpoint we must be careful to note which part of cycle time the customer actually sees. Because of this we are careful to distinguish between manufacturing **cycle time** (the time an entity spends in the system) and customer **lead time** (the time between when a customer order is placed and when it is received). Our Little's law example addresses manufacturing cycle time. We will treat customer lead time more carefully in Chapter 9.

2.3   Measuring Variability

Because of applications like those given above, Little's law is an essential tool in the arsenal of every operations or supply chain professional. However, it falls well short of painting a complete picture of a operations system. Writing Little's law in yet another form

$$\text{TH} = \frac{\text{WIP}}{\text{CT}}$$

suggests that it is possible to have two systems with the same throughput but where one has high WIP and long cycle time, while the other has low WIP and short cycle time. Of course, any manager would prefer the system with low WIP and short cycle times—such a system is more "efficient" in the sense of its ability to convert WIP into throughput. But in practice, operations and supply chain systems can exhibit dramatic differences in efficiency. Why? The answer—and this is a fundamental insight of the science of operations—is **variability**!

Variability is a fact of life. Heights of individuals, SAT scores, lightbulb lifetimes, daily barometric pressure readings, highway travel times, soil acidity levels, service times at a bank teller, fraction of people who vote in presidential elections, and millions of other everyday phenomena are subject to variability. Any collection of numerical measures that is not perfectly uniform is said to be variable. In operations systems, many important quantities are variable, including process times, equipment uptimes, equipment downtimes, product demands, yield rates, number of workers who show up on a given day, and a host of others. Because of the prevalence of variability and its disruptive influence on system performance, understanding it is critical to effective operations management. This involves two basic steps: (1) specification of consistent and appropriate measures of variability and (2) development of the cause-and-effect roles of variability in operations systems.

We begin with measures. First, we note that a quantitative measure whose outcomes are subject to variability is termed a **random variable**. The set of all possible realizations of a random variable is called its **population**. For example, the height of a randomly chosen American adult male is a random variable whose population consists of the set of heights of all American adult males.[2] Often, we do not have data for the entire population of a random

---

[2]A more mundane example of a random variable is the numerical outcome of the throw of a single die. The population for this random variable is the set
$S = \{1, 2, 3, 4, 5, 6\}$.

variable and therefore consider a subset or **sample** of the possible outcomes. For instance, we might estimate the height characteristics of the American male adult population from a sample of 10,000 randomly chosen individuals.

One way to describe either a population or a sample is by means of **summary statistics**. A statistic is a single-number descriptor calculated as a function of the outcomes in a population or sample. The most common statistic is the **mean**, which measures the average or central tendency of a random variable.[3] Second most common is the **standard deviation**, which measures the spread or dispersion of the random variable about its mean.[4]

For example, the mean and standard deviation of the scores on the 1999 SAT test were 1,017 and 209, respectively. For most random variables, a high percentage (e.g., 95 percent or so) of the population lies within two standard deviations of the mean. In the case of SAT scores, two standard deviations around the mean represents the range from 599 to 1,435. Because roughly 2 percent of test takers scored above 1,435 and 2 percent scored below 599, this interval contains about 96 percent of test scores, which is termed "normal" behavior.

Standard deviation is a commonly used measure of variability. However, it is not always the most suitable one. To see why, suppose we are told that heights of American males average 68 inches with a standard deviation of 4 inches. Which are more variable, heights of American males or SAT scores? We cannot answer questions like these on the basis of standard deviation alone. The reason is that standard deviations have units, indeed the same units as the mean (e.g., inches for heights, points for SAT scores). We cannot compare a standard deviation measured in inches with one given in points.

Because of this, a more appropriate measure of variability is the **coefficient of variation (CV)**, which is defined as

$$CV = \frac{\text{standard deviation}}{\text{mean}}$$

---

[3]The mean of a set of outcomes, $x_1, \ldots, x_n$, is computed by summing them and dividing by their number, that is, $\bar{x} = \frac{x_1 + \cdots + x_n}{n}$. Note that "x-bar" is commonly used to depict the mean of a sample, while the Greek letter μ ("mu") is commonly used to depict the mean of a population.

[4]The **variance** of a set of outcomes, $x_1, \ldots, x_n$, is computed as $s^2 = \frac{(x_1 - \bar{x})^2 + \cdots + (x_n - \bar{x})^2}{n-1}$. Note that this is almost the average of the squared deviations from the mean, except that we divide by $n - 1$ instead of n. The standard deviation is the square root of the variance, or s. Note that s is commonly used to denote the standard deviation of a sample, while the Greek letter σ ("sigma") is generally used to represent the standard deviation of a population.

Because mean and standard deviation have the same units, the co-efficient of variation is unitless. This makes it a consistent measure of variability across a wide range of random variables. For example, the CV of heights of American males is $4/68 = 0.06$, while the CV of SAT scores is $209/1,017 = 0.21$, implying that SAT scores are substantially more variable than are heights. Because the coefficient of variation provides a unitless measure of variability, we can use it to classify random variables. Random variables with CVs substantially below 1 are said to have **low variability**, while those with CVs substantially above 1 have **high variability**. Random variables with CVs around 1 (say between 0.75 and 1.33) have **moderate variability**.

We now consider variability specifically as it relates to operations systems. As we noted above, there are many sources of variability in production and service systems, some of which will be considered in more detail later. However, at the level of a single process, there are two key sources of variability: (1) interarrival times and (2) effective process times. **Interarrival times** are the times between the arrival of entities to the process. If arrivals occur at uniform intervals (e.g., cars on an assembly line arrive at a workstation every 58 seconds), then variability is very low. But interarrival times can be affected by vendor quality, scheduling policies, variability in upstream processes, and other factors. For example, if the assembly line is shut down due to a quality problem, then the time between the last arrival and the next one could be 30 minutes or more. When compared with the 58-second norm, this would constitute significant variability.

Effective process times are measured as the time from when an entity is ready for processing (i.e., is no longer behind any other entities) and when it is completed.[5] Notice that under this definition, effective process times include **detractors**, such as machine failures, setup times, operator breaks, or anything that extends the time required to complete processing of the entity, in addition to the actual processing time. For example, consider the experience of donating blood. Our cycle time represents the entire time we are at the clinic, waiting in queue, having our blood drawn, and so forth. Our process time represents only the time we spend actually giving blood. But our effective process time represents the time from when we reach the front of the line and when we finish giving blood. If, after finishing with the donor in front of us, the nurse takes a break,

---

[5]If there were always a queue at the process, effective process times would correspond to interoutput times. But because the process may be idle at times, this is not quite the case. The time a process waits idle for the next arrival to occur is not part of effective process time.

FIGURE 2.1

High- and low-variability arrivals

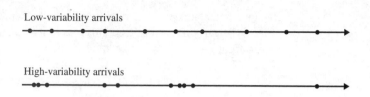

Low-variability arrivals

High-variability arrivals

cleans the space, or goes out to replenish materials, then this extra time is included in our effective process time. The reason is that there is no operational difference between our spending 20 minutes donating blood and spending 10 minutes waiting for the nurse to take care of her other duties and then spending 10 minutes donating blood. (There may be a medical difference, but because this is an operations book we ignore it.) If we have to wait for a long cleaning cycle before beginning our actual donation, then our effective process time could be substantially longer than those of the donors who preceded us. As a result, effective process times in the clinic could be highly variable, even if the actual donation time is fairly uniform.

We can characterize the variability in both interarrival times and effective process times via the coefficient of variation. For interarrival times, we could envision doing this by standing in front of the process with a stopwatch and logging the times between arrivals. If two entities arrive at the same time (e.g., as would be the case if two customers arrived to a fast-food restaurant in the same car), then we record the interarrival time between these as zero. With these data, we would compute the mean and standard deviation of the interarrival times, and take the ratio to compute the coefficient of variation. Figure 2.1 shows two arrival time lines. The top line illustrates a low-variability arrival process (CV = 0.07), while the bottom line illustrates a high-variability arrival process (CV = 2). Notice that low-variability arrivals are smooth and regular, while high-variability arrivals are "bursty" and uneven. Interestingly, in cases where we have a large number of independent customers arriving to a server (e.g., toll booths, calls to 911, customers to a bank) the CV will usually be close to 1.[6] Such arrival processes are called **Poisson** and fall right between the high-variability (CV > 1) and low-variability (CV < 1) cases.[7]

---

[6]This is known as the Palm-Khintchine theorem. For a proof and discussion, see Heyman and Sobel (2003, Section 5.8).

[7]To empirically verify that an arrival process is indeed Poisson, we can do two things. First, we check to see whether the mean and standard deviation of a sample of observed interarrival times are close to each other, so that the CV is approximately equal to 1. Second, we plot the interarrival times in a frequency histogram and observe that they follow an exponential distribution. For a discussion of the relationship between the exponential and Poisson distributions, see Ross (2002, Chapter 5).

TABLE 2.1   Effective process times from various
processes

Trial	Process 1	Process 2	Process 3
1	22	5	5
2	25	6	6
3	23	5	5
4	26	35	35
5	24	7	7
6	28	45	45
7	21	6	6
8	30	6	6
9	24	5	5
10	28	4	4
11	27	7	7
12	25	50	500
13	24	6	6
14	23	6	6
15	22	5	5
Mean	25.1	13.2	43.2
Standard Deviation	2.5	15.9	127.0
CV	0.1	1.2	2.9
Level of Variability	low	medium	high

We could collect data on effective process times in a similar
fashion by recording the time between when the entity enters the
process and when it leaves. For example, consider a CNC (computer
numerical control) turning center that machines complex metal
parts. To measure each effective process time, we would start our
stopwatch as soon as the machine finished processing one part and
had another one ready to start; we would stop it when the next part
finished processing. As we did for interarrival times, we would
compute the mean and standard deviation of these intercompletion
times and take the ratio to find the coefficient of variation. Table
2.1 illustrates three cases. Process 1 has effective process times
that vary slightly about 25 minutes, so that the CV is 0.1. This low-
variability process is representative of automated equipment and
might characterize our CNC machine as long as it operates without stoppages. Process 2 has short process times around 6 minutes
punctuated by an occasional 40-minute time. This results in moderate variability with a CV of 1.2 and might be representative of
our CNC machine if every so often we must shut the machine down
to change the tools in the magazine and reprogram its instructions.
Finally process 3 is identical to process 2 except that the twelfth
observation is much longer. This behavior, which results in a high-
variability process with a CV of 2.9, could be the result of a long

failure of our CNC center. The key conclusion to draw from these examples is that low-, moderate-, and high-variability effective process times are all observed in operations systems. Depending on factors like setups, failures, and other disruptive elements, it is possible to observe CVs ranging from 0 to as high as 10 or more.

2.4   Influence of Variability

Now that we have defined an appropriate measure of variability and have identified the key types of variability at the level of an individual process, we turn to the cause-and-effect relationships between variability and performance measures in an operations system. These are characterized through the science of **queueing theory**, which is the study of waiting line phenomena.[8] In a operations system, entities queue up behind processes, so that

$$\text{cycle time} = \text{waiting time} + \text{process time}$$

where **waiting time** represents the time entities spend in the system not being processed. As we will see, there are several causes of waiting. One of the most important is **queueing**, in which entities are ready for processing but must wait for a resource to become available to start processing. The fundamental cause of queueing is a lack of coordination between arrivals and processing. If arrivals were synchronized to occur only when the process has finished with the previous entity, there would be no queueing. But if there is variability in either the interarrival times or effective processing times, then arrivals may occur before the process is ready for them and a queue may build up. Figure 2.2 illustrates schematically how arrival and process variability lead to queueing and also lists some of the most common sources of each type of variability.

We can characterize the fundamental behavior of queueing at a station with the following principle:

Principle (Queueing).   *At a single station with no limit on the number of entities that can queue up, the waiting time* (WT) *due to queuing is given by*

$$WT = V \times U \times T$$

---

[8]*Queueing* is also the only word we know of with five consecutive vowels, which makes it handy in cocktail party conversation, as well as supply chain management. Introductory texts on queueing theory include Cooper (1990) and Gross and Harris (1998). Texts that relate queueing theory specifically to production and service systems include Buzacott and Shanthikumar (1993) and Hall (1991).

FIGURE 2.2

Lack of coordination between arrivals and processing due to variability causes queueing

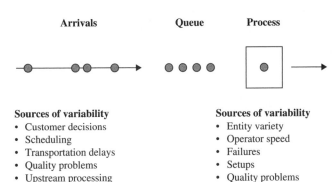

Arrivals   Queue   Process

Sources of variability
- Customer decisions
- Scheduling
- Transportation delays
- Quality problems
- Upstream processing

Sources of variability
- Entity variety
- Operator speed
- Failures
- Setups
- Quality problems

where

$$V = a\ variability\ factor$$

$$U = a\ utilization\ factor$$

$$T = average\ effective\ process\ time\ for\ an\ entity\ at\ the\ station$$

The variability factor V is an increasing function of both the CV of interarrival times and the CV of effective process times. The utilization factor U is an increasing function of utililization, which grows to infinity as utilization approaches 100 percent. The above expression, which we term the **VUT equation**, tells us that waiting time due to queueing will be VU multiples of the actual processing time T. Because an entity at a station is either waiting or being processed, we can write the following as a corollary to the queueing principle:

$$CT = WT + T = VUT + T$$

These equations are major results in supply chain science because they provide basic understanding and useful tools for examining the primary causes of cycle time.[9]

The first insight we can get from the VUT equation is that variability and utilization interact. High variability (V) is most damaging at stations with high utilization (U), that is, at bottlenecks. So, through a combination of activities that lower utilization and/or reduce variability we can reduce queueing. Furthermore, variability reduction is most effective at bottlenecks.

To draw additional insights, we need to further specify the factors that determine the U and V factors.

---

[9]For further detail on the VUT equation and its components, see Hopp and Spearman (2000, Chapter 8).

FIGURE 2.3

Impact of
utilization and
variability on
waiting time at a
station

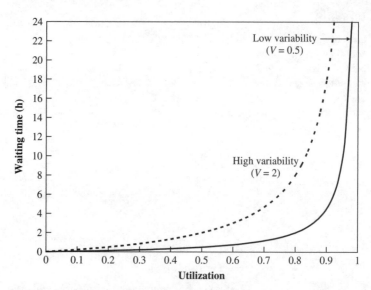

The utilization factor is a function of station utilization (fraction of time station is busy). While exact expressions do not exist in general and approximations vary depending on the nature of the station (e.g., whether the station consists of a single process or multiple processes in parallel), the utilization factor is proportional to $1/(1-u)$, where u is the station utilization. This means that as utilization approaches 100 percent, waiting time due to queueing approaches *infinity*. Furthermore, as illustrated in Figure 2.3, it does so in a highly nonlinear fashion. This gives a mathematical explanation for the utilization principle introduced in Chapter 1. The main conclusion we can draw here is that unless WIP is capped (e.g., by the existence of a physical or logical limit), queueing becomes extremely sensitive to utilization as the station is loaded close to its capacity.

The variability factor is a function of both arrival and process variability, as measured by the CVs of interarrival and process times. Again, while the exact expression depends on station specifics, the V factor is generally proportional to the **squared coefficient of variation (SCV)** of both interarrival and process times.

Figure 2.3 also illustrates the impact of increasing process and/or arrival variability on waiting time at a station. In this figure we illustrate what happens to waiting time at two stations that are identical except that one has a V coefficient of 0.5 and the other has a V coefficient of 2. By the queueing principle, the waiting time will be four times higher for any given level of utilization in the latter system than in the former. As we see from Figure 2.3, this has the effect of making waiting time in the system with $V = 2$ "blow up" much more quickly. Hence, to achieve the same level of waiting time in these two systems, we have to operate the system with $V = 2$ at a much lower level of utilization than we are able to maintain in the system with $V = 0.5$.

From this discussion we can conclude that reductions in utilization tend to have a much larger impact on waiting time than do reductions in variability. However, because capacity is costly, high utilization is usually desirable. According to the VUT equation, the only way to have high utilization without long waiting time is to have a low variability factor. For this reason, variability reduction is often the key to achieving high efficiency operations systems.

Insight by Analogy

A Restaurant

A restaurant is a service system that is subject to both demand and supply variability. On the demand side customer arrivals are at least somewhat unpredictable, and on the supply side the time it takes to feed a customer is also uncertain. This variability can degrade performance in three ways: (1) customers can be forced to wait for service; (2) customers can balk (go away) if they feel the wait will be too long, which causes a lost sale and possibly loss of customer goodwill; and (3) capacity (waiters, tables, etc.) can experience excessive idleness if the restaurant is sized to meet peak demand. Because the restaurant business is very competitive, the manner in which a particular establishment copes with variability can mean the difference between success and failure.

Because customer expectations are not the same for all types of restaurants, specific responses vary. For instance, in a fast-food restaurant, customers expect to be able to drop in unannounced (so arrival variability is high) and receive quick service. To respond, fast-food restaurants do whatever they can to keep process variability low. They have a limited menu and often discourage special orders. They keep food on warming tables to eliminate waiting due to cooking. They use simple cash registers with pictures of food items, so that all employees can process orders quickly, not just those who are adept at operating a keypad and counting out change. But even with very low variability on the supply side, the variability on the demand side ensures that the V coefficient will be quite high in a fast-food restaurant. To remain fast, such establishments typically retain excess capacity. For example to respond to peaks in demand, fast-food restaurants are generally overstaffed during slow periods. Furthermore, they frequently shift capacity between operations to respond to surges in demand (e.g., employees move from food preparation activities in the back to staff the front counter when lines get long).

Contrast this with an upscale restaurant. Because customers do not expect walk-in service, the restaurant can greatly reduce arrival variability by taking reservations. Even though the broader menu probably results in higher process variability than in a fast-food restaurant, lower arrival variability means that the upscale restaurant has a substantially lower overall V coefficient. Hence, the upscale restaurant has a waiting time curve that resembles the one labeled $V = 0.5$ in Figure 2.3, while the fast-food restaurant has one that resembles the $V = 2$ curve. As a result, the upscale restaurant is able to achieve higher utilization of its staff and facilities (a good thing, because pricey chefs and maitre d's are more expensive to idle than are fast-food fry cooks). Despite their higher utilization, upscale restaurants typically have lower waiting times as a percentage of service times. For example, one might wait on average 2 minutes to receive a meal that takes 20 minutes to eat in a fast-food restaurant, which implies that $V \times U = 0.1$ (waiting time is one-tenth of service time). In contrast, we might wait 5 minutes for a reserved table to eat a 100-minute meal, which implies $V \times U = 0.05$. Clearly, the variability reduction that results from taking reservations has an enormous impact on performance.

To illustrate the behavior described by the VUT equation, let us consider a simple station where the average effective process time for an entity is $T = 1$ hour and the CV for both interarrival times and process times is 1 (which for this system implies that $V = 1$). Then the capacity of the process is 1 per hour and utilization (UTIL) is given by

$$\text{UTIL} = \frac{\text{rate in}}{\text{capacity}} = \frac{\text{rate in}}{1} = \text{rate in}$$

Suppose this process receives arrivals at a rate of 0.5 entities per hour, so that utilization equals 0.5. In this simple system, the utilization factor (U) is given by

$$U = \frac{\text{UTIL}}{1 - \text{UTIL}} = \frac{0.5}{1 - 0.5} = 1$$

Hence, the waiting time due to queueing experienced by entities is

$$\text{WT} = V \times U \times T = 1 \times 1 \times 1 = 1 \text{ hour}$$

and

$$\text{CT} = WT + T = 1 + 1 = 2 \text{ hours}$$

If we were to double the variability factor to $V = 2$ (i.e., by increasing the CV of either interarrival times or process times), without changing utilization, then waiting time would double to 2 hours.

However, suppose that we increase arrivals to this process up to a rate of 0.9 entities per hour, so that utilization is now 0.9. Then, the utilization factor becomes

$$U = \frac{\text{UTIL}}{1 - \text{UTIL}} = \frac{0.9}{1 - 0.9} = 9$$

and waiting time due to queueing is

$$\text{WT} = V \times U \times T = 1 \times 9 \times 1 = 9 \text{ hours}$$

and

$$\text{CT} = WT + T = 9 + 1 = 10 \text{ hours}$$

Furthermore, doubling the variability factor to $V = 2$ doubles the waiting time to 18 hours (19 hours for cycle time). Clearly, as we noted, highly utilized processes are much more sensitive to variability than are lowly utilized ones.

Examples of the above relationship between variability, utilization, and waiting abound in everyday life. A common but dramatic instance is that of ambulance service. Here, the process is the paramedic team, while the entities are patients requiring assistance.[10] In this system, short waiting time (i.e., the time a patient must wait for treatment) is essential. But, because the very nature of emergency calls implies that they will be unpredictable, the system has high arrival variability and hence a large variability factor. The only way to achieve short waiting time is to keep the utilization factor low, which is precisely what ambulance services do. It is not unusual to find an ambulance with overall utilization of less than 10 percent, due to the need to provide rapid response.

A sharply contrasting example is that of a highly automated production process, such as an automatic soft drink filling line. Here, cans are filled quickly (i.e., a second or less per can) and with a great deal of regularity, so that there is little process variability. The filling process is fed by a conveyor that also runs at a very steady rate so that there is little arrival variability. This implies that the variability factor (V) is extremely tiny. Hence, it is possible to set the utilization close to 1 and still have little waiting time.

---

[10]Notice that it makes no difference logically whether the process physically moves to the entities or the entities move to the process. In either case, we can view the entities as queueing up for processing and hence the VUT equation applies.

However, we must be careful not to overinterpret this example and assume that there are many situations where utilization close to 1 is possible. If the automatic filling process is subject to failures, requires periodic cleaning, or is sometimes slowed or stopped due to quality problems, then the variability factor will not be near zero. This means that entities will have to build up somewhere (e.g., in the form of raw materials at the beginning of the filling line perhaps) to ensure high utilization and will therefore be subject to waiting time. If there is limited space for these materials (and there always is for a very fast line), the line will have to shut down. In these cases, the utilization will ultimately be less than 1 even though *planned* releases were designed to achieve utilization of 1.

Principles in Practice

Toyota

The Toyota Production System (TPS) has had a profound impact on manufacturing practice around the globe. Many specific practices such as kanban, kaizen, and SMED (single-minute exchange of die) have received considerable attention in popular management publications. But if one looks closely at the early publications on TPS, it is apparent that the queueing principle is at the core of what Toyota implemented. For instance, in his seminal book, Taiichi Ohno, the father of the TPS, begins his description of the system with a write-up replete with sections entitled "Establishing a Production Flow," "Production Leveling," and "Mountains Should be Low and Valleys Should be Shallow" (Ohno 1988). All of these drive home the point that the only way for production processes to operate with low waiting time (and by Little's law, low inventory) is for them to have low variability. Eliminating arrival variability at stations is the very foundation of the Toyota Production System (as well as just-in-time, lean, and the rest of its descendants).

While Ohno recognized the need for smooth flow into processes, he also recognized that variability in demand is a fact of business life. To compensate, Toyota placed tremendous emphasis on production smoothing. That is, they took a forecast of demand for a month and divided it up so that planned production volume and mix were the same for each day, and indeed each hour. If monthly demand required producing 75 percent sedans, then the plant should produce 75 percent sedans each and every hour. This avoided the pulsing through the line that would occur if different body types were produced in batches (e.g., a stream of sedans followed by a stream of hardtops followed by a stream of wagons).

Of course, feeding one station with a steady arrival stream only ensures that the next station receives steady arrivals if the upstream station has low process variability. So, Toyota also placed great emphasis on reducing variability in process times. Standard work procedures, total quality control, total preventive maintenance, setup reduction, and many other integral parts of the TPS were firmly directed at reducing process variability. With these in place along with the production smoothing measures, Toyota achieved exceptionally low arrival variability at stations throughout its production system. By the logic depicted in Figure 2.3 this enabled Toyota to run its processes at high levels of utilization and low levels of waiting time and inventory. Moreover, because the myriad methods Toyota used to drive variability out of its processes were notoriously hard to copy, Toyota maintained a competitive edge in its operations for decades—despite being the most intensely benchmarked company on the planet.

Questions for Thought

1. An insurance company processes 15,000 claims per year. The average processing time is 3 weeks. How many claims on average does the company have in process?

2. A consulting firm sells $50 million in consulting services per year. Their accounts receivable average $8 million. What is the average billing to collection time?

3. A manager states that inventory in her division turns four times a year. She also claims that everything the division buys is used and sold within 8 weeks. Are these statements consistent? (Hint: Recall that turns can be defined as throughput divided by WIP, provided that throughput is measured in cost of goods sold.)

4. An airline allows customers to check in either at its counter with an agent or at an electronic kiosk. Check-in times at the counter average 4 minutes with a standard deviation of 3 minutes. Check-in times at a kiosk average 2 minutes with a standard deviation of 0.5 minute. Which check-in process is more variable? What implications might this have for the number of agents and kiosks the airline should provide?

5. A supermarket has 30 checkout lanes, all of which have been traditionally staffed during peak time on Saturday morning. However, recent cost-cutting efforts have led to a reduction to only 29 cashiers on duty during peak time. The result was that average customer waiting time increased from 4 to 4.5 minutes. The store manager, seeking further cost reductions, has proposed reducing staffing to 28 cashiers. He argues that this will only increase wait times from 4.5 to 5 minutes, which will not irritate customers too much. Do you agree with his reasoning? (Hint: Look carefully at Figure 2.3.)

3   BATCHING

Delay due to batching (eventually) increases proportionally in the lot size.

3.1   Introduction

Many operations are done in **batches**. A painting process may paint several red cars before switching to blue ones. A secretary may collect a bundle of copying jobs before going to the copy room to process them. A foundry may place a number of wrenches into a furnace simultaneously for heat treating. A forklift operator may allow several machined parts to accumulate before moving them from one operation to another. The number of similar jobs processed together, either sequentially or simultaneously, is known as the **batch size** or **lot size** of the operation.

Why is batching used? The answer is simple: capacity. It is often more efficient to process a batch of entities than to process them one at a time. There are three basic reasons why batching increases efficiency:

1. *Setup Avoidance.* A setup or changeover is any operation that must be done at the beginning of a batch (e.g., cleaning out the paint gun, walking to the copy room, etc.). The larger the batch size, the fewer the setups required, and hence the less capacity lost to them.

2. *Pacing Improvement.* In some operations, particularly manual ones, it is possible to get into a good "rhythm" while processing a number of like jobs in a row. For instance, a secretary may handle

copying jobs quicker if they are part of a batch than if they are done separately. The reason is that repetition of motion tends to eliminate extraneous steps. We can think of the extraneous motions as setups that are done at the beginning of a batch and then dropped. But because these motions are not as obvious as a setup due to cleaning and may take several repetitions to disappear, we distinguish pacing improvement from setup avoidance.

3. *Simultaneous Processing.* Some operations are intrinsically batch in nature because they can process a batch of entities as quickly as they can process a single entity. For instance, heat treating may require 3 hours regardless of whether the furnace is loaded with one wrench or a hundred. Similarly, moving parts between operations with a forklift may require the same amount of time regardless of whether the move quantity is one part or a full load. Obviously, the larger the batch size, the greater the capacity of a simultaneous operation.

Because they are physically different, we distinguish between **simultaneous batches**, where entities are processed together, and **sequential batches**, where entities are processed one at a time between setups. Although the source of efficiency from batching can vary, the basic mechanics are the same. Larger batch sizes increase capacity but also increase **wait-for-batch time** (time to build up a batch), **wait-in-batch time** (time to process a batch), or both. The essential trade-off involved in all batching is one of capacity versus cycle time.

3.2 Simultaneous Batching

We begin by examining the trade-offs involved in simultaneous batching. That is, we consider an operation where entities are processed simultaneously in a batch and the process time does not depend on how many entities are being processed (as long as the batch size does not exceed the number of entities that can fit into the process). This situation is illustrated in Figure 3.1. Examples of simultaneous batching include heat treat and burn-in operations, bulk

FIGURE 3.1

Mechanics of simultaneous batching

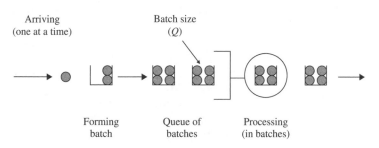

Arriving
(one at a time)

Batch size
(*Q*)

Forming
batch

Queue of
batches

Processing
(in batches)

transportation of parts between processes, and showing a training video to a group of employees. Regardless of the application, the purpose of simultaneous batching is to make effective use of the capacity of the process.

Note that simultaneous batching characterizes both **process batches** (number of entities processed together at a station) and **move batches** (number of entities moved together between stations). From an operations perspective, heat treating wrenches in a furnace and moving machined parts between processes is essentially the same. Both are examples of simultaneous batch operations.

The fundamental relationship underlying simultaneous batching behavior is the effect of batch size on utilization. Utilization, the fraction of time a process is busy, can be computed as

$$\text{utilization} = \frac{\text{rate in}}{\text{capacity}}$$

Because a batch process takes a fixed amount of time regardless of the batch size, capacity is equal to

$$\text{capacity} = \frac{\text{batch size}}{\text{process time}}$$

Hence,

$$\text{utilization} = \frac{\text{rate in} \times \text{process time}}{\text{batch size}}$$

For the system to be stable, utilization must be less than 100 percent, which requires

$$\text{batch size} > \text{rate in} \times \text{process time}$$

While this enables us to compute the minimum batch size needed to keep up with a given throughput rate, it usually makes sense to run simultaneous batching operations with batch sizes larger than the minimum. The reason is that, as the above analysis makes clear, utilization decreases in the batch size. Because we know from chapters 1 and 2 that cycle time increases in utilization, we would expect increasing batch size to decrease cycle time. This is exactly what happens as long as larger batch sizes do not cause entities to wait while forming a batch. For instance, if the entire batch arrives together, then none of the entities has to wait and cycle time unambiguously decreases with batch size. However, if parts arrive one at a time to a simultaneous batch operation, then cycle time may increase. For example, if arrivals to the operation are slow and the batch size is fixed and large, then the first entities to arrive must wait a long time for a full batch to form. In this case, even though reducing the batch size will increase utilization it might well reduce average cycle time by reducing the time entities wait to form a batch.

A more effective way to avoid excessive wait-for-batch time is to abandon the fixed batch size policy altogether. For instance, if whenever the operation finishes a batch we start processing whatever entities are waiting (up to the number that can fit into the operation, of course), then we will never have an idle process with entities waiting. But even this does not entirely eliminate the wait-for-batch time.

To see this, let us consider a batch operation with unlimited space. Suppose the process time for a batch is PT minutes, regardless of the number processed. So, we will start a new batch every PT minutes, consisting of whatever entities are available. If the arrival rate is ARATE, then the average number of parts that will be waiting is ARATE × PT, which will therefore be the average batch size. On average, these parts will wait PT/2 minutes (assuming they arrive one at a time over the PT-minute interval), and so their entire cycle time for the operation will be PT/2 + PT = 3PT/2. By Little's law, the average WIP in the station will be ARATE × 3PT/2. Note that the average batch size, average cycle time, and average WIP are all proportional to the process time PT. Speeding up the process by decreasing PT will allow smaller batches, which in turn will decrease WIP and cycle time.

As an example, consider a toolmaking plant that currently heat treats wrenches in a large furnace that can hold 120 wrenches and takes 1 hour to treat them. Suppose that throughput is 100 wrenches per hour. If we ignore queueing (i.e., having more than 120 wrenches accumulated at the furnace when it is ready to start a new batch) then we can use the above analysis to conclude that the average batch size will be 100 wrenches, the average cycle time will be 90 minutes, and the average WIP at (and in) heat treat will be 150 wrenches.

Now, suppose that a new induction heating coil is installed that can heat treat one wrench at a time in 30 seconds. The capacity, therefore, is 120 wrenches per hour, which is the same as the furnace and is greater than the throughput rate. If we again ignore queueing effects, then the average process time is 0.5 minutes or 0.00833 hours. So, by Little's law, the average WIP is 100 × 0.00833 = 0.833 wrenches. Even if we were to include queueing in the two cases, it is clear that the WIP and cycle time for this one-at-a-time operation will be vastly smaller than that for the batch operation. This behavior is at the root of the "lot size of one" goal of lean production.

3.3   Sequential Batching

A sequential batch operation is one that processes entities sequentially (one at a time) but requires time to setup or change over before moving to a different type of entity. This situation is illustrated in Figure 3.2. A classic example is a punch press that can stamp identical parts from sheet metal at a very fast rate but may be idle for a significant amount of time while the die is changed to produce a different part type. The decision of how many parts of a certain type to process before switching to a different type is a batch (or lot) sizing decision that involves a trade-off between capacity and cycle time.

As in the case of simultaneous batching, there exists a minimum sequential batch size necessary to ensure sufficient capacity to keep up with demand. To compute this, we define

ARATE = arrival rate of entities (number per hour)
PT   = process time for a single entity (hours)
ST   = setup time (hours)
BSIZE = batch size

Because it takes $ST + BSIZE \times PT$ time units to process a batch of BSIZE entities, the capacity (in units per hour) of a sequential batch operation is

$$\text{Capacity} = \frac{\text{BSIZE}}{\text{ST} + \text{BSIZE} \times \text{PT}}$$

Hence, utilization is

$$\text{Utilization} = \frac{\text{rate in}}{\text{capacity}} = \frac{\text{ARATE}(\text{ST} + \text{BSIZE} \times \text{PT})}{\text{BSIZE}}$$

FIGURE 3.2 Mechanics of sequential batching

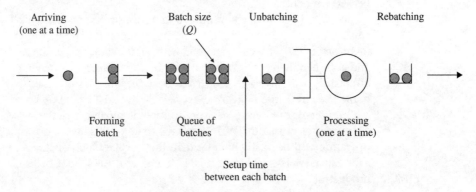

Arriving
(one at a time)

Batch size
(Q)

Unbatching

Rebatching

Forming
batch

Queue of
batches

Processing
(one at a time)

Setup time
between each batch

and for utilization to be less than 100 percent we require

$$\text{BSIZE} > \frac{\text{ARATE} \times \text{ST}}{1 - \text{ARATE} \times \text{PT}}$$

But as with simultaneous batching, it is frequently appropriate to set the batch size larger than the minimum level. The reason is that it may be possible to reduce cycle time by striking a better balance between capacity and delay. To see this, let us divide cycle time at a station into the following components:

Cycle time = wait-for-batch time + queue time + setup time
+ process time

Wait-for-batch time is the time it takes to form a batch in front of the operation. For simplicity, we assume that entities arrive one at a time and that we do not start processing until a full batch is in place. Under these conditions, the time to form a batch increases in proportion to the batch size.

From Chapter 1, we know that queue time increases in utilization. Because larger batches mean fewer setups, and hence lower utilization, queue time decreases (nonlinearly) as batch size increases.

Finally, if we assume that we must process the entire batch before any of the entities can depart from the operation, the setup plus process time for a batch is $\text{ST} + \text{BSIZE} \times \text{PT}$, which clearly increases in proportion to the batch size.

Adding all of these times together results in a relationship between cycle time and batch size like that shown in Figure 3.3. This figure illustrates a case where the minimum batch size required to keep up with arrivals is larger than 1. Below this minimum batch size, the system must do so many setups that it does not have time to process the jobs. If batch size is only slightly above the minimum, production is feasible, but cycle times are long because frequent setups lead to high utilization, which leads to long queue times. So, for a while, increasing batch size reduces total cycle time by lowering utilization and hence queue time. But the beneficial impact of larger batches on queue time eventually diminishes and is offset by larger wait-for-batch and process times. Hence, increasing batch size eventually increases total cycle time. As a result, there is some intermediate batch size, BSIZE*, that minimizes cycle time.

The main points of our discussion of batching leading up to Figure 3.3 are captured in the following principle.

FIGURE 3.3

Effect of
sequential
batching on
cycle time

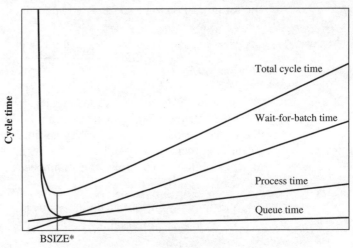

Batch size

Principle (Batching).   *In a simultaneous or sequential batching environment:*

  1. *The smallest batch size that yields a stable system may be greater than one.*
  2. *Delay due to batching (eventually) increases proportionally in the batch size.*

In sequential batching situations, the batching principle assumes that setup times are fixed and batch sizes are adjusted to accommodate them. However, in practice, reducing setup times is often an option. This can have a dramatic impact on cycle times. To see this, consider a milling machine that receives 10 parts per hour to process. Each part requires 4 minutes of machining, but there is a 1-hour setup to change from one part type to another.

We first note that the minimum batch size that allows the operation to keep up with the arrival rate is

$$\text{BSIZE} > \frac{\text{ARATE} \times \text{ST}}{1 - \text{ARATE} \times \text{PT}} = \frac{10 \times 1}{1 - (10 \times (4/60))} = 30$$

So, batch size must be at least 30. However, because utilization is still high when batch size is 30, significant queueing occurs. Figure 3.4 shows that for this case, cycle time is minimized by using a batch size of 63. At this batch size, total cycle time is approximately 33 hours.

A batch size of 63 is very large and results in significant wait-for-batch delay. If we cut setup time in half, to 30 minutes, the

FIGURE 3.4

Effect of setup
reduction on
sequential
batching and
cycle time

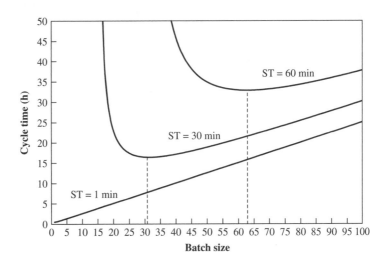

minimum batch size is also halved, to 15, and the batch size that
minimizes cycle time falls to 31. Total cycle time at this batch size
is reduced from 33 hours to 16.5 hours.

Further reduction of setup time will facilitate smaller batch
sizes and shorter cycle times. Eventually, a batch size of 1 will
become optimal. For instance, if setup time is reduced to 1 minute,
then, as Figure 3.4 illustrates, a batch size of 1 achieves a cycle
time of 0.5 hours, which is lower than that achieved by any other
batch size. Clearly, setup reduction and small batch production go
hand in hand.

Finally, we note that there is no intrinsic reason that the process
batch must equal the move batch. For instance, in the above milling
machine example with a 30-minute setup time, the fact that we use
a process batch size of 31 to balance capacity with batching delay
does *not* mean that we must also move lots of 31 items to the
next process downstream. We could transfer partial lots to the next
station and begin processing them before the entire batch has been
completed at the milling station. Indeed, if material handling is
efficient enough, we could conceivably move completed parts in
lots of 1.

Figure 3.5 illustrates the impact on the cycle time versus batch
size relationship of using move batches of size 1. The top curve represents the 30-minute setup case from Figure 3.4, while the bottom
curve represents the case where parts are moved downstream indi-
vidually as soon as they are finished at the milling station. Because
parts do not have to wait for their batch-mates, total cycle time is
reduced by this practice of **move batch splitting**. In systems with

FIGURE 3.5

Effect of move
batch splitting
on cycle time

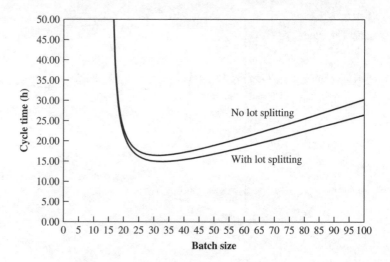

lengthy setup times and large process batch sizes, reducing move
batch sizes can have a significant effect on overall cycle time.

Insight by Analogy

An Intersection

What happens when a power failure causes the stoplight at a busy
intersection to go out? Temporary stop signs are installed and traffic
backs up for blocks in all directions.

Why does this happen? Because traffic etiquette at an intersection
with stop signs calls for drivers to take turns. One car goes through the
intersection in the east-west direction and then one goes in the north-
south direction. The batch size is 1. But, there is a setup (i.e., reaction
and acceleration) time associated with each car. So a batch size of 1
is too small. The excess setup time overloads the system and causes
traffic to pile up.

The opposite of the failed traffic light problem is the situation of a
traffic light that stays green too long in each direction. Again traffic
backs up. But this time it is because cars have to wait a long time for
a green light. The batch size is too large, which causes a substantial
delay while the batch builds up.

Optimally timing a traffic light so as to minimize average waiting
time is very much like the problem of finding a batch size to minimize
cycle time through a batch operation. The trade-off is essentially the
same as that depicted in Figure 3.3. Fortunately, traffic engineers know
about this trade-off and (usually) time traffic lights appropriately.

3.4   Multiproduct Batching

The above discussions make the fundamental point that batching is primarily about balancing capacity and delay. If all entities are identical, then the problem is simply to find a uniform batch size that strikes a reasonable balance. However, in most systems, entities (products, customers, data packets, etc.) are not identical. Therefore, in addition to balancing capacity and delay, we must also address the question of how to differentiate batch sizes between different entity types.

A common approach to the batching problem is the so-called **economic order quantity (EOQ) model**.[1] This model, which is presented in Chapter 7, tries to strike a balance between holding cost (which is proportional to inventory and hence cycle time) and setup cost. In purchasing situations, where the cost to order a batch of items is essentially fixed (i.e., does not depend on the size of the order) and orders are independent (e.g., come from different suppliers), the EOQ model can be very useful in setting lot sizes.

However, in production settings, where the setup "cost" is really a proxy for capacity, EOQ can lead to problems. First of all, there is no guarantee that the batch sizes produced by the EOQ model will even be feasible (i.e., utilization might exceed 100 percent). Even if they are feasible from a capacity standpoint, it may be very difficult to construct an actual production schedule from them. For instance, demand may not be neat multiples of the batch sizes, which means we will wind up with "remnants" in inventory. Finally, even if the batch sizes are feasible and lead to a schedule, the schedule might be such that a customer has to wait a long time for a particular entity type to "come around" on the schedule.

The problem with EOQ is not in the details of the model; it is in the fundamental approach of thinking about the problem in terms of setting batch sizes. A more effective way to approach the multiproduct sequential batching problem is in terms of allocating setups to product types. That is, suppose we know the processing rate, setup time to start a batch, and the quantity that must be processed over a fixed interval (e.g., to meet demand for the upcoming month). Then, if we allocate N setups to a given product, we will make N runs of it during the month and the size of each batch will be

$$\text{Batch size} = \frac{\text{demand}}{N}$$

[1] Details on the EOQ model can be found in almost any elementary textbook on operations management, including Hopp and Spearman (2000, Chapter 2), Nahmias (1997, Chapter 4), and Silver, Pyke, and Peterson (1998, Chapter 5).

TABLE 3.1 Data for multiproduct sequential batching example

Product	Basic	Standard	Deluxe	Supreme
Demand (units/mo)	15,000	12,000	500	250
Process Rate (units/h)	100	100	75	50
Setup Time (h)	8	8	6	4
Demand ÷ Process Rate (h/mo)	150	120	6.7	5

The problem thus becomes one of how many setups to allocate to each product.

To illustrate how this might be done, let us consider an example in which a plant produces four products: basic, standard, deluxe, and supreme. The same process is used to produce all four products, but a time-consuming setup is required to switch from one product to another. Demand for the upcoming month, production rate in units per hour, and setup time for each product are given in Table 3.1. We also compute the total amount of process time required to meet demand for the month as

$$\text{Total process time} = \frac{\text{demand}}{\text{process rate}}$$

In this example, a total of $150 + 120 + 6.7 + 5 = 281.7$ hours are required to meet monthly demand for all four products.

Suppose that the process is scheduled to run 18 hours per day for 22 days during the month. This means that a total of $18 \times 22 = 396$ hours are available. If we were to run the products with no setups at all (which is impossible, of course), utilization would be

$$\text{UTIL(zero setups)} = \frac{281.7}{396} = 71.1 \text{ percent}$$

Because any realistic schedule involves some setups, actual utilization must be higher than UTIL(zero setups). For example, if we were to set up and run each product only once during the month, we would require $8 + 8 + 6 + 4 = 26$ hours of setup time plus 281.7 hours of processing time, for a total of 307.7 hours. This would translate into a utilization of

$$\text{UTIL} = \frac{307.7}{396} = 77.7 \text{ percent}$$

Clearly, the actual utilization must lie between UTIL(no setups) and 100 percent. A reasonable target for many situations is

$\sqrt{\text{UTIL(zero setups)}}$, which in this case is $\sqrt{0.711} = 84.3$ percent. This means that we should schedule $396 \times 0.843 = 333.8$ hours, which allows for $333.8 - 281.7 = 52.1$ hours of setup time. The problem now is to allocate this setup time to the various products so as to make each product "come around" on the schedule as frequently as possible.

Although we could use various criteria to measure the responsiveness of a given schedule, a very simple one is the **maximum run length**. The run length of a product is simply the time it takes to run a batch. That is, if a product is run N times, then

$$\text{Run length} = \text{setup time} + \frac{\text{demand}}{N \times \text{process time}}$$

To see the implications of this choice, let us return to the example and start by allocating one setup to each product. As we can see from the following table, this uses up 26 hours of the 52.1 hours available for setup time.

Product	Basic	Standard	Deluxe	Supreme	Total
Demand	15,000	12,000	500	250	
Setup time	8	8	6	4	
Process time	100	100	75	50	
No. setups (N)	1	1	1	1	
Total setup time	8	8	6	4	26
Batch size	15,000	12,000	500	250	
Run length	158	128	12.7	9	

Note that the longest run length (bottom line in table) occurs for the basic product (158 hours). So, an additional setup would do the most good if applied to this product. Adding a second setup during the month for the basic product gives:

Product	Basic	Standard	Deluxe	Supreme	Total
Demand	15,000	12,000	500	250	
Setup time	8	8	6	4	
Process time	100	100	75	50	
No. setups (N)	2	1	1	1	
Total setup time	16	8	6	4	34
Batch size	7,500	12,000	500	250	
Run length	83	128	12.7	9	

We have used only 34 hours of setup time, so because the standard product now has the longest run time (128 hours), we allocate another setup to this product:

Product	Basic	Standard	Deluxe	Supreme	Total
Demand	15,000	12,000	500	250	
Setup time	8	8	6	4	
Process time	100	100	75	50	
No. setups (N)	2	2	1	1	
Total setup time	16	16	6	4	42
Batch size	7,500	6,000	500	250	
Run length	83	68	12.7	9	

Now the basic product again has the longest run time (83 hours). Because we still have time available to allocate to setups, we add a setup to this product:

Product	Basic	Standard	Deluxe	Supreme	Total
Demand	15,000	12,000	500	250	
Setup time	8	8	6	4	
Process time	100	100	75	50	
No. setups (N)	3	2	1	1	
Total setup time	24	16	6	4	50
Batch size	5,000	6,000	500	250	
Run length	58	68	12.7	9	

Because we have used up 50 of the 52.1 hours available for setups, we cannot add another setup without violating our 84.3 percent utilization target. In this final solution, we set the batch sizes so that the basic product runs three times in the month, the standard product runs twice, and the deluxe and supreme products each run once.

In Figure 3.6 we illustrate the schedule assuming we run all of the products in sequence at the beginning of the month and then rotate between the basic and standard products. By running these latter products more frequently, we minimize the wait a customer order for them would experience. Of course, the deluxe and supreme products are only run once per month, so if an order just misses this month's production, it will have to wait for next month. But, because many more customers order the basic and standard products, this is a reasonable way to allocate setup time to improve responsiveness to the majority of customers.

FIGURE 3.6

Batching
schedule to
minimize
maximum run
length

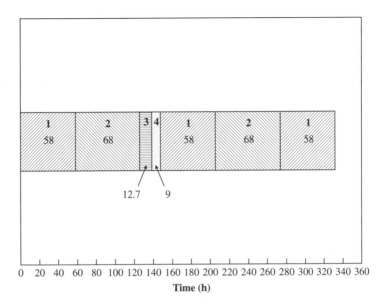

Notice that if we were able to reduce setup times, we could run the products more frequently given the same utilization target. For example, if we were to cut all the setup times in half in the previous example, then our setup allocation procedure would result in the following batch sizes:

Product	Basic	Standard	Deluxe	Supreme	Total
Demand	15,000	12,000	500	250	
Setup time	4	4	3	2	
Process time	100	100	75	50	
No. setups (N)	6	5	1	1	
Total setup time	24	20	3	2	49
Batch size	2,500	2,400	500	250	
Run length	29	28	9.7	7	

Because setups are half as long, we can do twice as many. However, because run lengths are still longer for the basic and standard products, it makes sense to add the extra setups to these products rather than increasing the number of setups assigned to the deluxe and supreme products. (Indeed, because the run lengths are still shorter for these less popular products, we might even consider running them every other month and keeping some inventory on hand to enable us to fill some orders between runs.) The resulting schedule is illustrated in Figure 3.7. Note that the shorter run lengths

FIGURE 3.7

Batching
schedule with
setups cut in
half

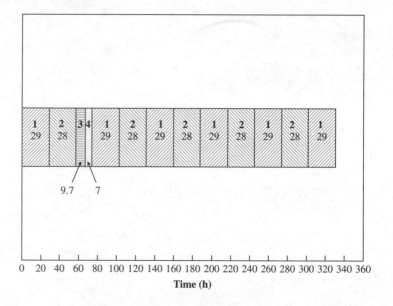

make the basic and standard products come up more frequently
during the month, implying that customers will have shorter waits.

Principles in Practice

TrusJoist MacMillan

TrusJoist MacMillan (TJM) makes an engineered lumber product
called Parallam® by chipping wood into thin narrow strips and then
compressing them with glue in a microwave curing press. The result is
a uniformly strong beam called a "billet" that can be sawed into structural members of various widths, thicknesses, and lengths. To avoid
waste, TJM cuts the end products out of different width billets. However, to change the width of the billet being produced requires cleaning
and resetting the press, a lengthy procedure. Therefore, to avoid losing
excessive capacity to setups, TJM runs a substantial batch of one width
(typically several days' worth) before switching the press to another
width.

The problem of deciding how much of each product to run between
setups matches almost exactly the multiproduct batching situation discussed in this chapter. While TJM could use a cyclic schedule (i.e.,
establish a product sequence and produce some of each product in this
sequence before going back to the beginning of the list and starting
over), our discussion above suggests that this would be inefficient. For

instance, suppose that TJM is thinking about running two cycles in a month, so that two batches of each billet width will be run during the month. But further suppose that only a small quantity is needed of one of the widths. Then it seems logical to run the entire month's demand for that width billet in a single batch and avoid the extra setup. This setup could be used to make three runs of one of the high-demand widths to reduce the inventory buildup it causes during the month or it could be left off altogether to reduce press utilization. The bottom line is that thinking in terms of distributing setups among products is likely to lead to a better schedule than thinking in terms of setting batch sizes for the product runs.

The TJM system has an interesting wrinkle that presents an opportunity for further reducing setups. Because Parallam is a construction product, its demand is seasonal. During the winter months, total demand is below capacity. But during the spring and early summer, demand significantly outstrips capacity. As a result, TJM builds up inventory in the off-season so that it can keep up with demand during the peak season. Conventional wisdom would dictate building up inventory of the most popular products because those are the most likely to sell. However, because of the strong effect of setups on the schedule, there may be reason to go against conventional wisdom.

To see how, suppose that the sum of the demand for products that are cut from one of the billet widths represents a fairly small fraction of total demand. If TJM were to produce a large percentage (e.g., 75 or 80 percent) of the amount of each of these products forecasted to be needed during the peak season, then it would be able to avoid running any billet of this size until well into the season. That is, it would fill orders for these products from stock. By eliminating the need to change over to this billet size, TJM could avoid some lengthy setups and use the extra time to produce much needed product of the other types.

In a cost-competitive industry like lumber and building products, intelligent use of batching can make a significant difference in profitability and long-term viability.

Questions for Thought

1. In old-fashioned computer systems, jobs were run in batch mode. That is, users brought in their programs (on decks of cards), they were queued up with a large number of other programs, and run as a large batch. Two days later, users would get the results (which often showed that a syntax error crashed out the entire program). While punch cards are a thing of the past, batch processing still exists in modern computers. In many situations, a computer can run several jobs in sequence faster than it can run them simultaneously (i.e., by doling out cycles of computing time to

the various jobs in process). Why do you think this is the case and how does it relate to the science of batching?

2. A "chip shooter" can place SMT (surface mount technology) components on circuit boards in 15 seconds. However, when the machine is changed from one product family to another, the components in the magazine must be changed. This takes 10 minutes.

   a. What is the minimum batch size needed for the chip shooter to run at a rate of 3 boards per minute?

   b. If management wants to run at a rate of 3 boards per minute but have utilization no higher than 80 percent (to keep queue time under control), what is the minimum batch size?

   c. What would batch size have to be to have utilization less than 75 percent (still with a run rate of 3 boards per minute)?

3. A large punch press stamps out sheet metal parts at a rate of 6 per minute. Changing the die to stamp out a different part currently requires 1 hour. If the desired rate of the process is 4 parts per minute, how much must the setup time be reduced to permit a lot size of 1?

P A R T

II LINE SCIENCE

4   FLOWS

A process flow is a sequence of processes and stock points through which entities pass to deliver a product or service to a customer.

4.1   Introduction

The performance of any operations system is evaluated in terms of an objective. This could involve making money (e.g., in a manufacturing system), serving people (e.g., in a public service system), or winning a war (e.g., in a military system). The fundamental link between a system's objective and its physical operations are the **process flows** that make up a production or supply chain system. For our purposes, we will define a flow[1] as follows:

Definition (Process Flow).   *A process flow (or flow, for short) is a sequence of processes and stock points through which entities pass to deliver a product or service to a customer.*

For example, a manufacturing line consists of several stations in tandem through which jobs flow. A hospital contains many connected sequences of operations (admission, in-room care, surgical prep, surgery, recovery, etc.) through which patients flow. A bank involves sequences of operations through which money flows. Understanding flows is fundamental to designing and managing effective operations systems.

---

[1]Throughout this book we use the terms *process flow, flow, routing,* and *line* interchangeably.

At the level of a flow, the following performance metrics relate most closely to overall system performance:

Throughput (TH): The rate of good (nondefective) entities processed per unit time. Tons of steel produced per day, cars assembled per shift, or customers served per hour are examples of throughput measures. Note that it is important not to count defective product, which must be reworked or remade, as part of throughput.

Cycle time (CT): Time between the release of an entity into a flow (routing) and its completion. In a flow that produces subcomponents, cycle time measures the time from when raw materials are drawn from a stock to when the component is placed in an intermediate crib inventory. In a flow that produces final products, cycle time measures the time from when the entity starts down the flow to when it is placed in finished goods inventory or shipped to the customer.

Work in process (WIP): Measurement of the inventory in a flow. Generally, WIP does not include raw materials or finished goods inventory. However, for flows that cut across multiple processes, it may include intermediate crib inventories. While there is some flexibility in defining the start and end of a flow, it is important that the same definitions be used for both WIP and CT to make these consistent.

We know from Chapter 1 that these measures are related by Little's law, so that $WIP = TH \times CT$. But how else are they related? For instance, how is TH affected by WIP? If we reduce WIP in a given flow (e.g., by implementing kanban) without making any other changes, what happens to output? Clearly, because WIP and TH are key performance measures, this is an important question.

Little's law, written in the form $TH = WIP/CT$, also suggests that the same throughput can be achieved with a large WIP and long CT or with a low WIP and short CT. How broad a range is possible? What factors make a system capable of achieving a high level of TH with a low WIP? Again, these are important questions that are at the root of lean production practices. To understand how to use these practices to design high-efficiency flows we must first understand the basics of how flows behave.

4.2   Characterizing Flows

The first step in understanding flows is to characterize their basic behavior as simply as possible. To do this, we compare flows to conveyors, because a stream of entities flowing through a sequence

FIGURE 4.1

The conveyor
model of a
process flow

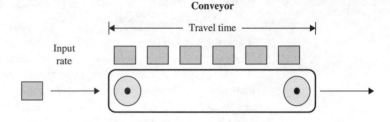

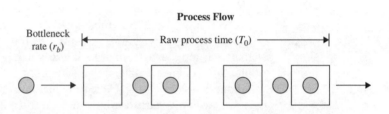

of processes behaves much like a stream of items being transported
down a moving conveyor (see Figure 4.1). The basic behavior of a
conveyor is described by two parameters: the *rate* at which items
are placed on the front and removed from the end of the conveyor,
and the *time* it takes an item to go down the conveyor. Analogously,
the behavior of a process flow depends on two parameters:

Bottleneck rate (BNR): Capacity of the flow (i.e., the rate of
the process with the highest utilization).

Raw process time (RPT): Total time entities spend being
processed in the flow (i.e., the average time it would take an
entity to traverse an empty flow).

It turns out that a wide range of performance is possible for a given
(BNR, RPT) pair. We examine how and why this occurs below.

4.3   Best-Case Performance

We start by considering the best possible performance for a line
with a given bottleneck rate (BNR) and raw process time (RPT).
We do this by making use of the simple production line shown in
Figure 4.2, which we refer to as the *Penny Fab*. This stylized line
produces large pennies for use in Fourth of July parades and consists
of four processes: head stamping (H-Stamp), which stamps the head
design on a penny blank; tail stamping (T-Stamp), which stamps
on the tail design; rimming (Rim), which places a rim around the
penny; and deburring (Deburr), which removes any sharp burrs.
Each operation requires exactly 2 minutes to perform.

FIGURE 4.2

The Penny Fab

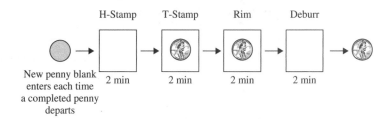

Notice that in this line, the processing rates of all stations are identical and equal to 1 penny every 2 minutes or 0.5 pennies per minute. Because all pennies pass through all operations, every station is a bottleneck and the bottleneck rate is BNR $= 0.5$ pennies per minute. The raw process time is the time it takes a single penny to traverse an empty line, which is RPT $= 8$ minutes.

We would like to characterize the Penny Fab performance in terms of three basic measures—throughput, WIP, and cycle time—and also examine the relationships among these measures. To do this, we perform a thought experiment in which we hold the WIP level in the line constant and observe the other two measures. For instance, for a WIP level of 1, we release 1 penny blank into the front of the line and wait until it is completely finished before releasing another. Because each penny takes 8 minutes to finish, throughput is 1 penny every 8 minutes or TH $= 0.125$ pennies per minute and the cycle time is CT $= 8$ minutes.

When we increase the WIP level to 2 pennies, we start by releasing two blanks into the system and then wait and release another blank each time a finished penny exits the line. Although the second blank must wait 2 minutes to get into the H-Stamp station (because it was released into the line simultaneously with the first blank), this is a transient effect that does not occur after the start of the experiment. It is easy to see that in the long run, the pennies will follow one another through the line, taking 8 minutes to get through and resulting in an output of 2 pennies every 8 minutes. Hence, TH $= 0.25$ pennies per minute and CT $= 8$ minutes.

Increasing the WIP level to 3 pennies causes throughput to rise to 3 pennies every 8 minutes, or TH $= 0.375$ pennies per minute. Again, after an initial transient period in which the second and third blanks wait at H-Stamp, there is no waiting at any station and therefore each penny requires exactly 8 minutes to complete. Hence, cycle time is still CT $= 8$ minutes.

When WIP is increased to 4 pennies, something special happens. Six minutes after the four blanks are released to the line, the first penny reaches the last station, and each of the four processes has 1 penny to work on. From this point onward, all stations are constantly busy. This means that a penny finishes at the last station every 2 minutes so TH $= 0.5$ penny per minute, which is the maximum output the line can achieve (i.e., the bottleneck rate BNR). In addition, because each machine completes its penny at exactly the same time, no penny must wait at a process before beginning work. Therefore, CT $= 8$ minutes, the minimum value possible (i.e., the raw process time RPT). This special WIP level, which results in both maximum throughput and minimum cycle time, is called the **critical WIP**.

In a balanced line (i.e., one where all processes require the same amount of time) made up of single server[2] stations, the critical WIP always equals the number of stations, because each station requires one job to remain busy. In lines with unbalanced capacities at the stations (e.g., where some of the stations consist of multiple servers in parallel), the critical WIP may be less than the total number of machines in the system. The critical WIP can be computed from the bottleneck rate and raw process time by using Little's law.

Definition (Critical WIP).   *The* WIP *level that achieves the maximum throughput* (BNR) *and minimum cycle time* (RPT) *in a process flow with no variability is called the critical* WIP *(CWIP) and is computed as*

$$CWIP = BNR \times RPT$$

If we increase the WIP level above the critical WIP, say to 5 pennies, then waiting (queueing) begins to occur. With 5 pennies in the line, there must always be 1 waiting at the front of the first process because there are only four machines in the line. This means that each penny will wait an additional minute before beginning work in the line. The result will be that while TH $= 1$ penny per minute, as was the case when WIP was 4 pennies, and CT $= 10$ minutes, due to the waiting time. Increasing the WIP level even more will not increase throughput, because TH $= 1$ penny per minute is the capacity of the line, but will increase the cycle time by causing even more waiting.

We summarize the TH and CT that result from WIP levels between 1 and 10 in Table 4.1. Notice that these data satisfy Little's law, WIP $=$ TH $\times$ CT. This is to be expected, because as we know from Chapter 2, Little's law applies to much more general systems than this simple Penny Fab.

---

[2]Recall that we use the term *server* to denote a machine, operator, or whatever resource is used to perform processing at the station.

TABLE 4.1   Results for best-case Penny Fab

WIP	TH	CT	TH × CT
1	0.125	8	1
2	0.250	8	2
3	0.375	8	3
4	0.500	8	4
5	0.500	10	5
6	0.500	12	6
7	0.500	14	7
8	0.500	16	8
9	0.500	18	9
10	0.500	20	10

TH and CT as functions of WIP are plotted in Figure 4.3. We refer to this as the **best case** because it represents a system with absolutely regular processing times. If we were lucky enough to manage such a line, it is clear that the optimal strategy would be to maintain WIP right at the critical level (4 pennies). This would maximize throughput while minimizing cycle time. Lower WIP levels would cause a loss of throughput, and hence revenue, while higher WIP levels would inflate cycle time with no increase in throughput. Unfortunately, virtually no real-world manufacturing line is as nicely behaved as this. Still, considering it gives us a baseline from which to judge actual performance.

We can sum up the best-case behavior shown in Figure 4.3 by observing that TH cannot be greater than the bottleneck rate BNR. Furthermore, Little's law, TH = WIP/CT, and the fact that CT ≥ RPT implies that TH cannot be greater than WIP/RPT. Likewise, CT can never be less than the raw process time RPT. Writing Little's law as CT = WIP/TH and noting that TH ≤ BNR implies that

FIGURE 4.3 Throughput and cycle time vs. WIP in the Penny Fab

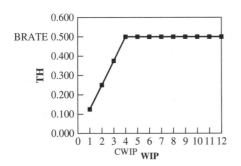
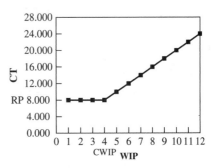

CT ≥ WIP/BNR. Hence, we can summarize the behavior shown in Figure 4.3 in the following principle for flows:

Principle (Best-Case Performance).   *Any process flow with bottleneck rate BNR, raw process time RPT, and work-in-process level WIP will have*

$$\text{TH} \leq \min \left\{ \frac{\text{WIP}}{\text{RPT}}, \ \text{BNR} \right\}$$

$$\text{CT} \geq \max \left\{ \text{RPT}, \ \frac{\text{WIP}}{\text{BNR}} \right\}$$

4.4   Worst-Case Performance

The Penny Fab example gives us an indication of how flows behave under the best of circumstances. But no real-world production system operates under these conditions. As we stressed in Chapter 2, virtually all processes involve some amount of variability, which degrades their performance. So a question of interest is, how bad can a flow perform? That is, what is the minimum TH and maximum CT that could occur for a specified WIP level, given the parameters BNR and RPT?

To answer this question, consider the production line shown in Figure 4.4, which we call the *Nickel Fab*. Similar to the Penny Fab, this line produces giant novelty nickels for use in Fourth of July parades. But unlike the Penny Fab, it uses a three-step process (H-Stamp, T-Stamp, Finishing) and is not a balanced line. H-Stamp and T-Stamp take 1 minute per nickel, while Finishing takes 2 minutes. Therefore, the bottleneck rate is BNR = 0.5 nickels per minute and the raw process time is RPT = 4 minutes. The critical WIP (CWIP) is

$$\text{CWIP} = \text{BNR} \times \text{RPT} = 0.5 \times 4 = 2 \text{ nickels}$$

Notice that unlike the Penny Fab, the critical WIP is not equal to the number of stations in the line. Unbalanced lines generally have

FIGURE 4.4

The Nickel Fab

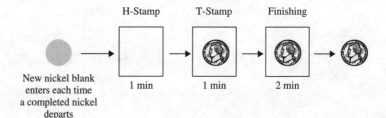

critical WIP levels below the number of stations because all stations do not need to be 100 percent busy to achieve full throughput under best-case conditions. In the Nickel Fab, 2 pennies are enough to fill up the line, because H-Stamp and T-Stamp can complete their operations during the time it takes Finish to process a nickel.

Now let us perform a thought experiment to answer the question of how bad performance can get for a given WIP level. As we did for the Penny Fab, we will suppose that the WIP level is held fixed by only allowing a new nickel to enter the line each time one is finished. Furthermore, we imagine ourselves riding through the line on one of the nickels. Clearly, the worst cycle time we could possibly experience would occur if each time we reach a station we find every other nickel in queue ahead of us (see Figure 4.5). One way this could happen would be if all the nickels in the line were moved together between stations (e.g., on a nickel forklift). Under these conditions, if there are w nickels in the line, the time to get through each station is w times the process time at that station; hence cycle time is w times the total processing time, or $w \times$ RPT. By Little's law,

$$ \text{TH} = \frac{\text{WIP}}{\text{CT}} = \frac{w}{w \times \text{RPT}} = \frac{1}{\text{RPT}} $$

FIGURE 4.5

Worst-possible performance of a process flow

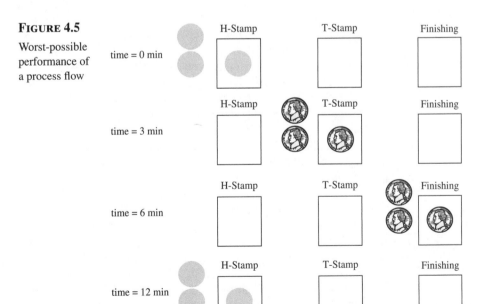

FIGURE 4.6 Throughput and cycle time vs. WIP in the Nickel Fab

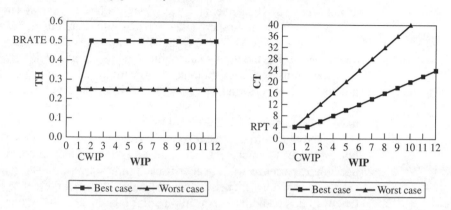

Because we cannot possibly do worse than this, we have identified another principle governing flows:

Principle (Worst-Case Performance).   *Any process flow with
bottleneck rate* BNR*, raw process time* RPT*, and work-in-process
level* WIP *will have*

$$TH \geq \frac{1}{RPT}$$
$$CT \leq WIP \times RPT$$

Figure 4.6 illustrates this worst-case performance for the Nickel
Fab and contrasts it with the best-case performance for this line.
Note that there is a huge difference between best- and worst-case
behavior. Interestingly, this difference has nothing to do with randomness or uncertainty in the process times; both the best and worst
cases have completely deterministic processing times. What causes
the performance of the worst case to be so bad is either *batching* or
variability, depending on how we view the mechanics of the worst
case.

On one hand, we can interpret the cause of the extreme queueing observed in the worst case as being that all entities are moved
between stations in a single batch. On the other hand, we can view
the queueing as being caused by highly variable process times; that
is, one entity has process time at station i of wt_i (where t_i is the
process time at station i and w is the WIP level) and all other entities have zero process times. Logically, the system with extremely
variable process times behaves the same as the system with extreme batching; the entities with zero process times will always
be waiting in queue behind the entity with the long process times.
But, of course, the physical causes of batching and variability are
different. Batching is due to setups and material handling issues,

while variability is the result of many factors, including quality, reliability, staffing, scheduling, and others. In practice, what this means is that either large batching or variability problems can push the performance of a process flow toward that of the worst case.

4.5 Practical Worst-Case Performance

The worst case is *so* bad, however, that it is not a very practical benchmark for evaluating actual systems. A process flow need not be close to the worst case to offer room for substantial improvement. To provide a more realistic point of comparison, we introduce the **practical worst case** (**PWC**). The PWC occurs for a line that satisfies the following three conditions:

1. *Balanced flow.* All stations in the flow have the same capacity. Because it is clear that increasing the capacity of any station can only help performance with regard to TH and CT, it follows that the worst behavior we can see for a given bottleneck rate, BNR, will occur when all stations work at this rate (and hence are bottlenecks too).

2. *Single-server stations.* All stations consist of one server, and hence can only work on one entity at a time. If a station had multiple servers working in parallel, then when one server experiences a delay, entities can continue to flow through the other servers. (This is why banks typically organize tellers in parallel to serve a single queue of customers; when one teller gets tied up on a long transaction, customers are automatically routed to other tellers.) Hence, process flows with single-server stations exhibit worse performance (higher CT) than flows with multiple-server stations.

3. *Moderately high variability.* Process times of entities at every station are so variable that the standard deviation of the process times equals the mean process time. Equivalently, the coefficient of variation (CV) of all process times equals 1. While this is not the worst possible situation (we could have CV > 1), it is a fairly high level of variability for most practical situations. As we noted in Table 2.1, it generally takes something more than the actual processing times (e.g., setup times, station failures, staffing outages, etc.) to cause effective process times to exhibit this much variability.

To see how the practical worst case behaves, consider a third example, the *Dime Fab*, which produces giant novelty dimes (no one knows why). The Dime Fab has four stations just like the Penny Fab (H-Stamp, T-Stamp, Rim, Deburr) with the same process times (2 minutes at every station). Thus, the bottleneck rate is BNR = 0.5

FIGURE 4.7 Throughput and cycle time vs. WIP in the Dime Fab

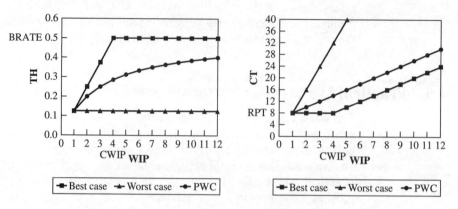

and raw process time is RPT = 8 minutes, just like the Penny Fab. However, unlike the Penny Fab, the process times in the Dime Fab are variable—indeed they are so variable that the CVs of the process times at all stations are equal to 1. Thus, the Dime Fab satisfies all three conditions of the practical worst case.

The performance of the Dime Fab is illustrated in Figure 4.7, along with the best-case and worst-case performance for this line. Notice that for each WIP level, the practical worst-case achieves more throughput than the worst case, but less than the best case. Because the three assumptions we made to define the practical worst case describe fairly inefficient behavior, we label the region between the PWC and the worst case as the "bad region." The region between the PWC and the best case is the "good region." To put it another way, a process flow operating in the bad region is one where significant improvement opportunities probably exist. One operating in the good region represents a case where improvements are likely to be small and hence we should probably look elsewhere for opportunities.

Qualitatively, we see from Figure 4.7 that the PWC is closer to the best case than the worst case. Hence, to be "good" a process flow should not be anywhere near the worst case. To give a precise definition of "good," we can use the following expression for the throughput of the PWC:[3]

Definition (PWC performance).   *The throughput of a process flow with bottleneck rate BNR and raw process time RPT that*

---

[3]For a derivation of the throughput of the practical worst case as a function of WIP, see Hopp and Spearman (2000, Chapter 7).

satisfies the conditions of the practical worst case is

$$TH_{PWC} = \frac{WIP}{WIP + CWIP - 1} BNR$$

where $CWIP = BNR \times RPT$ *is the critical* WIP.

4.6   Internal Benchmarking

The formula for TH_{PWC} provides a very simple **internal bench-mark** (i.e., comparison of performance against theoretical capability) of a process flow. Note that this is different from an **external benchmark**, which is a standard of comparison based on performance of another system. To evaluate this internal benchmark, we need only collect four parameters: bottleneck rate (BNR), raw process time (RPT), average work-in-process (WIP) level, and actual throughput (TH). With the first three of these we can compute TH_{PWC}. If $TH > TH_{PWC}$, then the flow is in the good region; otherwise it is in the bad region.

To illustrate the use of the PWC formula as an internal benchmarking tool, we consider the process flow illustrated in Figure 4.8, which represents the order-entry system for a manufacturer of institutional office cabinets. To get from a customer request to a factory order involves six distinct steps. The capacities and times required for each step are given in Figure 4.8. Notice that the capacity of a single station need not be the inverse of its average process time. For instance, Engineering Design requires 8 hours, but has a capacity of 2 per hour. The reason is that, while an individual designer requires an average of 8 hours to complete the task, there are 16 designers working in parallel, so the capacity is $16(1/8) = 2$ per hour.

The bottleneck of the order-entry system is Engineering Design, because it has the least capacity and all orders pass through all processes. This means that Engineering Design will have the highest utilization among the processes in the flow. Thus, the bottleneck rate is BNR $= 2$ orders per hour. The raw process time is the sum of the process times, which is RPT $= 10.73$ hours. This implies that the critical WIP is

$$CWIP = BNR \times RPT = 2 \times 10.73 = 21.46 \text{ jobs}$$

Now, suppose that over the past several months, the throughput of the order-entry system has averaged 1.25 jobs per hour and the

FIGURE 4.8 An order-entry system

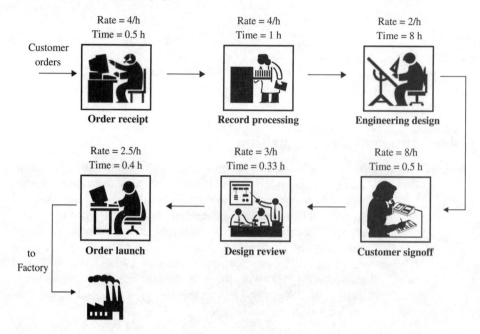

average number of customer orders in process (WIP level) has been 60. Is this good or bad performance?

To answer this question, we use the PWC formula to compute what the throughput would be for a flow that has the same parameters as those of order entry and satisfies the conditions of the practical worst case. This yields

$$\text{TH}_{\text{PWC}} = \frac{\text{WIP}}{\text{WIP} + \text{CWIP} - 1}\text{BNR} = \frac{60}{60 + 21.46 - 1}2 = 1.49$$

Hence, we can conclude that a PWC line would achieve higher throughput for a WIP level of 60 than does the actual line. This is a sign of serious problems. Either batching or variability is causing the system to be very inefficient in translating work-in-process into throughput.

One possible problem in this particular system could be high variability in the arrival of customer orders. This could be due to the manner in which customers schedule purchases (e.g., their planning process tends to make them all place orders at the beginning or end of the week). Or it could be due to the manner in which the firm quotes due dates (e.g., all orders placed during the week are given the same due date, thereby giving customers incentive to place orders on Friday). The result in either case would be periodic crushes of orders. While the system may have capacity to handle the volume in a steady flow, such crushes will temporarily overwhelm the system and result in delays and high WIP levels. If arrivals are indeed a major source of variability, then actions to smooth customer orders would significantly improve system performance.

4.7 Variability Propagation

Given the bottleneck rate, BNR, and the raw process time, RPT, there are two factors that degrade performance relative to the best case: *variability* and *batching*. The reason the PWC line achieves less throughput for a given WIP level than does a best-case line is that the PWC assumes highly variable process times. The reason the worst-case line achieves even less throughput for a given WIP level than does the PWC is that it uses extremely large (i.e., equal to the WIP level) move batches. We know from Chapters 2 and 3 that variability and batching degrade the performance of single stations. Not surprisingly, they also degrade the performance of flows.

However, the impact of variability and batching is more subtle in a flow than in a single station because these behaviors propagate between stations. In the case of batching, this is obvious. For instance, if all stations in a line process and move entities in batches, then the waiting time caused by batching will be the sum of the waiting times at the individual stations. The batches propagate from one station to the next and so does the waiting they cause.

The propagation of variability in a flow is not as obvious as the propagation of batches, but it is just as real and just as corrosive to performance. To see how it works, consider a station that experiences both **flow variability** (i.e., variability in the interarrival times of entities to the station) and **process variability** (i.e., variability in the process times at the station). The way this station will pass variability on to the next station in the flow is by generating variable interoutput times. Because these will be the interarrival times to the next station, variability in them will cause queueing delay at the downstream station.

As one would expect, the flow variability that comes out of a station depends on both the flow variability coming into it and the process variability created at the station itself. But how much it depends on each of these is a function of station utilization. Figure 4.9 illustrates this. The left side of Figure 4.9 shows the behavior of a very high utilization station. Because it is heavily utilized, a queue will generally be present in front of this station. Therefore, regardless of how arrivals come to the station, they will

FIGURE 4.9 Propagation of flow variability

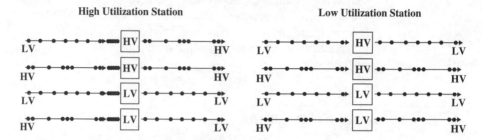

generally wait in queue before being processed. This means that the interoutput times will be almost identical to the process times. So, if the station is highly variable, the outputs will also be highly variable. If the station has low process variability, the outputs will also be of low variability.

The right side of Figure 4.9 shows the behavior of a very low utilization station. In this case, interarrival times are significantly longer on average than process times. To consider an extreme case, suppose arrivals come on average once per hour but process times average 1 minute. Such a station will be idle most of the time. So, interoutput times will be almost identical to interarrival times (lagged by 1 minute). Whether the process times are highly variable (e.g., they vary from 10 seconds to 3 minutes) or very predictable (e.g., they are exactly 1 minute) will make little difference in the interoutput times. So, in low-utilization stations, high-variability arrivals will translate into high-variability departures, while low-variability arrivals will produce low-variability departures.

In realistic stations, with utilization levels that are neither very close to 1, nor very close to 0, the departure variability will be a weighted sum of the arrival variability and process variability. The insight we can draw from this is that whenever we create variability in the system (e.g., through machine failures, setups, quality problems, operator behavior, information problems, or whatever), this variability will propagate to downstream stations by causing uneven arrivals and hence congestion.

To illustrate the effects of variability propagation, let us consider a two-station segment of an electronics assembly line. The first station (Inspect) consists of an automated machine that takes an average of 5.1 minutes to process a job. This machine exhibits moderate variability in processing times (due to differences in the product and the number of test cycles it goes through) and is also subject to failures, with a mean time to failure (MTTF) of 200 hours and a mean time to repair (MMTR) of 8 hours. The second station is a manual operation staffed by a single operator who takes on average 5.7 minutes to inspect each job. These inspection times are subject to moderate variability, but there are no failures at the second station. Jobs arrive to this segment of the line at a rate of 10 jobs per hour with moderate variability in the interarrival times.

To determine which machine is the bottleneck, we need to compare utilizations. The availability (AVAIL) at the first station is the fraction of uptime, or

$$AVAIL = \frac{MTTF}{MTTF + MTTR} = \frac{200}{200 + 8} = 0.962$$

The capacity of station 1 is therefore

$$capacity\ of\ station\ 1 = (1/5.1) \times 0.962 = 0.188\ jobs/min$$
$$= 11.3\ jobs/h$$

and the utilization is

$$utilization\ of\ station\ 1 = \frac{rate\ in}{capacity} = \frac{10\ jobs/h}{11.3\ jobs/h} = 88.4\ percent$$

The capacity of station 2 is

$$capacity\ of\ station\ 2 = (1/5.7) = 0.175\ jobs/min = 10.5\ jobs/h$$

so the utilization is

$$utilization\ of\ station\ 2 = \frac{rate\ in}{capacity} = \frac{10\ jobs/h}{10.5\ jobs/h} = 95\ percent$$

Because it has higher utilization, the second station is the bottleneck. Hence, we would expect the second station to experience more queueing and longer delays than the first station. And it does. Performance statistics for the system show that, on average, jobs spend about 6 hours at the second station, compared to about 3 hours at the first station. The average queue length is about 60 jobs at the second station, but only about 30 jobs at the first station.

But only part of the congestion at the second station is due to high utilization. Process variability created at the second station and flow variability that comes from the first station also add to the congestion. In fact, flow variability from the first station is very significant because that station has high process variability due to the long repair times and high utilization, which means that the process variability is converted into departure variability.

If we reduce the repair times at the first station from 8 hours to 4 hours, the average time at that station falls from 3 hours to

1.3 hours and the average number of jobs falls from 30 jobs to 13 jobs. This is hardly surprising, because from Chapter 2 we know that reducing variability improves performance. More interesting, however, is that halving repair times at the first station causes total time at the second station to fall from 6 hours to 3 hours and the average number of jobs to fall from 60 to 30. Reducing repair times reduced process variability at the first station, which reduced flow variability into the second station, which resulted in a dramatic improvement in the downstream station. We see that variability reduction at a nonbottleneck station can have a significant impact on the performance of the bottleneck and hence of the entire flow.

Finally, our discussion of flow variability has only noted that variability can propagate downstream. In "push" systems, where entities are processed without regard for the status of downstream stations, this is the only direction variability can move. However, in "pull" systems, where processing at an upstream station is governed by the needs of the downstream station, then variability can also propagate upstream. For example, in the penny (and nickel and dime) examples discussed earlier, a new job was not started until one was completed. This constant work-in-process (CONWIP) protocol is an example of a simple pull system. Because every time a job exited the last station a new one entered the first station, the departure variability from the last station becomes the arrival variability of the first station. We will discuss CONWIP and the general concepts underlying pull systems in Chapter 6. For now, we will simply stress that variability, along with batching, is the dominant factor that degrades performance of process flows relative to best-case performance. Therefore, understanding variability and finding ways to drive it out are at the core of many operations improvement methodologies.

Insight by Analogy

A Stadium Parking Lot

What happens at the end of a ballgame? Depending on the outcome there is some cheering or jeering in the stands. There might be some postgame entertainment (e.g., fireworks). But inevitably a crush of people descends on the parking lot and experiences a big traffic jam. At a big event it isn't uncommon to spend 30 minutes or more sitting in the car waiting for the congestion to clear.

Why does this occur? The quick answer is that the crowd overwhelms the capacity of the parking lot and adjacent streets. However, if we think about the situation a bit longer, we realize that it isn't simply a problem of capacity. We can view the stadium as a giant process that puts out people during the 3-hour (or so) duration of the game and sends them to the next process in the flow, the parking lot. But the stadium does not produce people smoothly. During the first 2 hours of the game almost no one leaves, so interoutput times might be 10 or 15 minutes. During the last hour, the flow starts to increase (particularly if the home team is getting hammered), so that interoutput times may drop below 1 minute. But then, all of a sudden, the flow spikes, to the point that interoutput times are a fraction of a second. In the terms of this chapter, the stadium is a highly variable process that feeds a second process of limited capacity. The result is that the parking lot experiences high variability and hence high delay.

What can be done to improve performance in this system? A theoretical option would be to smooth the flow to the parking lot. If people were to leave the stadium at uniform intervals over the 3-hour game there would be virtually no delay in the parking lot. However, because fans are unlikely to react well to being told that they must leave at specified times (imagine being stuck in the section that must leave during the first inning), this option is of limited use. Postgame activities that delay the departure of some fans may help, but the parking lot still gets hit with a crush of people at the end of the game. Another option is to try to increase the capacity of the parking lot. Many stadiums do exactly this, by opening many alternate exit routes, altering stoplights, and blocking off streets. But because capacity is still limited and arrival variability to the parking lot is very high, delays still occur.

Parking lot delay may be one of the prices we must pay to participate in sporting and other mass entertainment events. However, having a production or supply chain system that sends bursts of work to downstream operations is usually avoidable. Machines with long setups or failures, schedules that run products in batches, and staffing policies that periodically idle certain operations are examples of voluntary steps that serve to feed work to downstream processes in uneven waves. The consequence of these waves is the same as those in the stadium parking lot—congestion and delay. Moderating the waves, by reducing setups, speeding repairs, or modifying batching and scheduling policies, will reduce these negative consequences.

4.8   Improving Performance of Process Flows

The previously described benchmarking procedure using the PWC formula only captures one category of inefficiency. That is, it can only tell us how efficient a line is *given* the parameters BNR and RPT. It cannot tell us whether the bottleneck rate or raw process time could be improved. But, because these parameters incorporate detractors (downtime, setups, yield loss, etc.) they may also be amenable to improvement.

This suggests two routes for enhancing performance of a process flow:

1. *Improve system parameters.* Increase the bottleneck rate BNR or decrease the raw process time RPT. Speeding up the bottleneck increases BNR, while speeding up any nonbottleneck process reduces RPT. Processes can be sped up by either adding capacity (e.g., replacing a machine with a newer, faster one) or via more subtle means such as improving reliability, yield, staffing, or quality.

Figure 4.10 illustrates the effect on performance from changes that improve the parameters of a process flow. Part (a) illustrates the effect of increasing the bottleneck rate from 0.5 to 0.67 in the Penny and Dime Fabs. Part (b) illustrates the effect of reducing the process times at two of the stations from 2 minutes to 1.5 minutes and one of the stations from 2 minutes to 1 minute, so that raw process time is reduced to RPT $= 6$, while the bottleneck rate remains unchanged at BNR $= 0.5$. Notice that the effect of increasing the rate of a bottleneck is much more dramatic than that of increasing the rate of a nonbottleneck, both for an ideal system (Penny Fab) and a system with variability (Dime Fab). The reason is that speeding up the bottleneck adds capacity to the system, while speeding up a nonbottleneck does not. However, speeding up a nonbottleneck does have a beneficial effect, especially in systems with variability, because faster nonbottlenecks are better able to feed the bottleneck.

2. *Improve performance given parameters.* Alter the performance curves in Figure 4.6 to move away from the worst case and toward the best case. The two primary means for doing this are to (1) reduce batching delays at or between processes by means of setup reduction, better scheduling, and/or more efficient material handling; and (2) reduce delays caused by variability via changes in products, processes, operators, and management that enable smoother flows through and between stations.

Figure 4.11 illustrates the effect on performance that improves a flow's efficiency for a given set of parameters. Specifically, this figure illustrates the effect of reducing the variability at all stations in the Dime Fab such that the CV is reduced from 1 to 0.25. Notice that the capacity of the system is unchanged. However, because stations are less variable, they starve less often and hence the system achieves higher throughput for a given WIP level.

The specific steps required to achieve these improvements will depend on the details of the operations system. Furthermore, as we noted in Chapter 0, the desired balance of performance measures

FIGURE 4.10

Improving
system
parameters

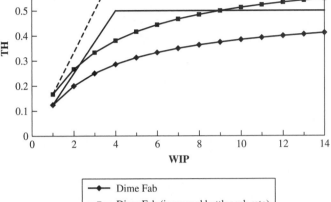

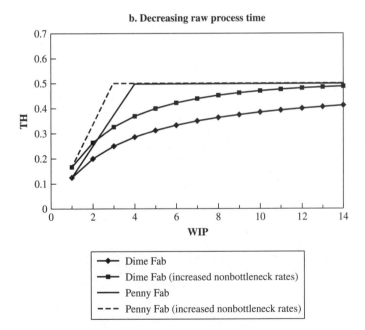

FIGURE 4.11

Improving
efficiency given
system
parameters

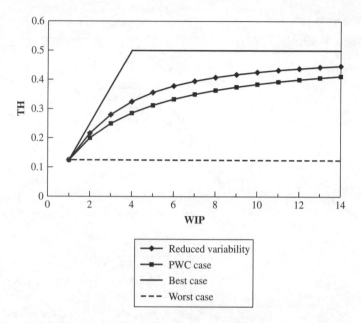

(TH, CT, WIP, service, flexibility, cost) depend on the business strategy. We will explore these trade-offs more extensively in Chapter 5 in the context of variability buffering.

Principles in Practice

IBM

In the early 1990s IBM operated a plant that made raw (unpopulated) circuit boards. One operation near the end of the line, called Procoat, applied a protective plastic coating to the boards so that their delicate circuitry would not be damaged in later assembly (board stuffing) operations. But Procoat was having serious throughput problems and as a result the plant was using an (expensive) outside vendor to provide the needed capacity.

With some simplification, the Procoat process consisted of the following steps:

Coating: Uncured coating in liquid form was applied to both sides of the board.

Expose: Photographically exposed portions of the coating were removed to allow attachment of surface-mount components.

Develop: The exposed portions of the coating were developed off.

Bake: The remaining coating was baked into a hard plastic.

Inspect: Any defects in the coating were detected and repaired.

Capacity calculations showed that Expose, with a capacity of about 2,900 boards per day, was the bottleneck. The raw process time, estimated as the sum of the average times for a job to go through each of the above steps, was about half a day. WIP in the line averaged about 1,500 boards. (Note that this is only about a half day's worth of production; because many of the operations consisted of connected conveyors, there was little space to build up excess WIP.) But—and this was the major problem—throughput was averaging only about 1,150 boards per day.

Even though it was blatantly obvious to the managers in charge that the performance of Procoat was not acceptable, we can document this with the internal benchmarking technique given in this chapter. Using BNR = 2,900 and RPT = 0.5 (so that CWIP = BNR × RPT = 2,900 × 0.5 = 1,450) we can compute the throughput that would result in a Practical Worst Case line with WIP = 1,500 to be

$$\text{TH}_{\text{PWC}} = \frac{\text{WIP}}{\text{WIP} + \text{CWIP} - 1}\text{BNR}$$

$$= \frac{1,500}{1,500 + 1,450 - 1}2,900 = 1,475 \text{ boards/day}$$

Because actual throughput of 1,150 per day is significantly less than this, we can conclude that Procoat is ripe for improvement.

The place to start the search for improvement options is at Expose, because it is the bottleneck. One opportunity, suggested by the operators themselves, was to have people from Inspect take over the Expose operation during lunch breaks. Because the line ran three shifts a day, this added 90 minutes per day of additional time at the bottleneck. Management was able to further supplement capacity at Expose by having the most productive operators train the other operators in the most effective procedures.

Further improvements required looking beyond the bottleneck. The Coater was subject to periodic failures that lasted an average of 4 hours. In the terms of this chapter this meant that the Coater subjected Expose to a highly variable arrival process. Normally this would have produced a large queue in front of Expose. However, because Expose was inside a clean room with very limited space for WIP, this was not possible. Instead, the failures would cause Expose to use whatever WIP it had and then starve. Because the time lost to starvation could never be made up (because Expose was the bottleneck), the result was a serious degradation in throughput. Therefore, to address the problem the maintenance staff adopted new procedures to make sure repairs started promptly and stocked field-ready replacement parts to facilitate faster completion of them. The shorter downtimes smoothed the flow of work into Expose and made it more likely that it would be able to keep running.

The net effect of these and a few other changes was to increase capacity to about 3,125 panels per day (so that CWIP = BNR × RPT = 3,125 × 0.5 = 1,562.5) and actual throughput to about 2,650 per day with no additional equipment and virtually no change in WIP level. Comparing this to the practical worst case benchmark of

$$TH_{PWC} = \frac{WIP}{WIP + CWIP - 1} BNR$$

$$= \frac{1,500}{1,500 + 1,562.5 - 1} 3,125 = 1,531 \text{ boards/day}$$

we see that performance after the improvements significantly exceeded that of the PWC. Even more important, these changes permitted IBM to save the substantial cost of having boards coated by the outside vendor.

Questions for Thought

1. Consider Figure 4.12. The mean process times represent the time for a single server to process an entity. Each entity must visit all four stations, but needs to be processed by only one server at that station.

   a. What are the bottleneck rate (BNR), raw process time (RPT), and critical WIP (CWIP) for this line?

   b. How does the critical WIP compare to the total number of servers (larger or smaller)? How can the line stay fully busy with this number of entities in it?

   c. Is the fourth server at station 2 necessary? Why or why not?

2. A supply chain for producing personal computers consists of three basic processes carried out in separate plants in close proximity to one another. The first process is the Panel Plant, which produces raw circuit boards. The second is the ECAT (Electronic Card Assembly and Test) Plant, which attaches the electronic components to the integrated circuit boards.

FIGURE 4.12

Sample process flow with parallel servers

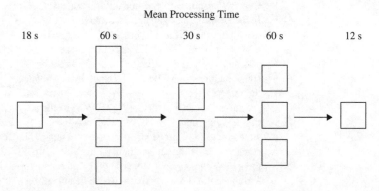

Mean Processing Time

| 18 s | 60 s | 30 s | 60 s | 12 s |

The third is the Box Plant, which assembles the populated (stuffed) circuit boards into the computers.

The capacities of the Panel, ECAT, and Box plants are 1,000, 1,000, and 950 per day measured in PC equivalents (e.g., if a PC requires two circuit boards, then a plant that produces 1,000 PC equivalents per day produces 2,000 circuit boards per day). Using current batch sizes and accounting for time to move parts from one plant to another, the raw process times (minimum average times for a batch to go through the plant and be delivered to the next plant) for the Panel, ECAT, and Box plants are 8 hours, 16 hours, and 12 hours. All three plants work 24 hours per day, 7 days per week.

a. Suppose there is no yield loss at any of the plants. What are the bottleneck rate (BNR), raw process time (RPT), and critical WIP (CWIP) for this system?

b. Now suppose that there is a 10 percent yield loss after ECAT. (That is, the last operation in the ECAT process is a test, which indicates 10 percent of the boards are defective.) How does this change the bottleneck rate (BNR)? If defective boards can go through the Panel and ECAT plants a second time (with the same process times as the first pass) and yield on the second pass is 100 percent, what is the raw process time (RPT)? (Hint: Remember that RPT is the average time for an entity to go through the flow with no waiting [queueing] time.)

c. Compute the critical WIP (CWIP) for the line with yield loss. Why is this number higher than that for the line without yield loss?

3. Suppose we are examining a flow and have determined that BNR = 500 units per day and RPT = 12 hours (half a day).

a. What is the minimum amount of WIP that could be in the system for it to run at full capacity?

b. If the system behaves like the best case, what would the throughput be if WIP is set at 250 units?

c. If the system behaves like the worst case, what would the throughput be if WIP is set at 250 units?

d. If the system behaves like the practical worst case, what would the throughput be if WIP is set at 250 units?

e. How much WIP would be required to achieve a throughput of 475 per day if the system behaves like the practical worst case?

4. Consumer loan applications are processed in several steps. Suppose we have estimated BNR = 20 applications per day and RPT = 2 hours. In recent months, throughput has averaged 18 applications per day, while the average number of loans in process has averaged 60. What do you think of the efficiency of this process? (Hint: Apply internal benchmarking by comparing actual performance with that of the practical worst case.)

5 BUFFERING

*Variability in a production or supply chain system will be buffered by
some combination of inventory, capacity, and time.*

5.1 Introduction

In previous chapters, we have stressed repeatedly that variability
degrades performance of production and supply chain systems.
Variability is the reason that queues form at processes. Variability
is what drives behavior of a flow away from the best case and toward
the worst case. Variability is the reason you leave a little extra time
to drive to the doctor's office and variability is the reason the doctor
is running behind when you get there. Virtually all facets of life are
affected by variability.

The impact of variability on performance suggests that variability reduction is an important vehicle for improving production
and supply chain systems. Indeed, many of the improvement policies identified in earlier chapters can be classified under the heading
of variability reduction. But, because performance is not measured
in a single dimension, the relationship between variability and performance is not simple. We can understand it by examining the
ways in which variability can be buffered.

5.2 Buffering Fundamentals

It is common to think of buffering against variability by means of
inventory. For instance, a factory will often carry stocks of repair

parts for its machines. The reason is that the demand for these parts is unpredictable because it is caused by machine failures. If failures (and part delivery times) were perfectly predictable, then spare parts could be ordered to arrive exactly when needed and hence no safety stock would be required. But because failures are unpredictable (variable), safety stocks of repair parts are required to facilitate quick repair of machines.

Note, however, that inventory is not the only means for buffering variability. In the machine maintenance situation, we could choose not to stock repair parts. In this case, every time a machine failed it would have to wait for the needed parts to arrive before it could be repaired. The variability in the failure events and the variability in the arrival of repair parts would still be buffered, but now they would be buffered by time instead of inventory.

Alternately, we could choose not to stock repair parts but instead maintain backup machines to pick up the slack when a failure occurs. If we have enough backup machines then failures will no longer cause delays (no time buffer) and we will not need stocks of repair parts (no inventory buffer). This amounts to buffering the variability caused by unpredictable failures entirely by capacity.

These three dimensions—inventory, capacity, and time—are the *only* ways variability can be buffered. But each need not be used exclusively. For instance, if we had limited backup capacity we might experience a delay if enough machines failed and we had to wait for repair parts from the vendor. Hence, the variability due to failure times would be buffered by a combination of time and capacity. If we chose to carry some stock, but not enough stock to cover for every possible delay, then the variability would be buffered by a combination of time, capacity, and inventory.

We can summarize the fundamental principle of variability buffering as follows:

Principle (Variability Buffering).   *Variability in a production or supply chain system will be buffered by some combination of inventory, capacity, and time.*

The appropriate mix of variability buffers depends on the physical characteristics and business strategy of the system. Because variability is inevitable in all systems, finding the most appropriate mix of buffers is a critical management challenge.

Newspapers, Fires, and Organs

Newspapers

Demand for newspapers at a newsstand on any given day is subject to uncertainty and hence is variable. Because the news vendor cannot print newspapers, capacity is not available to buffer this variability. Customers are unwilling to wait for their papers (e.g., place an order for a paper in the morning and pick up the paper in the afternoon), so time is also unavailable as a buffer. As a result, news vendors must use inventory as their exclusive variability buffer. They do this by typically stocking somewhat more papers than they expect to sell during the day.

Emergency Fire Service

Demand for emergency fire service is intrinsically unpredictable and therefore variable. A fire station cannot use inventory to buffer against this variability because services cannot be inventoried. Further, the very nature of *emergency* fire service implies that time is an inappropriate choice. Hence, the primary buffer used in such systems is capacity. As a result, fire engines are utilized only a small fraction of time to ensure that they are available when needed.

Organ Transplants

Both supply and demand for human organ transplants are subject to variability. Because organs are perishable, they cannot be inventoried for any length of time. In addition, organs only become available when donors die, so capacity cannot be augmented (ethically anyway). With inventory and capacity largely unavailable as variability buffers, time is the only viable option, which is why people in need of organ transplants typically have to wait a long time to receive them.

5.3   The Role of Strategy

The appropriate mix of variability buffers is not determined by the physical system alone. As an example of physically similar systems that made use of different buffer types, consider McDonald's and Burger King in the 1970s. Both had menus consisting largely of hamburgers, fries, and drinks. Both made use of similar, though not identical, production processes. And both were subject to unpredictable demand, bacause fast-food customers do not make reservations. But, because the two companies had slightly different strategies for targeting customers, they developed different operations systems.

As the first nationwide fast-food hamburger chain, McDonald's established its reputation on the basis of delivery speed. To support this key component of its business strategy, it used a policy of stocking inventories of finished food products on a warming table. Because staff needed only to bag the food to fill an order, they were able to respond quickly to variable demand.

In contrast, Burger King elected to distinguish itself from McDonald's in the marketplace by offering customers more variety. Its "have it your way" advertising campaign encouraged customers to customize their orders. But this gave Burger King a much broader effective product line (i.e., because holding the pickles or the lettuce resulted in different end products). As a result, Burger King could not duplicate the McDonald's practice of stocking finished hamburgers without building up excessive inventory and incurring the resulting spoilage loss. Instead, it assembled burgers to order from the basic components. Of course, to be effective in the marketplace, Burger King had to ensure that its assembly speed was suffiently fast to avoid excessive delays that would not be tolerated by customers of fast-food restaurants. To do this, Burger King probably had to maintain more hamburger production capacity than did McDonald's. In effect, Burger King substituted a combination of time and capacity buffers in place of inventory buffers to provide its customers a higher product mix, albeit with slower delivery times. Given Burger King's business strategy, its choice of operations system made perfect sense.

The fact that the production or supply chain system depends on the business strategy and physical environment leads us to the following insights:

1. *Design of the physical production environment is an important aspect of management policy.* Because what is practical operationally depends on what is possible physically, design decisions, such as layout, material handling, process reliability, automation, and so on, can be key. In the Burger King system, a rapid cooking/assembly process was essential to making assemble-to-order feasible. Similarly, in manufacturing systems, flow-oriented cellular layouts are used to make low inventory production practical.

2. *Different operations systems can be used for different products.* Because conditions and objectives can differ among products, it can make sense to treat them differently. For instance, by the

1980s, the McDonald's product line had grown too large to allow it to stock all products on the warming table. Therefore, it only built inventories of the most popular items, such as Big Macs and Quarter Pounders. For lower-volume items, such as Filet-o-Fishes, it used a make-to-order strategy like Burger King's. This made sense, because precooking and stocking the high-volume products would speed delivery on the majority of orders. Furthermore, because they turn over rapidly, these products were much less subject to spoilage than the low-volume products. In the 1990s, General Motors used an almost identical approach to manufacture and distribute Cadillacs. The relatively few configurations that represented 70 percent of demand were stocked in regional distribution centers, to allow 24-hour delivery, while the many configurations representing the remaining 30 percent of demand were made to order with much longer lead times.

3. *The appropriate operations system for a given application will change over time.* Because both the physical environment and business strategy fluctuate and/or evolve over time, the operations system needs to adjust as well. An example of short-term fluctuation is the daily demand seen by McDonald's. During the lunch-hour rush, demand is high and therefore the make-to-stock policy of holding popular items on the warming table makes sense. However, during low demand times (e.g., the middle of the night), there is not enough demand to justify this strategy. Therefore, McDonald's switches to a make-to-order policy during these times. As an example of a long-term strategy shift, consider the example of Peapod. A pioneer in online grocery sales, Peapod initially invested in a localized "pick and pack" model for distributing goods (i.e., employees went to neighborhood grocery stores to gather items and then delivered them to customers). This was well suited to low-volume markets catering to customer convenience. However, as additional entrants to the online grocery market forced Peapod to compete more on price, it built central warehouses with automation to lower the cost of delivering goods to customers.

5.4   Buffer Flexibility

In practice, variability buffering often involves more than selecting a mix of buffer types (inventory, capacity, time). The nature of the buffers can also be influenced through management policy. A particularly important aspect of buffers is the extent to which they are *flexible*. Flexibility allows buffers to "float" to cover variability in different places (e.g., at different entities, stations, or flows).

Because this makes the buffers more effective at mitigating the negative effects of variability, we can state the following principle:

Principle (Buffer Flexibility).   *Flexibility reduces the amount of buffering required in a production or supply chain system.*

To make the concept of buffer flexibility concrete, consider the following specific examples:

1. *Flexible inventory:* Stock that can be used to satisfy more than one type of demand. One example of such inventory is the undyed sweaters produced by clothing maker Benetton. The sweaters are "dyed-to-order" to fill demand for any color. Another example is the supply of spare parts maintained at a central distribution center by Bell & Howell to meet repair requirements of its mail sorting machines at customer sites all over the United States. In either case, less generic stock (undyed sweaters or centralized parts) is required to achieve the same service achieved with specialized stock (dyed sweaters or localized parts).

2. *Flexible capacity:* Capacity that can be shifted from one process to another. A common example of this is an operator who has been cross-trained to perform multiple tasks so that he/she can float to stations where work is piling up. Another example is a flexible manufacturing system, which can switch quickly from producing one product to another. The ability to work on multiple processes means that flexible capacity can be more highly utilized than fixed capacity, and therefore achieve a given level of performance with less total capacity.

3. *Flexible time:* Time that can be allocated to more than a single entity. For example, a production system that quotes fixed lead times to customers (e.g., all deliveries are promised within 10 weeks of ordering) is making use of a fixed time buffer. However, a system that quotes dynamic lead times (e.g., based on work backlog at the time of an order) is using a flexible time buffer. In the flexible case, weeks of lead time can be shifted between customers, so that a customer who places an order during a slack period receives a short lead time quote, while one that places an order during a busy period receives a longer quote. Because dynamic lead times allocate time to customers where it is needed most, the system with flexible lead times achieves the same level of customer service (i.e., fraction of orders filled on time) as the system with fixed lead times, but with a shorter average lead time.

All buffers are costly, so minimizing them is key to efficient operation of production and supply chain systems. Indeed, as we will discuss below, this is the essence of the lean production movement. For this reason, creative use of flexibility in buffers is a vital part of effective operations management.

5.5   Buffer Location

How well a buffer compensates for the effects of variability is strongly influenced by its location. The reason is that the throughput, cycle time, and WIP in a process flow are largely determined by the bottleneck process. Therefore, a buffer that impacts a bottleneck generally has a larger effect on performance than one that impacts a nonbottleneck.

To make this observation precise, consider a flow with a fixed arrival rate of entities. Because what comes in must come out (subject to yield loss) the throughput is fixed as well. For such a flow, we can state the following result.

Principle (Buffer Position).   *For a flow with a fixed arrival rate, identical nonbottleneck processes, and equal-sized WIP buffers in front of all processes,*

- *The maximum decrease in WIP and cycle time from a unit increase in nonbottleneck capacity will come from adding capacity to the process directly before or after the bottleneck.*
- *The maximum decrease in WIP and cycle time from a unit increase in WIP buffer space will come from adding buffer space to the process directly before or after the bottleneck.*

To illustrate the above principle, consider the flow shown in Figure 5.1. In this simple system, all stations have average processing times of 1 hour, except station 4, which is the bottleneck with an average processing time of 1.2 hours. All stations have moderate variability ($CV = 1$) and there are zero buffers. The lack of buffers means that a station becomes *blocked* if it finishes processing before the next station downstream becomes empty. We assume an infinite supply of raw materials, so that station 1 runs whenever it is not blocked. We are interested in the effect of adding WIP or capacity buffers at the various stations.

Figure 5.2 shows the relative impact on throughput from adding a unit buffer space in front of stations 2 through 6. Notice that as predicted, the increase is largest adjacent to the bottleneck. In this case, the biggest increase in throughput occurs when a buffer space is added in front of the bottleneck, rather than in back of it. Because there are more stations prior to the bottleneck, and hence more chance for starving the bottleneck than blocking it, buffering

FIGURE 5.1

A sample flow
with buffers

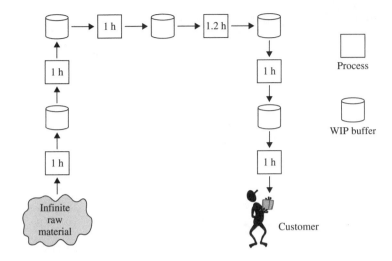

before the bottleneck is more effective than buffering after it. But,
as we would expect, the further upstream (or downstream) away
from the bottleneck the buffer space is placed, the less effective it
becomes. The symmetry of this example gives the curve in Figure
5.2 a regular pattern that would not occur in most situations. But the
general behavior that WIP buffering is most effective when used at
or near the bottleneck is universal.

Note that the above principle only implies that buffering is best
at processes adjacent to the bottleneck when all buffers (capacity
and WIP) are identical. A station with more capacity requires less
downstream WIP buffering, while a station with more variability
requires more downstream WIP buffering to protect the bottleneck.

FIGURE 5.2

Relative impact
of adding WIP
buffer spaces at
different
stations

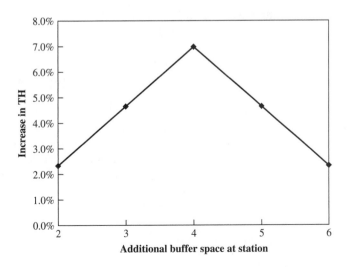

FIGURE 5.3

Diminishing
returns to
additional buffer
spaces in front
of the bottleneck

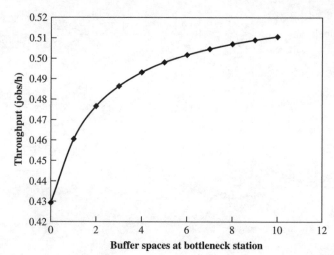

Buffer spaces at bottleneck station

Furthermore, because there are diminishing returns to additional buffers, we can reach a point where the most attractive place to add a buffer may not be at the bottleneck. To see the effect of diminishing returns, consider Figure 5.3, which shows the increase in throughput from adding additional buffer spaces in front of the bottleneck. After adding enough buffer space in front of the bottleneck to reduce starvation to a low level, it becomes more attractive to add buffer space after the bottleneck to prevent blocking.

For example, let us reconsider the line from Figure 5.1. Suppose, as shown in Figure 5.4, that we have already added four buffer spaces in front of station 4 and are considering adding a fifth space. From the buffer position principle, we know that the most attractive place for a buffer would be in front of the bottleneck, if all of the stations had the same amount of existing buffer space. However, because there are already four buffer spaces in front of the bottleneck, and none anywhere else, we must take into account the impact of diminishing returns. It turns out that if we add it in front of station 4 (to bring the buffer to five spaces), throughput will increase to 0.498 jobs per hour.[1] However, if we leave station 4 with four buffer spaces and add the extra space in front of either station 3 or station 5, throughput increases to 0.512, a 4.6 percent larger increase. Hence, while the objective is to buffer the effect of variability at the bottleneck, placing buffers at stations other than the bottleneck is sometimes the best solution.

---

[1]These numbers were computed using a computer simulation of the line in Figure 5.4 whose details are beyond the scope of this discussion.

FIGURE 5.4

Options for adding a buffer space to a sample flow

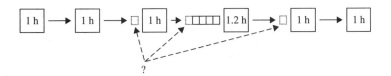

Note that the behavior of capacity buffers in a system like this is entirely analogous to that of WIP buffers. For instance, if we had a unit of additional capacity that could be added to any nonbottleneck station, the biggest increase in throughput would be achieved by adding it to station 3 immediately in front of the bottleneck. By allowing this machine to move material more rapidly to the bottleneck, this increase in nonbottleneck capacity will reduce the amount of time the bottleneck is starved. As in the WIP buffering case, capacity buffers will exhibit diminishing returns to scale and hence increases in capacity at other stations will eventually become attractive means for increasing throughput.

5.6   The Science of Lean Production

Lean production is the contemporary term for the just-in-time approach popularized by Toyota and other Japanese firms in the 1980s (Womack, Jones, and Roos 1991). In most accounts, lean is described in terms of waste reduction (see, e.g., Conner 2001, Jordan and Michel 2001). But this description is imprecise because it depends on the definition of waste. While obviously unnecessary operations can unambiguously be classed as waste, many sources of inefficiency are more subtle.

To provide a rigorous definition of lean it is useful to think in terms of buffers. After all, it is the fact that it must be buffered that makes variability so damaging to performance. For example, if a quality problem causes variability in the system, it will show up on the balance sheet via excess inventory, lost throughput (capacity), and/or long, uncompetitive lead times (which eventually lead to lost sales). Hence, we have the following definition of lean, to provide a clear link between operations policies and system performance:

Definition (Lean Production). *Production of goods or services is lean if it is accomplished with minimal buffering costs.*

This definition encompasses the more common definition of lean as production with minimal waste. Pure waste, such as excess inventory due to poor scheduling or excess capacity due to unnecessary processing steps, serves to inflate buffering costs and hence prevents a system from being lean. But this definition also highlights less obvious forms of inefficiency, such as those due to the variability caused by machine outages, operator inconsistency, setups, quality problems, and so forth. By thinking of waste as the result of buffers against variability, we can apply all of the principles of this book toward identifying levers to make a production system lean.

One immediate consequence of this definition of lean is that it broadens the focus beyond inventory. Some discussions of lean imply that the lone goal is low WIP production. While it is true that excessive inventory is inconsistent with lean, simply lowering inventory does not necessarily make a system lean. The reason is that other buffers, capacity for instance, could still be excessive. Certainly we would not want to regard a low-WIP production system with all equipment operating at less than 10 percent utilization as lean. To be truly lean, a system must be efficient with respect to its use of capacity and time, as well as inventory.

A second consequence of the above definition is that it implies that the choice of buffering mechanisms can have an impact on how lean is implemented. Ultimately, of course, a system has to reduce variability to become lean. That is the only way to drive buffering costs to low levels. But a reduction program is almost never accomplished overnight and never completely eliminates variability. Hence, management has a choice of which form of buffering—inventory, capacity, and/or time—to use. Of these, inventory tends to be the worst, because it obscures problems in the system and thus hinders efforts to drive out variability.

An important, and generally overlooked, aspect of the evolution of the Toyota Production System is that very early on Toyota instituted a two-shift operation (8 hours on, 4 hours off, 8 hours on, 4 hours off) that was in sharp contrast to the three-shift operations used by other major automobile manufacturers. The 4-hour down periods between shifts were designated for preventive maintenance (PM). But in reality they also served as capacity buffers. If a shift fell short of its production quota, the PM period could be used for overtime. This schedule enabled Toyota to dampen out the effects of variability within the system (e.g., due to quality or workpace problems), so they were able to drive down inventory in both the manufacturing system and the supply chain. By focusing for many years on rooting out the many sources of variability, Toyota developed a production system that has yielded lasting competitive advantage despite being the most heavily benchmarked system in the world. As a result, in 2004, Toyota began making use of a three-shift schedule in some of its European plants. Evidently, variability was low enough (and sales were high enough) to justify eliminating the capacity buffer inherent in the two-shift schedule.

FIGURE 5.5

Lean implementation steps at Toyota

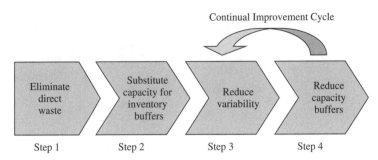

We can summarize the continual improvement path implied by our definition of lean production and used so successfully by Toyota with the diagram shown in Figure 5.5. The first step is to eliminate obvious sources of waste, such as redundant operations, outages due to unreliable equipment, delays due to operator errors, and so forth. This is as far as many lean implementation programs go. But to achieve the truly world-class performance exemplified by Toyota, we must go further. Step 2 is to make sure there is a sufficient capacity buffer in the system to enable a significant reduction in inventory without sacrificing customer service. Then, using the enhanced visibility made possible by the low-WIP environment, step 3 is to drive out variability. Finally, as variability is reduced, it becomes possible, in step 4, to operate resources closer to their capacity. Variability is never completely eliminated, but it is important to establish variability reduction as an ongoing process to steadily reduce buffering costs. The result will be an organization that grows leaner, and smarter, over time.

Principles in Practice

Whirlpool Kitchens

In 1986, Whirlpool acquired the St. Charles Manufacturing Company, a maker of cabinetry and related equipment. One of their product lines was a series of sheet metal cabinets for institutional applications (e.g., schools and hospitals). The company, renamed Whirlpool Kitchens, described its offerings in a catalog that also cited a 10-week lead time for delivery for all models. However, because on-time delivery was poor, and a competitor was offering 4-week lead times, management undertook a review of ways to improve responsiveness.

A process flow analysis revealed that a substantial amount of the lead time consisted of premanufacturing steps (order entry and engineering design). There were two reasons for this. First, because the catalog quoted a 10-week lead time measured from the last day of a 2-week interval or "bucket" for all orders placed in that interval, customers tended to place their orders at or near the last day of the bucket (every other Friday). This caused a huge overload of work at order entry and hence a delay at getting orders into the system. Second, because the cabinet systems were customized for the application, order-specific design work was required. The designers experienced periodic bursts of work (passed on to them from order entry), so this already time-consuming task took even longer.

When they discovered this, management quickly shifted their focus from the manufacturing process itself to the premanufacturing steps. In the language of this chapter, the problem they faced was a consequence of orders arriving to the system in a highly variable fashion, occuring in biweekly bursts rather than a steady stream. The system was buffering this variability by a combination of time (backlog of orders awaiting processing) and inventory (queue of jobs in design). Hence, a logical first step was to eliminate the order buckets and quote lead times from the day a customer placed an order. This change removed the incentive for customers to "aim" for the last day of the bucket, and hence served to smooth out orders and reduce delay at order entry and design. Note that if management had been willing to move to a variable lead time (e.g., quote customers longer lead times when the order backlog was large and shorter ones when the plant was lightly loaded), they could have achieved an *average* lead time shorter than 10 weeks with the same on-time performance. But this change would have required a change of policy (and catalog).

This and other improvements in the flow of work through the pre-manufacturing phase enabled the firm to meet its 10-week lead time more reliably, and even positioned it to reduce lead time quotes. However, it was not sufficient to reduce lead times close to the competition's 4-week standard. The reason was that the competition made use of modular product designs. Rather than making cabinets from sheet metal, they produced basic cabinet components to stock and assembled these into the final products for the customer. The customer only saw the assembly time, not the time to fabricate components, so lead times were substantially shorter. To match these lead times, Whirlpool Kitchens would have had to further reduce system variability and then maintain excess capacity to buffer the variability it could not eliminate (e.g., the variability caused by fluctuations in customer demand). Alternatively, it could have moved to an assemble-to-order strategy of its own.

Ultimately, however, Whirlpool decided that such a transformation was not consistent with the firm's capabilities and sold the division. Reconfigured under new ownership, the company refocused its strategy on the residential market where customization was a more central aspect of business strategy.

Questions for Thought

1. In each of the following, identify the main sources of variability and the resulting (inventory, capacity, and time) buffers.
   a. A hospital emergency room.
   b. An online retailer.
   c. A movie theater.
   d. The supply of sheet steel to an automotive stamping plant.
   e. The delivery of insulin by a pharmaceutical company to diabetic customers.

2. The Gap (a mass retailer of clothing) and Givenchy (a haute couture designer of custom clothing) are superficially similar. Both sell clothing to customers who exhibit variable demand. But managers of the two firms would certainly consider their businesses very different.
   a. Contrast the strategies (i.e., value propositions to the customer) of the two firms.
   b. Describe how you think the two firms buffer demand variability and note how their operations policies are linked to their strategic priorities.

3. Automakers make extensive use of platform architectures in which many different vehicles are built on a common platform consisting of common components that are largely unseen by customers (e.g., chassis, suspension, basic electrical components, etc.). Describe how this facilitates flexibility in both capacity and inventory buffers and list the cost savings at different levels in the supply chain.

4. Consider the system illustrated in Figure 5.6, which shows a flow with multiserver stations that have unbalanced capacity. Assuming that there is no yield loss or rework, station 4 is the bottleneck, because it has the smallest capacity and will therefore have the highest utilization. Suppose that (i) all processes, as well as demand, are subject to variability; (ii) lead times currently being quoted to customers are long by industry standards and on-time delivery performance is poor; (iii) utilization of station 4 is below 90 percent; and (iv) additional capacity at station 4 is prohibitively expensive.
   a. How is this system making use of time buffers? Do you think these are good choices as variability buffers?

FIGURE 5.6

Buffering the bottleneck in a flow

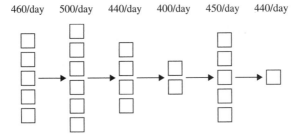

460/day   500/day   440/day   400/day   450/day   440/day

b. Describe how capacity and/or inventory could be substituted for time as variability buffers.

c. What information would you need to determine whether an additional capacity or time buffer should be located upstream or downstream from the bottleneck? (Hint: Think about the mechanics of blocking and starving of the bottleneck.)

d. Suppose capacity at all nonbottleneck machines is equally costly (but much cheaper than capacity at the bottleneck) and all nonbottleneck processes are equally variable. Under these conditions, at which station would you expect an additional machine to have the largest impact on reducing lead times and improving customer service?

e. What advantage might there be to substituting a capacity buffer, rather than an inventory buffer, for the current time buffer before making a longer term effort to reduce variability? (Hint: Think about the logic behind Figure 5.5.)

6   PUSH/PULL

The magic of pull is the WIP *cap.*

6.1   Introduction

The just-in-time (JIT) movement of the 1980s made the term *pull* practically a household word, primarily as a description of the kanban system introduced by Toyota. On the surface, pull is an appealingly simple concept. Rather than "pushing" parts from one process to the next, each process "pulls" (requests) them from an upstream process only when they are imminently needed. From this follow many operational benefits.

But is pull really this simple? When we buy a hamburger from a fast-food restaurant, is the system that produces it push or pull? What about the system that puts goods (e.g., jeans) in a retail store? How about an ATM station? Or a moving assembly line, such as that used to build automobiles? While most people claim to understand the meaning of pull, they frequently disagree on how to classify systems such as these. Often, they equate pull with make-to-order (i.e., systems that only produce products for which customer orders exist). But Taiichi Ohno cited American supermarkets, which are quintessential make-to-stock systems, as his inspiration for the Toyota kanban system, so there must be something wrong with this definition. At the same time, because the Toyota Production System is demonstrably effective, there must be something to pull that is worth understanding.

6.2   What Is Pull?

To be able to consistently classify systems as push or pull and to discover how pull produces operational benefits, we need a precise definition of pull. The following definition highlights the fundamental distinction between push and pull that is responsible for why pull works:

Definition (Push and Pull).   A pull system *is one in which work is released based on the status of the system and thereby places inherent limit on* WIP. A push system *is one in which work is released without consideration of system status and hence does not inherently limit* WIP.

Figure 6.1 illustrates this definition. In the push station, entities (jobs, parts, customers, etc.) enter according to an exogenous arrival process. The key aspect of these arrivals that makes the station "push" is that there is nothing that ties them to the status of the process in a way that limits their number in the system. For example, systems in which customers arrive to a service station when they want, jobs arrive to a machining station when they are completed by an upstream process, telephone calls arrive at a switching station as they are placed, are all instances of push systems, because arrivals are not influenced by what is going on in the process and there is no inherent limit on the WIP in the system.

In the pull station (illustrated in Figure 6.1 as a kanban system) entities can only enter when they are authorized to do so (i.e., by a kanban card). Moreover, this authorization is not arbitrary. Entities

FIGURE 6.1

Prototypical
push and pull
workstations

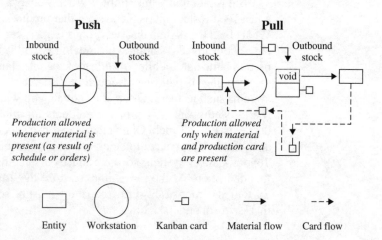

are allowed into a pull station specifically to replenish an *inventory void* created by removal of outbound stock (by a customer or a downstream process). Kanban cards are signals of voids, although other signals are also possible (e.g., electronic indicators of inventory level, physical spaces in an inventory buffer, etc.). The key is that, because releases into the system are only allowed when completions create voids, releases are tied to completions in a pull system.[1]

The above definition is straightforward and consistent with the early systems at Toyota and elsewhere. However, over time pull has been variously defined, sometimes in misleading ways. So, to be precise, it is useful to define what pull is not:

1. *Pull is* not *kanban.* Kanban is certainly one type of pull system, because it does indeed link releases to system status to limit WIP. But other systems can accomplish this as well. So, defining pull to be equivalent to kanban is too restrictive.

2. *Pull is* not *make-to-order.* It has become common in the practitioner literature to associate pull with producing to order, as opposed to producing to forecast. In this view, a customer order "pulls" a job into the system. But, while make-to-order may well be preferable to make-to-forecast, this definition seriously misses the point of pull. A classic MRP system in which the master production schedule is made up entirely of genuine customer orders is make-to-order. But, because MRP does not take system status into consideration when generating releases, there is no intrinsic bound on WIP level. Hence, MRP systems can become choked with inventory and as such usually do not exhibit any of the benefits associated with pull.[2]

3. *Pull is* not *make-to-stock.* Although most pull systems authorize releases to fill stock voids, this is not quite the same thing as being a make-to-stock system. A make-to-stock system replenishes inventories without a customer order. For example, in a supermarket, groceries are restocked to fill shelves rather than to fill orders. However, while Ohno's kanban system made use of the stock void replenishment feature of the make-to-stock supermarket system, there is nothing to prevent the kanban system from releasing orders that are already associated with customers. Hence, it is possible for

---

[1] For a more complete description of the classical Toyota-style kanban system see Hall (1983) or Schonberger (1982).

[2] This is why most MRP users do not allow their MRP system to have complete control over work releases. By supplementing MRP with other mechanisms that do consider system status in the conversion of planned order releases into actual releases, these users have introduced an element of pull into what is otherwise a classic push system.

kanban, a pull system, to be either make-to-order or make-to-stock. Hence, neither of these terms defines pull.

The bottom line is that *a pull system systematically limits work releases to limit the total amount of work in the system.* As we will see below, it is the cap on WIP achieved by a pull system that leads to its operating benefits, not the specifics of how WIP is capped. This is good news from a practical standpoint, because it means we have considerable flexibility on how to implement pull.

6.3   Examples of Pull Systems

The above definition gives a precise theoretical description of the concepts of push and pull. However, in practice, virtually all real-world systems exhibit some characteristics of pull. The reason is that physical space or other limitations usually establish some kind of limit on the WIP that can be in the system. So, even in the purest MRP implementation, there exists a point at which new releases are stopped due to system overload. Because this serves to couple work releases to system status we could regard it as a pull system. But the WIP limit is not explicitly set as a management parameter and is typically reached only when performance has degraded seriously, so it makes more sense to regard such a system as push.

To give a more practical sense of what constitutes "essentially push" and "essentially pull" systems, let us consider a few typical examples.

• A pure MRP system in which work releases are set entirely on the basis of customer orders (or forecasts) and not on system status is a push system. But, if actual releases are held back (e.g., because the system is too busy), an MRP system begins to look more like a pull system. If the planned order releases from MRP are regarded as a plan only, with actual releases being drawn into the system to fill inventory voids (e.g., via a kanban system), then the system is clearly pull.

• A retail store in which shelf stock is monitored and replenished is a pull system. The shelf space (plus possibly backroom space) establishes a specific limit on inventory and releases (i.e., replenishment orders) are made explicitly in response to a shift in system status (i.e., a void in a stock level). Taiichi Ohno drew his inspiration for the kanban system at Toyota from the workings of an American supermarket precisely because it is such a clean example of the concept of pull.

• Most doctors' offices operate essentially as push systems. That is, patients arrive according to their scheduled appointment times, not according to any information about system status (e.g., whether the physician is running late). However, the author has a personal physician whose office staff calls patients (well, at least the author, who is a notorious complainer about having to wait for a scheduled appointment) when the doctor is behind schedule. This allows the patients to delay their arrival and hence reduce the time they spend in the waiting room. Conceptually, the doctor has reduced the waiting cycle time of his patients by making use of a simple pull mechanism.

• We usually think of pull systems as resulting from a conscious choice. For instance, installing a kanban system in a manufacturing plant or a patient feedback system in a doctor's office are examples of deliberately designed pull systems. However, pull systems can also result from the physical nature of a process. For example, a batch chemical process, such as those used for many pharmaceutical products, consists of a series of processes (e.g., reactor columns) separated by storage tanks. Because the tanks are generally small, capable of holding only one or possibly two batches, processes in such systems are easily blocked by downstream operations. This implies that releases into the system cannot be made until there is space for them. Hence, these systems establish a well-defined limit on WIP and explicitly link releases to system status. So, they are pull systems even if their designers never gave a thought to just-in-time or pull.

From these examples we see that the concept of pull is flexible enough to implement in a variety of ways. Certainly the well-publicized kanban system of Toyota is one way to link releases to system status. But physical space limitations such as those in a retail outlet or a pharmaceutical process, or a simple feedback mechanism like the phone calling on the part of a physician's staff, can achieve the same effect. Hence, managers need not imitate Toyota; they can obtain the benefits of pull from a policy that is well suited to their specific environment.

6.4   The Magic of Pull

Having defined pull as the act of linking releases to system status so as to limit WIP, we are now ready to ask the important question, What makes pull so good? Early descriptions of the Toyota Production System stressed the act of pulling as central. Hall (1983) cited a General Motors foreman who described the essence of pull: "You don't never make nothin' and *send* it no place. Somebody has to come get it." But was this really the secret to Toyota's success? To see, let us examine the benefits commonly attributed to the use of pull systems:

1. *Reduced costs*—low WIP and less rework.
2. *Improved quality*—pressure for internal quality and better detection of problems.
3. *Better customer service*—short cycle times and predictable outputs.
4. *Greater flexibility*—work is pulled into the system only when it is ready to be worked on.

If we examine these closely, we see each benefit stems from the fact that a pull system establishes a **WIP cap**. Because releases are synchronized to completions, a pull system cannot build up excessive amounts of inventory. This restraint keeps WIP low and prevents excessive rework (i.e., because shorter queues mean that fewer defects are produced between the time a problem occurs and the time it is detected). The reduced inventory promoted by a WIP cap also puts pressure on the system for good quality, because a low-WIP system cannot function with frequent disruptions from quality problems. Low WIP also makes detection of quality problems easier because it shortens the time between problem creations and inspection operations. By Little's law, lower WIP shortens cycle time. Furthermore, the stabilization of WIP levels induced by a WIP cap produces more predictable outputs, which in turn allows shorter lead time quotes to the customer. Finally, the WIP cap delays releases into the system until they are imminently needed. By keeping orders on the work backlog as long as possible, the system preserves flexibility to make changes in orders or products.

For these reasons, the specific pull mechanism is not central to the benefits of lean production, but the WIP cap is. From an implementation standpoint, this is good news. It means that any mechanism that places an explicit upper bound on the amount of inventory in a production or supply chain system will exhibit the basic performance characteristics of lean systems. This bound can be established by using kanban cards, physical buffer spaces, electronic signals, or just about any mechanism that provides feedback on the inventory level of the process and links releases to it. Depending on the physical characteristics of the process, the information system available, and the nature of the workforce, different options for achieving a WIP cap will make practical sense.

Insight by Analogy

Air Traffic Control

How often has the following happened to you? You're on a plane. The doors have been sealed, the flight attendants have made their announcements, your personal belongings have been safely stored in the overhead bin, and the plane has just pulled back from the jetway. An on-time departure! Then the plane stops. The captain comes on the intercom and announces that there will be a delay of approximately 30 minutes due to air traffic control.

This sequence of events occurs on a daily basis. Why? Because airport runways are heavily utilized resources. Any disruption can cause them to become seriously backed up.

For example, suppose you are flying from New York to Chicago and there were thunderstorms in Chicago earlier in the day. All the planes that were unable to land were delayed. When these finally landed, they took the scheduled landing times of other planes, which were delayed to still later landing times. As a result, the time slot for your flight has now been preempted by another plane. Of course, your plane could take off as scheduled. But if it does, it will wind up circling around Lake Michigan, waiting for an opening on the runway, wasting fuel, and compromising safety. So, instead, air traffic controllers hold the flight on the ground at La Guardia until the anticipated load on the runway at O'Hare 2 hours from now will permit the plane to land. You will land at the same time (late, that is) in Chicago, but without the waste of fuel and the risks associated with additional flying time. Furthermore, if the weather in Chicago should take a turn for the worse, resulting in the flight being further delayed or canceled, you will be on the ground in your city of origin, New York, rather than being rerouted to some random city whose weather would permit the plane to land.

Note that what air traffic control does is impose a WIP cap on the number of flights in the air headed for Chicago O'Hare. Flights are only released into the air when the runway has capacity to handle them. This is completely analogous to what a WIP cap does in a production system. Jobs are released into the system only when the bottleneck process has capacity to work on them. As a result, the system does not waste effort holding and moving the job while it waits to be processed. Moreover, if the customer order associated with the job is canceled or changed, the fact that it has not yet been released gives the system the flexibility to respond much more efficiently than if the job were already being processed. Just like in the air traffic control system, a WIP cap in a production system or supply chain promotes both efficiency and flexibility.

FIGURE 6.2

Pure push and
CONWIP
systems

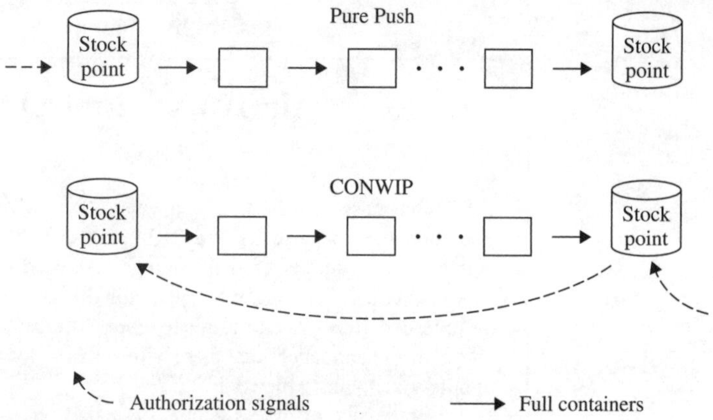

Pure Push

CONWIP

Authorization signals   Full containers

6.5   Comparisons of Push and Pull

To appreciate how pull achieves its logistical benefits and why they
are so closely linked to the idea of a WIP cap, let's compare the basic
performance of push and pull systems. To do this, we compare two
flows, one that operates in pure push mode (i.e., releases into the
flow are completely independent of system status) and the other that
operates in CONWIP mode (i.e., releases occur only at completion
times, so that the WIP level is held constant[3]). These two systems
are illustrated schematically in Figure 6.2.

We use CONWIP as our pull system because it is the simplest
form of WIP cap for an individual flow. Note, however, that in
CONWIP all stations are not pull. Except for the first station in
the flow, for which releases are triggered by completions at the
last station in the flow, all other stations operate in push mode.
That is, releases into them are triggered by completions at the
upstream station. But, the overall flow is pull, because releases
into it are authorized by system status. In addition to allowing us
to use simple CONWIP to understand the workings of pull, this
insight points out that we need not pull at every station to achieve
the operational benefits of pull. So, it may not be necessary to deal
with the additional complexity of setting WIP levels (card counts)
for every station in a flow to make it a pull system. Setting a single
WIP level for the entire line may be sufficient.

---

[3]Recall that we invoked CONWIP as part of a thought experiment to control the
coin fabs in Chapter 4. There we used it to regulate WIP so that we could observe how
throughput varies with WIP. But now we note that because CONWIP establishes a
WIP cap on a flow (either a line in a production/service system or a routing in a supply
chain system) it is a perfectly viable pull system.

With this, we can examine the three essential advantages of pull over push:

1. *Observability.* Pull systems control WIP, which is easily observable, while push systems control releases relative to capacity, which must be estimated rather than observed directly.
2. *Efficiency.* Pull systems achieve a given level of throughput with a smaller investment in inventory.
3. *Robustness.* Pull systems are less sensitive to errors in setting the WIP level than push systems are to errors in setting the release rate.

The first advantage is obvious; we can count WIP, but we can only approximate capacity. As we noted in Chapter 1, true capacity is a function of many things (equipment speed, failures, setups, operator outages, quality problems, etc.), all of which must be estimated to provide an estimate of overall system capacity. Because it is much easier to overlook a detractor than to overstate one, and we humans tend toward optimism, it is very common to overestimate the capacity of production and service processes.

The second advantage is less obvious, but still straightforward. In a push systems, work releases are not coordinated with system status. As a result, sometimes no releases occur when the system is empty (potential throughput is lost) and many releases are made when the system is completely full (inventory builds up with no additional throughput). In contrast, a pull system synchronizes releases with system status specifically to prevent this. During periods when the system runs slower than normal (cold streaks), the pull mechanism draws in less work and therefore keeps WIP under control. During periods when the system runs faster than normal (hot streaks), it draws in more work and therefore facilitates higher throughput. This reasoning lies behind the first principle of pull production:

Principle (Pull Efficiency).   *A pull system achieves higher throughput for the same average* WIP *level than an equivalent push system.*[4]

This principle also implies that a pull system can achieve the same throughput with a lower average WIP level than an equivalent push system.

---

[4]By "equivalent" we mean that the processes in the push and pull systems are identical.

The third advantage is the most subtle, and the most important. To understand it, we consider a simplified profit function:

$$\text{Profit} = r \cdot \text{TH} - h \cdot \text{WIP}$$

where r represents unit profit (considering all costs except inventory costs), h represents the cost to hold one unit for a year and, as usual, TH and WIP represent throughput and work-in-process, respectively. To make the units consistent, throughput is measured in entities per year.

In a push system, we choose the release rate, which directly determines the throughput (i.e., what goes in must come out, as long as releases are below capacity), but which indirectly determines the WIP level (i.e., through queueing behavior). In a pull system, we set the WIP (CONWIP) level directly, which in turn indirectly determines the throughput rate. In both cases, we can adjust the control (TH in the push system, WIP level in the pull system) to maximize the profit. From the Pull Efficiency Principle, it is apparent that the pull system will achieve higher profits (i.e., because for any throughput level pull will have smaller inventory costs than push).

But in realistic settings the controls will never be truly optimal because they must be set with respect to approximate parameters, the system may be changing over time, and implementation of the controls will be imperfect. So it is of great practical importance to know how the system performs when controls are set suboptimally. That is, what happens when the release rate (TH) is too high or too low in a push system, or the WIP level is too high or too low in a pull system.

Because the controls for push and pull have different units, we cannot compare them directly. However, we can compare them if we consider the ratio of the actual control to the optimal control. That is, suppose that the optimal release rate (TH) for the push system is 20,000 units per year, while the optimal WIP level for the pull system is 1,000 units. Then a push system with a release rate of 22,000 units would have a ratio of $22,000/20,000 = 1.1$, which indicates a level that is 10 percent too high. Likewise, a pull system that has a WIP level of 900 units will have a ratio of $900/1,000 = 0.9$, which indicates a level that is 10 percent too low. A ratio of 1 indicates an optimal control level.

If we plot the profit versus this ratio for both the push and pull system on the same graph, we get something like Figure 6.3.[5]

---

[5]For a more technical discussion of the models used to derive these curves, see Hopp and Spearman (2000, Chapter 10).

FIGURE 6.3

Robustness of
push and pull
systems

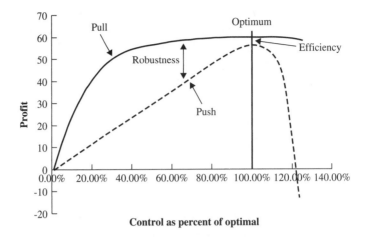

Control as percent of optimal

Notice that in the push system, profit diminishes substantially if
the release rate is set 20 percent too low, and drastically if it is
set 20 percent too high. In contrast, profit of the pull system is
relatively insensitive to a 20 percent error, high or low. The reason
is that, as we discussed in Chapter 1, WIP (and therefore holding
cost) is very sensitive to release rate, particularly when releases
approach capacity. But as we saw in Chapter 4, when we examined
the behavior of CONWIP lines in the form of coin fabs, throughput
changes gradually as WIP levels are adjusted, particularly at higher
WIP levels as TH approaches capacity. We can summarize this
behavior in the second principle of pull production:

Principle (Pull Robustness).   *A pull system is less sensitive to
errors in* WIP *level than a push system is to errors in release rate.*

This observation is at the heart of the success of kanban and
other pull systems. Because WIP levels need only be approximately
correct, pull systems are (relatively) easy to set up. WIP levels do
not need to be finely adjusted in response to changes in the system
(e.g., learning curves that alter capacity over time), so pull systems
are (relatively) easy to manage. Finally, because of their stability,
pull systems promote a focus on continual improvement, rather
than a mode of firefighting to deal with short-term problems.

This observation also underlies the decline of material requirements planning (MRP) as a work release mechanism. In its original form, MRP was an almost pure push system, with releases
set to an exogenous schedule. Because most users would load the
schedule close to (or over) capacity, MRP systems became synony-
mous with high WIP and poor service. In response, manufacturing

execution systems and finite capacity scheduling systems were developed to replace the standard MRP release mechanism. By linking releases to system status, these had the effect of introducing an element of pull into a fundamentally push system. Today, classical MRP logic is used almost exclusively for planning rather than execution.

6.6   Pull Implementation

The fact that the magic of pull is in the WIP cap is good news; it implies that the benefits of pull can be obtained through a variety of mechanisms. Toyota-style kanban, as diagrammed in Figure 6.1, is one. CONWIP is another. Even simple feedback loops that take WIP status into account when scheduling can prevent "WIP explosions" and help achieve the efficiency and robustness associated with pull.

CONWIP is probably the simplest method for implementing a WIP cap, because it just establishes a WIP level and maintains it. In many environments, direct CONWIP is eminently practical. But in others it may make sense to use a more sophisticated form of pull. For instance, there may be managerial or communication reasons for defining CONWIP loops that cover less than the entire line. Figure 6.4 illustrates how CONWIP can be viewed as a continuum of designs, ranging all the way from simple CONWIP covering the entire line to pure kanban, which uses pull at every station. If different segments of the line are under separate management or are physically distant, it may make sense to decouple them by defining separate CONWIP loops for the segments. Also, if the act

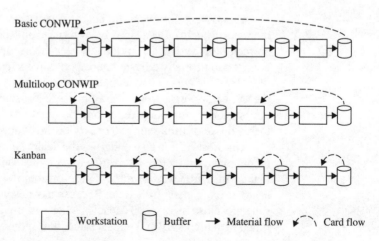

FIGURE 6.4

Variants on CONWIP

Basic CONWIP

Multiloop CONWIP

Kanban

☐ Workstation   ⬭ Buffer   → Material flow   ⤺ Card flow

FIGURE 6.5

Coupled and
uncoupled
CONWIP loops

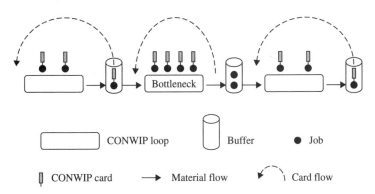

of pulling forces greater communication between stations, it may
be effective to move all the way to kanban to force every station to
authorize transfer of entities from upstream.

If separate CONWIP loops are used, they must be coupled
appropriately. Failure to do this could allow WIP between loops to
grow without bound and defeat the purpose of establishing a WIP
cap. For example, Figure 6.5 illustrates a series of tandem CONWIP
loops, where the center loop is uncoupled and the other loops are
coupled. This is achieved by releasing the kanban cards for the
uncoupled loop as soon as entities leave the loop (i.e., before they
enter the downstream stock point), but releasing the kanban cards
for coupled loops only when entities leave the downstream stock
point. As long as the center loop is a consistent bottleneck, it will not
be able to build up a large amount of WIP in its downstream buffer.
So uncoupling this loop will prevent it from ever being blocked
by downstream problems. However, if the bottleneck floats with
changes in product mix or other conditions, then leaving a line
uncoupled could lead to a WIP explosion. In such a system, it
would probably be better to have all loops coupled.

A natural place to split CONWIP loops is at assembly operations, as illustrated in Figure 6.6. In this system, each time an
assembly is completed a signal is sent to each of the fabrication
lines to start another component. Note that because the fabrication
lines may be of different length, the WIP levels in them need not
(should not) be the same. So, the components that are started when
given a signal from assembly may not be destined for the same final product. However, because assembly sets the pace for the line,
arrivals from the fabrication line will be well synchronized, which
will prevent the buildup of component inventory that occurs when
one or more components needed for assembly is missing.

Finally, we note that WIP need not be measured in pieces
in a pull system. In multiproduct systems in which different

FIGURE 6.6

A CONWIP
assembly
system

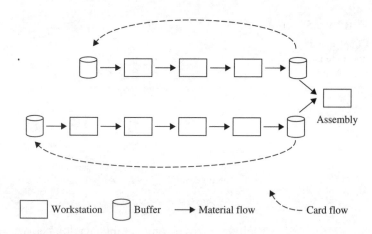

products have highly varied processing times, holding the total
number of pieces in a loop constant may actually allow the workload to fluctuate widely. When the system contains mostly simple
(i.e., light workload) pieces, workload will be small. When it contains mostly complex (i.e., heavy work content) pieces, workload
will be large. This suggests that CONWIP could be implemented
using other measures of workload. For instance, in a factory that
makes agricultural planting machines, where processing times are
proportional to the number of row units (wider planting machines
have more row units and hence more parts to fabricate and assemble), we might measure WIP in row units rather than in machines.
A printed circuit board plant, where processing time depends on
the number of layers (cores), might measure WIP in cores rather
than boards. In general, a system might measure WIP in terms of
hours at the bottleneck, rather than in pieces.

  To implement a pull system in which WIP is measured in units
other than pieces, physical cards are not practical. An alternative is
to use electronic signals to control CONWIP, as illustrated in Figure
6.7. In this system, whenever work is released into the system, its
work content (in complexity adjusted units, time at the bottleneck,
or whatever) is added to the running total. As long as this total is
above the CONWIP target, no further releases are allowed. When
entities are completed, their work content is subtracted from the
total. In addition to maintaining the workload, such an electronic
system can display the sequence in which jobs should be processed.
This sequence could be designed to facilitate batching efficiency, as
discussed in Chapter 3. As such, the CONWIP controller depicted
in Figure 6.7 acts as a link between the scheduling and execution
functions.

FIGURE 6.7

A CONWIP
controller

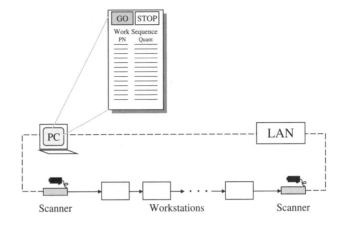

Scanner   Workstations   Scanner

Principles in Practice

Cisco Systems

In early 2000 Cisco Systems was flying high. Founded in December 1984 by two members of Stanford University's computer support staff, the company had gone public as a 250-person, $69 million company in 1990, and had ridden the Internet boom to become a $19 billion, 34,000-employee juggernaut by 2000. At that point, a market capitalization of $579 billion briefly made Cisco the most valuable company in the world.

Then came the Internet bust, which triggered a rapid decline in sales of switches, routers, and other networking equipment. In August 2001, Cisco announced the first negative earnings in its history. Worse, with no upturn in sales in sight, Cisco was forced to write off $2.25 billion in inventory and lay off 8,500 people. By the end of the year, market capitalization had fallen to $154 billion (*BusinessWeek* 2002).

What went wrong? Reams have been written on this question, as we would expect when one of the world's largest and most successful companies takes a major tumble. Many analysts have pointed to irrational optimism on the part of Cisco's leadership. Having never experienced anything but growth, management was unable to recognize the ominous signs of a downturn in late 2000. Furthermore, because production had been outsourced to contract manufacturers, who had no incentive to tell their prized customer its projections were wrong, there was no counterbalancing opinion to temper management's overly optimistic vision. So Cisco continued planning for growth until it was too late.

But, while optimism and outsourcing certainly played a role, they were not entirely responsible for the huge inventory write-off. At the root of the problem was the fact that Cisco's supply chain was run fundamentally as a push system. Component orders were driven by demand forecasts without any mechanism to limit the amount of inventory that could build up at various levels in the chain. Furthermore, rapid growth in the industry during the late 1990s had spurred a furious competition for materials and contract manufacturing capacity. In an effort to keep up with demand, Cisco purchased components and capacity in large quantities well in advance of actual demand. As a consequence, inventories of raw materials and subassemblies grew steadily right up to the bust.

Excess supply chain inventory was not a serious problem as long as robust growth continued. But when demand declined sharply, the uncapped inventory levels quickly became a huge liability. One reason for the speed of the decline was that many of Cisco's customers ordered equipment from both Cisco and its competitors simultaneously, planning only to buy from whichever firm delivered first. This served to artificially inflate demand, which made the drop even more dramatic when customers began canceling orders in 2001 as a cost-cutting response to the recession. The buildup of raw material and in-process inventory left Cisco extremely vulnerable to the rapid and unanticipated decline in demand.

After living through the pain of layoffs and shareholder wrath that resulted from this supply chain failure, Cisco set out to refine its systems to prevent inventories from ever getting so far out ahead of demand again. It began by creating a virtual logistics network by constructing links between its own Cisco IT infrastructure and the many third-party systems used by its suppliers and customers. By improving visibility of orders, inventories, and production plans throughout the supply chain, this system should facilitate more accurate forecasting and more effective communication between partners. As such, it should help Cisco detect impending problems more rapidly than in the past.

With this IT network in place, Cisco developed a new inventory management system called "Cisco Lean," that incorporates elements of pull. This system makes use of reorder points at each level of the supply chain. Only when stock of an item falls below its reorder point is a replenishment order generated. This places a cap on the amount of inventory that can build up at any stock point, because the on-hand plus on-order inventory can never exceed the reorder point (ROP) plus the order quantity (OQ). Hence, if a decline in demand occurs, the pull system will naturally limit the potential liability. Furthermore, because the greater visibility provided by the virtual logistics network should provide better advance warning of a decline, Cisco should be able to adjust these ROPs downward in advance of a precipitous decline and further mitigate the damage.

Questions for Thought

1. Identify the following systems as push or pull according to whether they regulate releases on the basis of system status in a manner that establishes a WIP cap.
   a. A server at Amazon.com.
   b. The drive-up window at a bank.
   c. The gas tanks at a filling station.
   d. The operating rooms at a hospital.
   e. A commercial printer's supply chain for paper stock if the printer orders stock needed for customer orders as the orders arrive.
   f. A commercial printer's supply chain for paper stock if the printer uses an order-up-to policy in which it reviews the inventory of paper stock each week and orders enough to bring the total up to a prespecified level.

2. Consider a three-station flow with single-server stations, each of which has processing times with an average of 1 hour and a CV of 1.

   If we operate this flow as a push system, we can use the VUT equation to compute the average WIP level that would result from any given throughput (TH). To do this, first note that because the processing rate of each station is 1 per hour, then utilization of all stations is

   $$\text{UTIL} = \frac{\text{rate in}}{\text{capacity}} = \frac{\text{TH}}{1} = \text{TH}$$

   as long as TH < 1 so that the stations can keep up with the release rate, which will therefore be equal to the throughput. Furthermore, if we assume that the arrival CV is 1, then, because all process CVs are also 1, the variability coefficient (V) in the VUT equation is also 1. Hence, we can compute the cycle time for any station as the sum of waiting time (WT) and process time (PT), where WT is given by the VUT equation:

   $$\text{CT}_{\text{station}} = \text{WT} + \text{PT} = \text{VUT} + 1 = U + 1$$
   $$= \frac{\text{UTIL}}{1 - \text{UTIL}} + 1 = \frac{1}{1 - \text{UTIL}}$$

   Using Little's law, we can convert this into the WIP at each station:

   $$\text{WIP}_{\text{station}} = \text{TH} \times \text{CT}_{\text{station}} = \text{UTIL} \times \text{CT}_{\text{station}} = \frac{\text{UTIL}}{1 - \text{UTIL}}$$

   Finally, because the three stations are identical, the total WIP in the line is given by

   $$\text{WIP} = \frac{3\text{UTIL}}{1 - \text{UTIL}} = \frac{3\text{TH}}{1 - \text{TH}}$$

If, instead, we were to operate this same line as a CONWIP system, we can compute the throughput that would result from any choice of WIP by using the practical worst-case formula

$$TH = \frac{WIP}{WIP + CWIP - 1} = \frac{WIP}{WIP + 2}$$

because we know that CWIP = 3 for a balanced three-station line.

a. Suppose in the push system we set TH = 0.9. What is the resulting average WIP level?

b. Suppose in the CONWIP system we set WIP equal to the answer from part (a). What is the resulting throughput (TH)? What does this show us about the relative efficiency of the push and CONWIP systems?

c. Consider the profit function 100TH − 0.1WIP.

   (i)   Use the above expression for WIP in the push system to compute the profit and confirm that it is maximized when TH = 0.945 (i.e., try some values above and below this level and note that profit is less).

   (ii) Use the above expression for TH in the CONWIP system to compute the profit and confirm that it is maximized when WIP = 43 (again, try some values above and below this level). Is profit higher or lower in the CONWIP case than in the push case?

   (iii) Compute the profit for the push case when TH = 0.992 (i.e., the release rate is 10 percent too high). Compute the profit for the CONWIP case when WIP = 45 (i.e., the WIP level is 10 percent too high). Which case suffers a greater decrease in profit relative to the optimal levels from (i) and (ii)?

3. Suppose we have a single-product kanban line consisting of five stations like that illustrated at the bottom of Figure 6.4. Suppose there are currently a total of 30 cards, allocated among the various stations, and the line is achieving a throughput of 50 jobs per hour.

   Now suppose that we convert the line to a CONWIP system like that shown at the top of Figure 6.4 and set the number of cards equal to 30.

   a. It can be shown mathematically that the throughput level in the CONWIP line will be at least as large, and possibly larger, than that in the kanban line. Explain why this occurs. (Hint: Note that the throughput of the line will be equal to the rate of the bottleneck station times the utilization of the bottleneck. Think about what causes blocking and starving of the bottleneck.)

   b. Given the result of part (a) and the fact that CONWIP is simpler to implement (i.e., because it only requires setting a single card count, rather setting card counts for each station), when would it make sense to use kanban instead of CONWIP?

P A R T

III NETWORK SCIENCE

7 INVENTORY

The appropriate amount of safety stock for an inventoried item depends on the item's unit cost, replenishment lead time, and demand variability.

7.1 Introduction

Inventory is the lifeblood of any production or supply chain system. Whether the entities moving through the system consist of materials, people, or logical transactions, the efficiency with which these are stored, processed, transported, and coordinated is central to the effectiveness of the overall system.

The basic trade-off involved in all inventory systems is one of *cost versus service*. Holding inventory entails cost in the form of lost interest on money tied up in stock, construction and maintenance of storage space, material handling expenses, quality assurance expenditures, and other inventory-related expenses. But holding inventory also facilitates service by enabling a process to match production with demand without delay. Striking an appropriate balance between cost and service is a key challenge in inventory management.

Figure 7.1 illustrates the basic mechanics that underlie the cost versus service trade-off associated with inventory. The essential function of any production or supply chain system is matching a supply/production process with a demand process. That is, customers generate requests (orders) for products or services and the production process uses its capacity to convert a supply of inputs

FIGURE 7.1 Role of inventory in matching production with demand

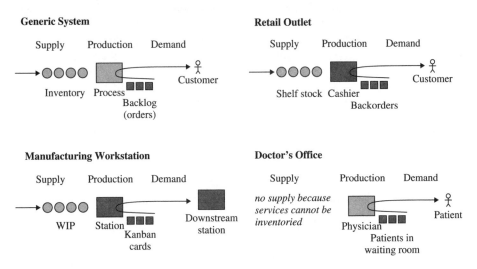

to satisfy these requests. If the supply, production, and demand processes were all completely predictable, and the production and supply processes had enough capacity to keep up with demand, then we could perfectly synchronize the three processes. Supplies of inputs would arrive just as they were needed and production of goods and services would be completed just as customers made their requests. The only inventory required in the system would be that actively being worked on in the production process or being transported in the supply process. Such a perfect system would be the supply chain equivalent of the best case we discussed in Chapter 4.

But, as we know from Chapter 2, there is always variability in operations systems. Moreover, as we discussed in Chapter 6, this variability is always buffered by some combination of capacity, inventory, and time. Figure 7.1 highlights these three buffers, and the role of inventory in particular. Whenever the inputs needed for the production process arrive before the production process is ready to use them, they must wait in stock (i.e., an inventory buffer). Analogously, whenever a customer demand occurs before the production needed to satisfy it has been completed, it must wait on a backlog (i.e., a time buffer). If the capacity of the production process exceeds demand (i.e., a capacity buffer), it will be able to work down the input stock and backlog levels more quickly and thereby operate with smaller inventory and time buffers.

The generic representation of a production process shown in Figure 7.1 can be used to represent virtually any operations system. For example, in a manufacturing workstation, the "customer" is the downstream workstation, the "orders" are signals of requirements (e.g., kanban cards in a pull system or scheduled production quantities in a push system), the "inventory" is WIP, and the backorders consist of unfilled requirements (e.g., waiting kanban cards or work remaining on the production schedule). In a retail outlet, we can view the process that connects supply with demand as the cash register; hence the "customer" really is a customer and "orders" really are orders, while "inventory" represents shelf stock and "backorders" represent unfilled customer demand. Finally, in a doctor's office, the production process is a service (i.e., health care activities by the physician and/or other personnel), so there is no supply of inputs.[1] In this system, "customers" are patients and "orders" represent people waiting to be seen by the doctor. Because the doctor provides a (nearly) pure service, there is no inventory-versus-speed trade-off in this system, and hence there are only two variability buffers—capacity and time.

Finding the best way to use inventory (and capacity and time) to match supply and production to demand is a complex problem. Environments differ in strategy, operations systems differ in structure, customers differ in priority, and supply entities differ in cost and other characteristics. As a result, no single management approach is appropriate for all operations systems. However, there are basic principles that underlie the behavior of inventory in production and supply chain systems. Understanding these is critical to making good management decisions.

In addition to being important, inventory is a very large and complex topic. Even the cursory treatment of it we provide in this chapter can make for pretty dense going. Nevertheless, because inventory control is so central to supply chain management, we introduce enough mathematical detail to enable us to highlight the key fundamentals. Those interested in a more comprehensive treatment of inventory modeling should consult Silver, Pyke, and

---

[1] Strictly speaking, a doctor does use a supply of physical inputs, such as medications, bandages, sutures, etc. So, in formal terms, the doctor's office looks much like the retail outlet, with the physician playing the role of the cashier. But realistically, in a retail outlet a customer will not go unserved for lack of service from the cashier, while a patient in the doctor's office will not go unserved for lack of materials. In both cases, the service portion of the customer product (i.e., the checkout activity in the retail outlet and the health care activities in the doctor's office) cannot be stocked. Because the service activity is the essence of the product in the doctor's office, increasing stocks of inventory generally has little effect on the speed with which patients are served.

Peterson (1998) for an elementary overview and Zipkin (2000) for a rigorous summary of the state of the art.

7.2   Classification

While the fundamental purpose of inventory in a production or supply chain system is to match production to demand, the specific role of inventory can vary depending on the circumstances. By describing the underlying reason for its presence, we can classify inventory into several different types:

Working stock: Inventory that is actively being processed or moved. Parts being cut on a machine, components being transported in a truck, and consumer loan applications being evaluated by a bank officer are all examples of working stock.

Congestion stock: Inventory that builds up unintentionally as a consequence of variability in the system. For instance, a queue that builds up behind a highly variable, highly utilized process is a form of congestion stock. Components waiting to be matched with their counterparts to form assemblies are another form of congestion stock.

Cycle stock: Inventory that results from batch operations. For example, when a purchasing agent orders office supplies in bulk (to obtain a price discount or to save on shipping costs) the excess beyond what is immediately needed becomes cycle stock. A heat-treat furnace that processes batches of wrenches produces a build up of cycle stock at the next downstream station as the batches wait to be split up into a one-piece flow.

Safety stock: Inventory that exists intentionally to buffer variability. Retail inventory held in outlets to accommodate variable customer demand is an example of safety stock.

Anticipation stock: Inventory that is built up in expectation of future demand. For instance, a plant might build up a stock of lawnmowers to satisfy a seasonal spike in demand. In general, this is done to level production in the face of uneven or cyclic demand to make better use of capacity.

Working stock is not generally a problem, because it is required for any production/supply chain system to operate. But the other forms of inventory are not strictly necessary and hence are often classified as "waste" (or "muda" by those with a penchant for Japanese terms). Managing these effectively is fundamental to achieving supply chain efficiency.

We have already dealt with the causes and cures of congestion stock in Part I. Anticipation stock is managed via scheduling and capacity planning as part of "aggregate planning."[2] Although significant in environments with long-term demand fluctuations, this type of inventory is not as ubiquitous as cycle stock and safety stock. Therefore, in this chapter, we will focus on the nature of cycle and safety stock, to develop basic inventory tools and insights.

The above classification is helpful in developing general management strategies and modeling approaches. But for detailed management purposes, a more practical and widely used categorization scheme is the **ABC classification**.[3] This approach divides items into categories based on dollar usage. Typically a small fraction of the items account for a large fraction of total annual dollar usage. Therefore, it makes sense to devote more attention to those items responsible for the majority of investment. To do this, the ABC classification ranks items by annual dollar usage and divides them into the following categories:

Class A items represent the first 5 to 10 percent of items that generally account for 50 percent or more of total annual usage measured in dollars. These should receive the most personalized attention and most sophisticated inventory management.

Class B items represent the next 50 to 70 percent of items that account for most of the remaining dollar usage. Like Class A items, these should be addressed with sophisticated inventory tools. But they are often too numerous to permit the individual management intervention that can be used for Class A items.

Class C items represent the remaining 20 to 40 percent of items that represent only a minor portion of total dollar usage. Management of these items should be as simple as possible, because time spent on such parts can have only a small financial impact on the system. However, when inexpensive Class C parts are essential to operations (e.g., lack of a fuse can cause an expensive delay) it makes sense to err on the side of ample inventory.

Variations on the ABC classification that consider part criticality, customer priorities, or other dimensions are possible for specific

---

[2]For descriptions of the aggregate planning problem and models used to address it, see Askin and Goldberg (2001, Chapter 5), Hopp and Spearman (2000, Chapter 16), and Nahmias (1997, Chapter 3).

[3]For more details on the ABC classification and its use in selecting appropriate management techniques, see Silver, Pyke, and Peterson (1998, Chapter 3).

environments. The goal is to focus the majority of attention on the minority of parts that are most essential to system performance.

7.3   Cycle Stock

As we noted in Chapter 3, many operations are done in batches. For instance, a purchasing agent buys bar stock in bulk, the plant makes it into wrenches that are treated in batches, and the distribution company ships the finished wrenches in truckloads. Because these batch operations result in inventory, which we call **cycle stock**, an important decision is how many items to make (or order or ship) at once.

The trade-off inherent in batching decisions is one of order frequency versus inventory. That is, the more frequently we order (or produce) an item, the less inventory we will have in the system. To see this, consider the sawtooth-shaped solid line shown in Figure 7.2, which illustrates the inventory level of a single item that experiences steady demand at a rate of D units per year and is replenished instantaneously in batches of size OQ (order quantity). The item will be replaced with a frequency of $D/$OQ times per year and the average inventory level will be OQ/2.

Now suppose we double the order frequency (by cutting the order quantity in half to OQ/2). As the shorter sawtooth path shown by the dotted line in Figure 7.2 shows, we now have half as much (OQ/4) inventory on average. Indeed, each time we double the order frequency (halve the order quantity) we will halve the average inventory, which implies that the relationship between inventory level and order frequency looks like Figure 7.3. From a practical perspective, this tells us that replenishing an item more frequently initially has a large impact on inventory, but the benefits of more frequent orders diminish rapidly as order frequency is increased.

If we assign costs to carrying inventory and placing replenishment orders then we can use the relationship shown in Figure 7.3 to strike an economic balance. Specifically, if we let h represent the

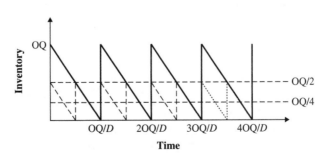

FIGURE 7.3

Inventory level
versus order
frequency

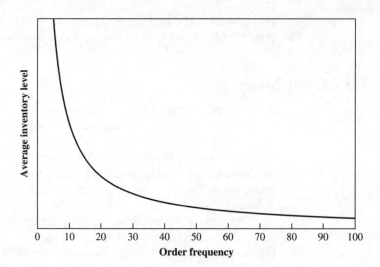

FIGURE 7.3

Inventory level
versus order
frequency

cost to carry a unit of inventory for one year and o represent the
cost to place a replenishment order, then the annual holding cost is
$h\text{OQ}/2$ and the annual order cost is $o D/\text{OQ}$. These are shown graphically as functions of the order quantity OQ in Figure 7.4. This figure shows that the total holding plus order cost is minimized at the
point where marginal holding cost equals marginal setup cost, that

FIGURE 7.4

Annual
inventory and
order costs as
functions of
order quantity

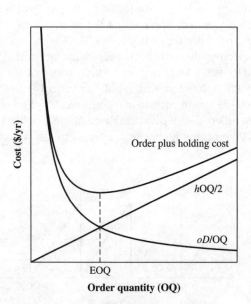

is $hOQ/D = oD/OQ$, which implies that the optimal order quantity, which we call the **economic order quantity (EOQ)**, is

$$OQ^* = EOQ = \sqrt{\frac{2oD}{h}}$$

Although EOQ is the optimal order quantity under these conditions, it turns out that the cost function is relatively flat near the optimum. This means that rounding off the order quantity to assure convenient quantities (e.g., full cases) or replenishment intervals (e.g., even numbers of weeks, so that different items can share delivery trucks) will not have a large impact on cost.

For instance, suppose a purchasing agent buys bar stock to make into wrenches. Each bar costs $18 and annual demand is very steady at 2,000 bars per year. The firm uses a 15 percent cost of capital to account for money tied up in inventory, and also charges a holding fee of $1 per bar per year to account for the annualized cost of storage space. Hence the holding cost is $h = 0.15(18) + 1 =$ $3.70. Finally, the cost of placing a purchase order is estimated to be $25 and the fixed (not variable) cost of a shipment of bar stock is $30, which implies a fixed order cost of $o = 25 + 30 = \$55$. With these, we can compute the order quantity that minimizes the sum of holding and order costs:

$$EOQ = \sqrt{\frac{2oD}{h}} = \sqrt{\frac{2(55)(2,000)}{3.7}} = 243.8 \approx 244$$

To order bar stock in batches of 244 we should place 2,000/ 244 = 8.2 orders per year, or roughly one every 6 weeks. But suppose it would make deliveries more convenient if we ordered exactly 10 times per year, so that bar stock can be delivered jointly with other materials on a regular schedule. Because of the insensitivity of the cost function of the EOQ model near the optimum, using an order quantity of $OQ = 2,000/10 = 200$ will have a relatively small effect on total cost. To see this, note that the total holding plus order cost under the optimal lot size of 244 is

$$\frac{hOQ}{2} + \frac{oD}{OQ} = \frac{3.7(244)}{2} + \frac{55(2,000)}{244} = \$902.20$$

while the total cost under the more convenient lot size of 200 is

$$\frac{hOQ}{2} + \frac{oD}{OQ} = \frac{3.7(200)}{2} + \frac{55(2,000)}{200} = \$920.00$$

Hence an 18 percent reduction in the order quantity (batch size) led to a 2 percent increase in cost.

In general, the EOQ formula is a practical means for setting order quantities when

- Demand is fairly steady over time.
- The cost to place an order (e.g., purchasing clerk time, fixed shipping expenses, etc.) is reasonably stable and independent of the quantity ordered.
- Replenishments are delivered all at once.

These conditions frequently describe situations for purchased parts. However, in many production settings, where the cost of a replenishment is a function of the load on the facility, other lot-sizing procedures, based on dynamic scheduling approaches, are more suitable than EOQ. Nevertheless, the EOQ formula provides a basic tool for economically controlling the cycle stock in many operations systems.

7.4   Safety Stock

Stock that is deliberately held with the intention of meeting unpredictable demand or protecting against unreliable supply is called **safety stock**. But even stock that is held for other reasons can act like safety stock. For instance, if input material arrives in batches to a process like those shown in Figure 7.1, then there will tend to be a supply of inventory that can be used to match production to demand. A customer whose order is filled immediately because of the presence of leftover cycle stock cannot tell that this stock was not intended to facilitate her demand. Because of this, we will ultimately need to take into account unintentional protection provided by other types of inventory when setting the intentional level of protection via safety stock.

Before we can do this, we must address two fundamental questions posed by the problem of using safety stock as protection against variability: (a) What policy should we use to control stock levels over time? and (b) Given a control policy, what level of safety stock is needed to achieve a desired level of customer service? To enable us to focus on the second issue, we begin our investigation by using a very simple replenishment policy that eliminates the need to consider cycle stock and its interaction with safety stock. In subsequent sections, we will turn to more sophisticated policies that allow us to treat cycle stock and safety stock in an integrated fashion, so that we can consider the dual role of cycle stock as excess from a batching process and protection against variability.

The simplest inventory replenishment system is the **base stock** system, in which a replacement is ordered each time an item is removed. A kanban system is essentially a base stock system, because cards represent replenishment orders that are triggered whenever an item is removed from an inbound stock point. Retail systems in which demand is too small to warrant batch replenishment (e.g., expensive jewelry, high-end automobiles, etc.) may also use a base stock system to regulate their stock.

To model a base stock system, we assume that demands occur one at a time at random intervals and are either met from stock (if there is inventory) or backordered (if the system is stocked out). Each time a demand occurs a replenishment order is placed to replace the item (also one at a time). Replenishment orders arrive after a fixed lead time, LT.

We define **net inventory** as on-hand inventory minus backorders (i.e., so that it becomes negative whenever we are out of stock and have outstanding customer backorders). We call the sum of net inventory plus replenishment orders the **inventory position** and note that it represents the total inventory either on hand or on order. Because a replenishment order is placed every time a demand occurs, the inventory position remains constant in a base stock system. We call this level the **base stock level (BSL)**. The base stock level can also be thought of as a target inventory level or "order up to" level. We place an order each time inventory position reaches BSL -1, so we call this the **reorder point (ROP)**.

Figure 7.5 illustrates the behavior of a base stock system with a reorder point of ROP $= 4$ (and hence a base stock level of BSL $= 5$). Notice that net inventory becomes negative when the system is stocked out. In such cases, it is possible to have more than BSL units on order. But even then, the inventory position, which represents the total unsold inventory in the pipeline, remains at BSL.

The key problem in a base stock system, as in all safety stock situations, is to strike an appropriate balance between service and inventory. Here, service is measured by **fill rate**, the fraction of demands that are met from stock. For the base stock system, we can calculate fill rate by considering the system at a moment when a demand has just occurred and thus a replenishment has just been ordered. This order will arrive after LT time units have elapsed. Because any other orders that were outstanding will also have arrived by this time, the replenishment order will arrive before it is demanded (i.e., will go into stock rather than fill a backorder) if

FIGURE 7.5 Mechanics of a base stock system

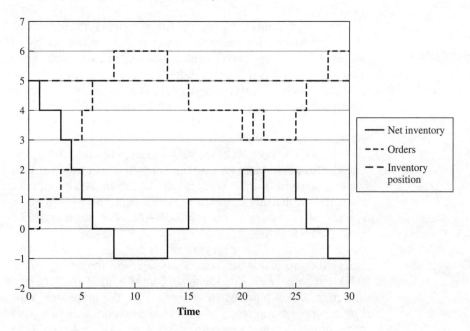

FIGURE 7.6

Finding a base stock level that attains fill rate *S*

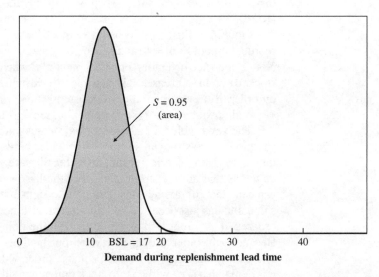

demand during this interval of length LT is less than BSL (i.e., less than or equal to ROP = BSL −1). The probability that an item will not be backordered, which is the same as the fraction of orders that will be filled from stock, is therefore equal to the probability that demand during replenishment lead time is less than or equal to ROP. Thus, if we can estimate the distribution of demand during replenishment lead time, we can find the base stock level that achieves a fill rate of S. Figure 7.6 graphically shows how to find the base stock level needed to achieve $S = 0.95$ for the case where demand during lead time is normally distributed with mean 12 and standard deviation 3.

If we approximate demand during replenishment lead time with a normal distribution with mean μ and standard deviation σ, the reorder point can be explicitly calculated from the formula

$$\text{ROP} = \mu + z\sigma$$

where z is a **safety factor** given by the Sth percentile of the standard normal distribution (which can be looked up in a table or computed in a spreadsheet; for example, if S is 0.95 then $z = 1.645$). In the example from Figure 7.6, we can compute the base stock level necessary to achieve 95 percent service as

$$\text{ROP} = 12 + 1.645(3) = 17$$

To increase service to a 99 percent level, we would need to increase the safety factor to 2.33, so the reorder point would increase to ROP $= 12 + 2.33(3) = 19$.

The **safety stock (SS)** is the amount of (net) inventory we expect to have when a replenishment order arrives.[4] Because we place an order whenever the inventory position (stock on hand or on order) reaches ROP and the expected demand during replenishment lead time is μ, the safety stock is given by

$$\text{SS} = \text{ROP} - \mu$$

In the case of normal demand, ROP $= \mu + z\sigma$, so the safety stock is given by $z\sigma$. Hence, the safety stock is determined by the safety factor z (which increases as the target fill rate increases) and the standard deviation of lead time demand σ. Safety stock is not affected by mean lead time demand μ.

We can see this graphically in Figures 7.7 and 7.8. Figure 7.7 shows that increasing the mean lead time demand from 12 to 36

---

[4]Note that safety stock could be negative if we expect to have items on backorder by the time a replenishment order arrives.

FIGURE 7.7

Effect on base
stock level of
increasing mean
lead time
demand

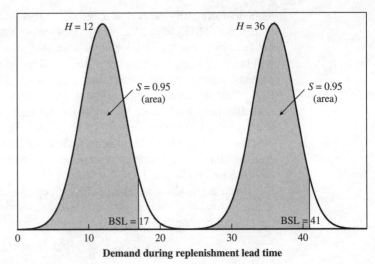

FIGURE 7.7

Effect on base
stock level of
increasing mean
lead time
demand

without changing the standard deviation causes the reorder point to
increase from 17 to 41 to maintain a fill rate of 95 percent. Because
the reorder point ROP and mean demand during replenishment
lead time μ both increase by the same amount, the safety stock
$SS = ROP - \mu$ is unchanged. In contrast, Figure 7.8 shows that
increasing the standard deviation from 3 to 4 without changing the
mean causes the reorder point needed to maintain the 95 percent fill

FIGURE 7.8

Effect on base
stock level of
increasing
standard
deviation of lead
time demand

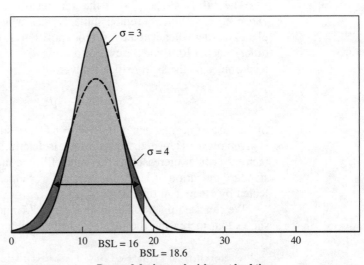

rate to increase from 16 to 18.6. Because ROP has increased by 2.6 units but μ has remained constant, the safety stock, $SS = ROP - \mu$ will also increase by 2.6 units.[5]

We can summarize the key results concerning safety stock with the following law:

Principle (Safety Stock).   *In a base stock system, safety stock increases with both the target fill rate and (for a sufficiently high target fill rate) the standard deviation of demand during replenishment lead time.*

The above analysis and insights can be extended to a host of practical inventory systems. We discuss some of the most fundamental cases below.

7.5   Periodic Review Systems

The EOQ model addresses situations involving only cycle stock (because it doesn't consider demand variability, which would necessitate safety stock), while the base stock model addresses systems involving only safety stock (because one-at-a-time replenishment does not build up cycle stock). But many realistic systems contain both cycle and safety stock. Because, as we noted earlier, cycle stock offers some variability protection, we need to consider both types of stock together to accurately assess their combined effect on service.

Although there are many variations, most inventory systems can be divided into two broad categories: **periodic review systems**, in which stock counts and replenishment orders are made at regular intervals (e.g., weekly), and **continuous review systems**, in which stock levels are monitored in real time and replenishment orders can be placed whenever needed. We discuss the periodic review case here and the continuous review case in the next section.

Examples of periodic review inventory systems abound in industry. For instance, retail stores, vending machines, and parking meters are examples of systems in which inventory is checked

---

[5]Note that the result that ROP increases with σ is based on the assumption that increasing σ causes the Sth percentile of the lead time demand distribution to increase. For the normal distribution, this is only true when S is greater than 50 percent. However, in practice, high fill rates are more prevalent than low fill rates, and changes in lead time variability are often due to variability in lead times (e.g., delays from suppliers), which affect the right tail of the distribution (i.e., the symmetric normal shape is not preserved), so more variability usually does mean that the Sth percentile increases.

and replenished at scheduled intervals.[6] While modern information systems have made it possible to monitor many inventories in continuous (or near continuous) time, there are still instances where such detailed monitoring is impossible or impractical. So, managing periodic review inventory systems is still an important production and supply chain function.

The simplest periodic review situation is where the distribution of demand is the same from period to period.[7] For example, suppose demand for an item occurs Monday through Friday. At the end of the day on Friday, the stock level is checked and a replenishment order is placed, which arrives in time for the start of the next week on Monday. If our forecast of weekly demand is the same every week (even though the actual demand may not be), then an **order-up-to policy**, in which inventory is brought up to the same specified level at the start of each week, is appropriate. The challenge is to determine the best order-up-to level.

The trade-off in setting an order-up-to level is between having too much inventory, which incurs holding cost, and too little inventory, which results in a backorder cost.[8] If the ordering period is a week, then we define h to represent the cost to hold one unit of inventory for one week and b represent the cost to carry one unit of customer demand on backorder for one week.[9]

If we consider the xth item in stock at the beginning of the week, then this item incurs a holding cost only if demand is less than x. Therefore, if D represents the (random) demand during a week, then the expected holding cost of the xth item is

$$hP(D < x)$$

---

[6]Note that "inventory" in a parking meter is actually space to hold the coins. Each time the meter is emptied, this empty space "inventory" is brought up to the capacity of the meter.

[7]Assuming a constant demand distribution is reasonable as long as there is no cyclicity of demand (e.g., high in the summer, low in the winter) or anticipated demand spikes (e.g., Christmas). When such demand patterns exist, it may still make sense to use an order-up-to policy, but with a different order-up-to level for different times of the year.

[8]Note that we are assuming that customers who encounter a stockout are willing to wait for backordered items. For systems, such as retail outlets where customers simply leave if they do not find an item in stock, we can still use our model with the backorder cost redefined as the cost of a lost sale (e.g., the lost unit profit plus any loss of future sales if a disappointed customer is less likely to return in the future).

[9]In practice, the backorder cost b is not a measurable quantity like the holding cost h. While h can reasonably be computed as ic, where i is the opportunity cost of money (discount rate) and c is the unit cost of an item in stock, b depends on intangibles such as loss of customer goodwill. Therefore, we view b as more of a "dial" in our model, which can be used to adjust the inventory/service trade-off to find a reasonable compromise.

where $P(D < x)$ represents the probability that demand is less than x. If, for simplicity, we ignore the discreteness of demand (which allows us to neglect the probability that $D = x$), then $P(D < x) = P(D \leq x)$.[10]

Similarly, the xth item incurs a backorder cost only if demand exceeds x, so the expected backorder cost of the xth item is

$$bP(D > x) = b[1 - P(D \leq x)]$$

To minimize total average cost, we should set the inventory level at the start of the week to a level where expected backorder cost just equals expected holding cost. That is,

$$hP(D \leq x) = b[1 - P(D \leq x)]$$

which yields

$$P(D \leq x) = \frac{b}{b + h}$$

We define the **order-up-to level (OUTL)** as the value of x that satisfies this condition. That is, if we order enough stock so that we start the week with OUTL on hand, our probability of meeting all demand during the week will equal $b/(b + h)$. Note that increasing the backorder cost b increases the target probability of meeting demand and hence the necessary order-up-to level, OUTL. Conversely, increasing the holding cost h decreases the target probability of meeting demand and hence the necessary order-up-to level.

If we approximate demand during the order period with a normal distribution with mean μ and standard deviation σ, then we can write the optimal order-up-to level as

$$\text{OUTL} = \mu + z\sigma$$

where z is a safety factor given by the $b/(b + h)$ percentile of the standard normal distribution, which can be looked up in a normal table or computed in a spreadsheet.

Notice that because we start the week with an inventory level of OUTL and the expected demand during the week is μ, the expected inventory level at the end of the week, which represents the safety stock (SS) is

$$\text{SS} = \text{OUTL} - \mu = \mu + z\sigma - \mu = z\sigma$$

---

[10]This approximation is very accurate when demand is large and is generally as accurate as the input data for the model. We use it here to keep the formulas simple.

FIGURE 7.9 Expected and actual inventory paths in a periodic review system

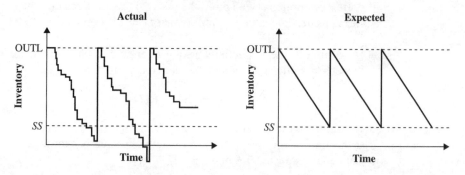

Figure 7.9 compares the expected and actual inventory paths in a periodic review system. In both paths, the inventory is brought up to the order-up-to level OUTL. In the expected path, inventory falls steadily to the safety stock (SS) level just before the replenishment order arrives. But in the actual path, inventory may fall past the safety stock level, or even become negative (if backorders are allowed).

To illustrate the use of this model in a periodic review inventory system, consider a hardware store that sells a particular model of cordless drill. The store receives weekly deliveries from the manufacturer and must decide each week how many drills to order. From experience, the owner knows that sales average 10 drills per week with a standard deviation of 3 drills per week. The retail price is $200, while the wholesale price is $150. The store uses a 26 percent annual carrying cost rate, so the holding cost per week is $0.26(150)/52 = \$0.75$. Because customers who do not find the drill in stock generally go elsewhere, we use in place of the backorder cost the lost profit or $200 - 150 = \$50$. Hence, from the earlier discussion, it follows that the store should order enough drills each week to bring inventory up to a level such that the probability of being able to meet all demand during the week is

$$\frac{b}{b+h} = \frac{\$50}{\$50 + \$0.75} = 0.9852$$

Clearly, because the cost of a lost sale exceeds the cost of holding a drill for another week, the optimal probability of meeting demand is very high for this case. To achieve it, we assume that demand can be approximated by a normal distribution and find (from a standard normal table) that the 98.52 percentile of the standard normal distribution is 2.18. Hence, the hardware store should bring the inventory of drills up to a level of OUTL at the beginning of each week, where

$$\text{OUTL} = \mu + z\sigma = 10 + 2.18(3) = 16.54 \approx 17$$

During an average week, the store will sell 10 drills and be left with 7 in stock when the next replenishment order arrives. These 7 drills represent safety stock that ensures a high percentage of customers (above 98 percent) will find the drill in stock.

Insight by Analogy

Soft Drink Machine

A classic example of a periodic review inventory system is a soft drink machine. At regular intervals a vendor visits the machine, checks the inventory levels, and refills the machine. Because the capacity of the machine is fixed, the vendor uses an order-up-to policy, where the order-up-to level is set by how much the machine can hold.

To begin with, suppose that the replenishment cycle is fixed (e.g., the vendor fills the machine every Friday). Clearly the factor that affects the fill rate (percent of customers who do not find the machine empty) is the average weekly demand rate (μ in the above notation). A machine in a prime location near the employee lunchroom is much more likely to stock out than a machine in a remote corner of an overly air-conditioned building.

Of course, to compensate for this, the vendor may visit the high-demand machine more frequently than the low-demand machine. For instance, suppose the lunchroom machine had average demand of 20 bottles per day and the remote machine had average demand of 4 bottles per day. Then if the vendor replenished the lunchroom machine every 2 days and the remote machine every 10 days, both would have average demand of 40 bottles during the replenishment cycle.

If the replenishment cycle is set so that average demand is the same, then other factors will determine the fill rate. The most important is the standard deviation of demand (σ in the above notation). For instance, suppose the lunchroom machine and a machine on a beach both sell on average 20 bottles per day. However, demand at the lunchroom machine is very steady, while demand at the beach machine varies widely depending on the weather. So, while the lunchroom machine sells very nearly 20 bottles every day, the beach machine might sell 40 one (hot) day and none the (cold, rainy) next. If the vendor visits these two machines on the same cycle, the beach machine will stock out much more frequently than the lunchroom machine. To achieve comparable customer service, the beach machine would either have to hold more bottles or be refilled more frequently.

Finally, another alternative to improve customer service without excess visits by the vendor would be to switch from periodic to continuous review. If vending machines were monitored via the Internet, then the vendor could check the stock levels of all machines in his/her region and only replenish machines when they were close to empty. With clever scheduling, the vendor should be able to visit machines less often and still achieve better customer service.

7.6   Continuous Review Systems

The periodic review approach was once the predominant basis for inventory management. However, in more recent years, modern information systems have made it increasingly possible to track inventory continuously and reorder at any point in time. In a continuous review inventory system the challenge is to determine both when and how much to order. Most systems make use of a reorder point approach, in which a replenishment order is placed whenever inventory drops to a specified level.

The basic mechanics of a reorder point system are illustrated in Figure 7.10. In this system, the reorder point (ROP) is equal to 3, while the order quantity (OQ) is equal to 4. Every time the inventory position (on-hand inventory plus replenishment orders minus backorders) reaches the reorder point of 3, a new replenishment order of 4 items is placed. We assume that the replenishment lead time is 6 days, so we see a jump in net inventory 6 days after the order is placed.

In this example, we start with 6 items on-hand, so net inventory is 6. Because there are no replenishment orders or backorders outstanding, inventory position is also equal to 6. Demands occur, reducing on-hand stock until net inventory (and inventory position) falls to the reorder point of 3. A replenishment order for 4 items is immediately placed, which brings inventory position up to 7 (OQ + ROP). But this order will not arrive for 6 days, so demands continue reducing net inventory and inventory position. On day 7, 4 more demands have occured, which causes inventory position to again hit the reorder point. So a second replenishment order of 4 is placed (which will not arrive until 6 days later on day 13). Note, however, that because the first replenishment order has not yet arrived, net inventory becomes negative. So, on day 8, on-hand inventory is 0, while the backorder level is

FIGURE 7.10 Mechanics of a continuous review system with OQ = 4, ROP = 3.

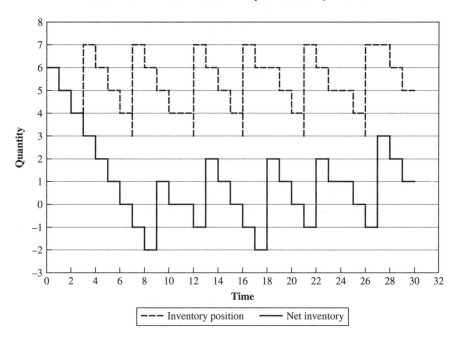

equal to 1. Because there are 8 units in outstanding replenishment orders,

$$\text{inventory position} = \text{on-hand inventory} + \text{replenishment orders} - \text{backorders}$$
$$= 0 + 8 - 1$$
$$= 7$$

which is what we see in Figure 7.10.

It is clear from Figure 7.10 that increasing either the reorder point, ROP, or the order quantity, OQ, will increase the average level of on-hand inventory. But increasing either ROP or OQ also reduces the average backorder level. So, the balance we must strike in choosing OQ and ROP is the usual one of inventory versus service. There exist mathematical models for optimizing this type of model. But because OQ and ROP interact with one another, such models are complex and require algorithms to solve (see Zipkin 2000 for the most comprehensive reference on inventory models and the algorithms for analyzing them). However, because all of the data for an inventory management system are approximate anyway (e.g., we can only estimate the demand rate), most practitioners resort to some kind of heuristic for setting the parameters in a reorder point system.

A reasonable heuristic for a continuous review system is to compute the order quantity and reorder point separately using the EOQ and base stock results. This means that to compute the order quantity we need to estimate the fixed cost of placing an order, o, the annual cost to hold an item in inventory, h, and the annual demand rate, D. Then the order quantity is given by the familiar square root formula

$$\text{EOQ} = \sqrt{\frac{2oD}{h}}$$

We compute the reorder point by estimating the annual cost of holding a unit of backorder, b, and setting

$$\text{ROP} = \mu + z\sigma$$

where z is the $b/(b + h)$ percentile of the standard normal distribution and, as in the base stock model, μ and σ represent the mean and standard deviation of demand during replenishment lead time.

As in the base stock model, the safety stock is the amount of stock we expect to have on hand when a replenishment order arrives. Because average demand during the replenishment lead time is μ, the optimal safety stock (SS) is equal to

$$\text{SS} = \text{ROP} - \mu = z\sigma$$

Hence, the optimal safety stock depends on the safety factor, z, and the standard deviation of lead time demand, σ. The parameter b depends on the service level we are trying to achieve (which will determine z) as well as the holding cost (which will be determined by the unit cost of the part). The standard deviation of lead time demand, σ, depends on the standard deviation of annual demand and the replenishment lead time, LT. So, from all this, we conclude that setting the safety stock to achieve a given level of service for a particular item should consider the unit cost, replenishment lead time, and variability (standard deviation) of demand. We will show later that failure to consider these factors can result in large inefficiencies.

To illustrate the use of this model in a continuous review inventory system, consider a plant that maintains a stock of a particular fuse to be used for equipment repairs. Annual usage of the fuse averages 100 units with a standard deviation of 10 units. New fuses are ordered from an outside supplier at a unit cost of $350 and have a lead time of 30 days. This means that average demand during replenishment lead time is

$$\mu = \frac{100}{365} \times 30 = 8.22$$

We will assume the standard deviation of demand during replenishment lead time is equal to the square root of mean demand.[11] This implies

$$\sigma = \sqrt{\mu} = \sqrt{8.22} = 2.87$$

Now, suppose the fixed cost of placing and receiving the order is estimated to be $o = \$50$ and the holding cost is computed using a 25 percent rate, so $h = 0.25(\$350) = \$87.50$. Finally, suppose that a shortage will cause a machine outage, which will cause lost throughput that will have to be made up on overtime at a cost of $250 per day. So, the annual cost of a unit backorder, assuming a 250-day work year, is $b = 250(\$250) = \$62,500$.

With these, we can use the EOQ formula to compute a reasonable order quantity to be

$$\text{EOQ} = \sqrt{\frac{2oD}{h}} = \sqrt{\frac{2(50)(100)}{87.5}} = 10.7$$

To compute the reorder point, we compute the target service level as the ratio

$$\frac{b}{b+h} = \frac{62,500}{62,500 + 87.50} = 0.9986$$

which is high because outages are so expensive. From a normal table, we find that the 99.86 percentile of the standard normal distribution is 2.99. Hence, the reorder point should be set as

$$\text{ROP} = \mu + z\sigma = 8.22 + 2.99(2.87) = 16.8$$

Thus, even though we expect demand of only 8.22 during the 30 days it will take to receive a replenishment order, we place this order when the stock of fuses drops to 16.8. The amount of inventory we expect to have when this order arrives, which is $16.8 - 8.22 = 8.58$, is the safety stock in this system. It is this high level of safety stock that produces such a high fill rate for fuses.

---

[11]The standard deviation of demand equals the square root of mean demand when demand follows a Poisson distribution, which is quite common and therefore often assumed when additional information about demand variability is not available.

FIGURE 7.11 Expected and actual inventory paths in a continuous review system

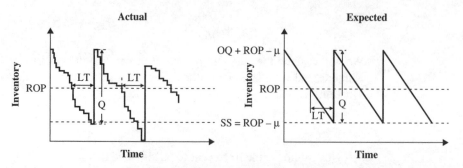

It is beyond the scope of this book to develop the exact formulas for computing the average on-hand inventory level that would result from using a given reorder point policy [see Hopp and Spearman (2000, Chapter 2) or Zipkin (2000, Chapter 6) for details]. But we can make a good estimate by using the simple approximation shown in Figure 7.11, which replaces the actual inventory path shown on the left, which is jagged and unpredictable due to demand uncertainty, with the expected inventory path shown on the right. In the expected inventory path, we assume that demand is smooth and constant. So, we will place a replenishment order each time the on-hand inventory level falls to the reorder point, ROP. During the lead time (LT) we wait for this order to arrive, demand will exactly equal the mean lead time demand (μ). Hence, the new order will arrive when stock is at the safety stock level, SS = ROP $-\mu$. Because the order quantity is OQ, the on-hand inventory level jumps to SS + OQ. It will then decline smoothly again until it reaches ROP and the process repeats. Because we are assuming that demand occurs at a steady rate, the average inventory level is halfway between the minimum and maximum points on this sawtooth diagram. Hence,

$$\text{Average on-hand inventory} \approx \frac{\text{SS} + (\text{SS} + \text{OQ})}{2} = \text{SS} + \frac{\text{OQ}}{2}$$

$$= \text{ROP} - \mu + \frac{\text{OQ}}{2}$$

For our example with OQ = 10.7 and ROP = 16.8, this becomes

$$\text{Average on-hand inventory} \approx \text{ROP} - \mu + \frac{\text{OQ}}{2} = 16.8 - 8.22$$

$$+ \frac{10.7}{2} = 13.93$$

which represents 13.93($350) = $4,875 tied up in fuse inventory.

It also turns out that the fill rate achieved by this policy is actually 99.989 percent.[12] The reason this is higher than the target we set of 99.86 percent is because the formula we used for setting the reorder point assumes that $OQ = 1$ (i.e., it is the base stock formula). But higher values of OQ mean that the reorder point is crossed less frequently and hence demands have a smaller chance of encountering the system in a state of stockout. Thus, the formulas given above for OQ and ROP are conservative. But, given the roughness of the data and the likelihood of inefficiencies not considered by the model (e.g., operator errors), this is not necessarily a bad thing.

Of course, in realistic settings, we do not usually use order quantities like 10.7 or reorder points like 16.8. As with the EOQ model, we generally round these to integers (e.g., $OQ = 11$ and $ROP = 17$). If we round up, then the rounding will improve the service level (at the expense of more inventory), although the effect will generally be small if OQ and ROP are fairly large numbers.

Finally, it is often the case that estimating o and b is difficult. As we noted in our discussion of EOQ, when replenishments are manufactured, the true cost of a setup depends on dynamic factors, such as equipment utilization, and so o is not really fixed. Estimating b is even harder, because the true cost of a backorder includes intangibles, such as the cost of lost goodwill. So, in practice, we often use the o and b parameters as "dials" to adjust OQ and ROP until the performance (in terms of both inventory and customer service) is acceptable. We discuss this approach further in the context of multi-item systems.

7.7   Multi-Item Systems

Most inventory systems involve multiple items. If the items do not interact, then the single-item approaches discussed above can be used to analyze each item separately. For instance, if a blood bank has ample storage, then it can compute stocking policies for each blood type independently. However, in a retail outlet with limited space, more inventory of one product means less space for another, and so the stocking policies for different items must be computed jointly. Similarly, in spare parts systems, more inventory of one item means fewer repair delays due to outages of that item, which may mean we can afford more delays due to outages of another

---

[12]Again, the exact formula for computing the fill rate in a continuous review inventory system is beyond the scope of this book, but can be obtained from either Hopp and Spearman (2000, Chapter 2) or Zipkin (2000, Chapter 6).

item. Striking an appropriate balance between inventory and total delay requires that the stocks of spare parts be set jointly.

Fortunately, the single-item models provide useful building blocks for the multi-item situation. The simplest case occurs when both fixed order costs and backorder costs can be assumed equal for all parts. For example, in purchasing systems where the paperwork is identical for all parts, the fixed order cost really is constant for all items. Backorder costs could be constant in a retail setting if customers are just as displeased to find the store out of $2 batteries as $500 televisions. Similarly, backorder costs would be constant across parts in a spare parts setting when a machine cannot run for lack of a $2 fuse or a $500 pump.

If the fixed order cost o is the same for all parts, then we can compute the order quantity for part i using the EOQ formula

$$\text{EOQ}_i = \sqrt{\frac{2oD_i}{h_i}}$$

where D_i and h_i are the annual demand and holding cost for part i. Note that high-demand and/or low-cost parts will tend to have larger lot sizes than low-demand and/or high-cost parts.

Similarly, if the annual cost of holding a unit of backorder b is the same for all parts, we can compute the reorder point for part i by using the base stock formula

$$\text{ROP}_i = \mu_i + z_i \sigma_i$$

where z_i is the $b/(b + h_i)$ percentile of the standard normal distribution and μ_i and σ_i represent the mean and standard deviation of demand during replenishment lead time for part i.

To illustrate how this would work, let us reconsider the spare part example from the previous section. Now, however, we assume that in addition to fuses, the plant stocks pumps, sensors, and controls. Each is used to repair equipment in the plant. The part costs, annual demand, replenishment lead time, and mean and standard deviation of demand during replenishment lead time are given in Table 7.1.

As in the earlier fuse example, we assume that the cost of placing and receiving a replenishment order is $o = \$50$, the holding cost rate is 25 percent, and the cost of having a unit of backorder is $250 per day so $b = \$62,500$ per year. We are assuming here that the fixed cost of placing an order is the same for all parts and,

TABLE 7.1   Multipart inventory example—Data

Part (i)	Unit Cost (c_i)	Annual Demand (D_i)	Lead Time (LT_i)	Mean LT Demand (μ_i)	Std Dev LT Demand (σ_i)
Fuse	350	100	30	8.2	2.9
Pump	1200	50	60	8.2	2.9
Sensor	350	25	100	6.8	2.6
Control	15000	10	15	0.4	0.6

because a shortage of any part prolongs an equipment outage, the backorder cost is also the same.

By using these values of o and b in the above expressions, we can compute order quantities and reorder points for each part, as shown in Table 7.2.[13] After computing OQ_i and ROP_i, we can compute the actual service, S_i (which will differ from the target service because of the approximations in the model), and the inventory investment, I_i (value of average on-hand inventory), for each part i. Formulas for these calculations are beyond the scope of this presentation but can be found in Hopp and Spearman (2000).

From these results we can make the following observations:

- Target and actual service are lowest for controls, because these are the most expensive components and so the model seeks to limit inventory of them.

- Fuses and sensors have the same target service because their cost is identical. However, because demand is greater for fuses, the model orders them in larger lots. Also, because demand during replenishment lead time is larger for fuses than for sensors, fuses have a higher reorder point as well.

- Average service across all parts (computed by weighting the service for each part by the fraction of total demand represented by that part) is 99.82 percent. The reason this is so high is that the backorder cost ($b = \$62,500$) is high. We could adjust the service level up or down by varying the value of b.

Table 7.2 shows that the continuous review model can be used to generate a stocking policy for the multi-item inventory problem.

---

[13]For simplicity, we have used the formulas without rounding. In practice it may make sense to round off the order quantity, OQ_i, and reorder point, ROP_i, to the nearest integers.

TABLE 7.2   Multipart inventory example—Results

Part (i)	Holding Cost ($h_i = 0.25c_i$)	Target Service ($b/(b+h_i)$)	Order Quantity (OQ_i)	Reorder Point (ROP_i)	Actual Service (S_i)	Inventory Investment (I_i)
Fuse	87.50	0.9986	10.7	16.8	0.99989	$4,870.40
Pump	300.00	0.9952	4.1	15.6	0.99895	$11,366.29
Sensor	87.50	0.9986	5.3	14.7	0.99981	$3,673.66
Control	3750.00	0.9434	0.5	1.4	0.97352	$1,9203.36
Total					0.99820	$39,113.71

But how do we know it is a good solution? To get a better sense of the leverage offered by a sophisticated inventory policy like this, we contrast it with an alternative often used in industry, namely the **days-of-supply** approach. Under this approach we set the safety stock equal to some number of days of demand. Specifically, we set the reorder point for part i as

$$ROP_i = \mu_i + \frac{kD_i}{365}$$

where $kD_i/365$ represents the safety stock and hence k is the number of days of demand covered by this stock.[14]

The reasoning behind the days-of-supply approach is that it provides a uniform level of protection across parts, because a high-demand part will have a larger safety stock than a low-demand part. But this reasoning is wrong! Because the formula for ROP_i does not consider the cost of the part or the replenishment lead time, this approach can result in serious inefficiencies.

To see this, let us reconsider the previous example. Suppose that order quantities are set as before using the EOQ model. However, reorder points are set using the above days-of-supply method. To make a fair comparison, we adjust the value of k by trial and error until the average service level equals 99.82 percent, the same as that achieved by the optimal approach. Doing this results in $k = 60$ days of supply for all parts. The resulting stocking parameters, service levels, and inventory investments are shown in Table 7.3.

The days-of-supply approach requires more than 50 percent additional inventory ($51,235.37 compared to $39,113.71) to achieve the same level of service as the optimal approach because it sets

---

[14]We divide k by 365 to convert to years because D_i represents annual demand.

TABLE 7.3   Multipart inventory example—Days-of-supply
approach

Part (i)	Order Quantity (OQ_i)	Reorder Point (ROP_i)	Actual Service (S_i)	Inventory Investment (I_i)
Fuse	10.7	24.8	1.00000	$7,677.33
Pump	4.1	16.5	0.99961	$12,403.85
Sensor	5.3	11.0	0.98822	$2,391.15
Control	0.5	2.1	0.99822	$28,763.04
Total			0.99820	$51,235.37

the reorder point too low for sensors and too high for everything
else. Sensors are an inexpensive part with comparatively low lead
time demand, so the service level for sensors can be increased at
relatively low cost. The optimal continuous review model does exactly this and then reduces inventory of the more expensive (or
longer lead time) parts to achieve the same service at lower total cost. Because the days-of-supply approach is not sensitive to
part costs or replenishment lead times, it has no way to strike this
balance.

The above discussion suggests that inventory is a complex
subject, and it is. There are entire books written on inventory theory
that make use of sophisticated mathematics to analyze the various
trade-offs involved [see, for example, Zipkin (2000)]. But while
the details are beyond the scope of our discussion here, the main
formulas are not. The above expressions for OQ and ROP are easily
implemented in a spreadsheet.[15] Moreover, the qualitative insight
that it is critical to consider part cost and replenishment lead time,
as well as mean and standard deviation of demand, is clear and
general. A multi-item inventory system with stocking parameters
that do not take these factors into account is a likely opportunity
for improvement.

---

[15]The expressions for service and inventory level are not simple and require macros
to implement in a spreadsheet. But these are not strictly necessary to make use of the
continuous review approach. We can estimate the *o* and *b* costs as accurately as
possible and make use of the simple formulas to get OQ and ROP. If in practice you
find that the lot sizes are too small (or replenishment orders are too frequent) then
increase *o*. Similarly, if you find that the average service level is too low, then
increase *b*. You can use the parameters *o* and *b* like "dials" to adjust the performance
of the inventory system to strike the desired balance among inventory, lot sizing, and
service.

Principles in Practice

Bell & Howell

Readers of the author's generation will undoubtedly remember Bell & Howell as the company that made the sturdy clicking movie projectors that were standard equipment in classrooms throughout the United States in the 1950s and 60s. But in recent years, Bell & Howell (Bowe, Bell & Howell since 2003) has licensed its brand to various electronics and optics products, but has focused its own efforts on mail and messaging solutions.

An important product line in Bell & Howell's portfolio is high-speed mail sorting equipment. These machines use optical character recognition technology to sort mail by zip code. In addition to their use in postal systems, these machines are purchased by companies that do high-volume mailings. By sorting their outgoing mail by zip code these companies are able to take advantage of lower rates offered by the U.S. Postal Service.

To support its customers, Bell & Howell offers parts and repair services. Failure of a machine in the field can impact a customer's revenue stream (e.g., it can interrupt mailing of invoices), so prompt repairs are a priority. For this reason, Bell & Howell carries inventories of spare parts.

In the early 1990s, the CEO raised the question of whether the spare parts were being stocked efficiently. At that time, the company maintained a central distribution center (DC) in Chicago with regional facilities across the company. Roughly half of the total spare parts inventory was held in the DC, with the remainder divided among the facilities where it would be closer to the customers. Repair technicians obtained their parts from the facilities, which were in turn replenished by the DC.

The CEO's intuition turned out to be right. Stock levels in both the DC and the facilities were being managed using a days-of-stock approach. That is, reorder points (and order quantities) were being set solely as a function of demand rate. No consideration was given to part cost, replenishment lead times, or demand variability, let alone subtler distinctions such as part criticality, demand trends, use of parts in batches or kits, or coordination of the inventory between the DC and facilities. An analysis like that given above for a multi-item continuous review model showed that inventory investment could indeed be reduced by as much as 40 percent with the same customer service. Alternatively, inventory could be reduced by a smaller amount while also improving customer service.

After contemplating an upgrade of their Chicago DC, Bell & Howell decided to move it to Wilmington, Ohio, where it adopted more sophisticated inventory rules and partnered with Airborne Express to deliver parts to customers. The combination of better stocking policies and more responsive delivery facilitated an upgrade in customer service with less investment in inventory.

Questions for Thought

1. Classify the inventory in the following settings as working stock, cycle stock, safety stock, congestion stock, or anticipation stock. (Note that some of the cases may involve multiple inventory types.)
   a. Chemicals in the reactor columns of a pharmaceutical plant.
   b. Gasoline in the tank of your car.
   c. Freight being transported in containers on a ship.
   d. Pints of blood in a hospital.
   e. Jeans on the shelf at a retail store.
   f. Luggage waiting to be unloaded from an airplane.
   g. Cars waiting in line at a car wash.
   h. Supplies of toys in the backroom of a department store prior to the Christmas season.

2. Consider a firm that purchases polystyrene as a raw material for use in a styrofoam plant. The plant runs 250 days a year. Polystyrene costs $1,500 per ton and the plant uses 125,000 tons per year. Delivery charges consist of a "per ton" charge, which is included in the material cost, plus a fixed charge of $225 for each delivery, which covers paperwork, receiving expenses, and so forth. The firm uses a 15 percent carrying cost rate for inventory.
   a. Use the EOQ model to compute the batch size that minimizes the sum of the holding plus ordering costs.
   b. How many days of supply does the above batch size represent?
   c. Suppose the firm decides for convenience to have polystyrene delivered every other day. What will the batch size be and how much will this cause the total (holding plus ordering) cost to increase?

3. A retailer sells handmade teak folding deck chairs at an average rate of 2 per week. The lead time from the craftsman is 8 weeks.
   a. What is the average demand during the replenishment lead time? If we set the base stock level (BSL) equal to average lead time demand, what would you expect the fill rate to be?
   b. Suppose that the standard deviation of demand during lead time is equal to the square root of average lead time demand (i.e., demand follows a Poisson distribution). What base stock level, BSL, is needed to achieve a fill rate of 95 percent? What is the reorder point, ROP, for this base stock policy?
   c. If we left ROP at the level in part (b) but ordered chairs in batches of 2, would the fill rate increase or decrease? Why?

4. An organic food market receives daily fruit deliveries at 8:00 A.M. Suppose demand for bananas averages 300 pounds per day with a standard deviation of 75 pounds.

   a. Why is a periodic review system an appropriate way to control inventory in this environment?

   b. Suppose, because of spoilage, the market estimates a holding cost of $0.05 per pound per day. Customers who do not find bananas in stock buy them elsewhere; the lost profit is $0.10 per pound. What probability of being able to meet demand should the market aim for? If the market starts the day with 100 pounds of bananas in stock, how many pounds should it have delivered on that day?

   c. If average demand for bananas is different on different days of the week (e.g., lower on Mondays and higher on Saturdays), how should the periodic review model be modified?

5. A distributor stocks electronic parts in a warehouse for shipment to various contract manufacturers. One specialized power supply costs $100 per unit and can only be purchased from the supplier in boxes of 24 with a lead time of 2 weeks. The distributor sells an average of 10 units per week with a standard deviation of 3 units. Because of the risk of obsolescence, the distributor uses an annual holding cost rate of 25 percent.

   a. If we use a continuous review ROP model and set the backorder cost to $b = \$25$ per year, what reorder point would the approximate model in this chapter set?

   b. If the order quantity, OQ, were equal to 1, what service level (fill rate) would result from the reorder point of part (a)?

   c. Because the order quantity is forced by the supplier to be 24, will the actual service level be higher or lower than that in part (b)? How might the distributor select an appropriate reorder point that considers the order quantity of 24?

6. Suppose a firm sells flow monitors and related equipment to chemical plants and refineries. Some of their products are critical to the operation of their customers' plants, while others are not. The firm uses a continuous review ROP approach to control stocks of finished goods.

   a. Why is it inappropriate to use the same backorder cost for all products, as we did in the example shown in Table 7.2?

   b. How could the multi-item inventory model discussed in this chapter be adapted to controlling both critical and noncritical products?

8 RISK

Combining sources of variability so that they can share a common buffer reduces the total amount of buffering required to achieve a given level of performance.

8.1 Introduction

Exposure to negative consequences of uncertain events is called **risk**. Up to this point, we have dealt with uncertainty in the form of routine variability, such as fluctuations in supply and demand. The logical protection against the risk posed by routine variability is the use of inventory, capacity, and time buffers. But supply chain systems face risk from events beyond normal levels of variability. Hurricanes, political disruptions, acts of terrorism, currency crises, technological breakthroughs, and many other unpredictable events can have substantial influence on supply chains. Dealing with such risks, therefore, is an important part of supply chain management.

While conventional buffers are very effective for reducing risk from routine variability, they are less helpful as protection against rarer and more consequential events (e.g., disasters). For instance, a week's worth of safety stock will not insulate a firm from the consequences of a fire that takes a supplier plant off-line for 6 months. Of course, the firm could carry a 6-month supply of safety stock, but because such serious disruptions are rare, this is almost certainly uneconomical. Hence, to manage risks from significant but rare events, we must supplement buffering with other strategies.

FIGURE 8.1

Layers of
protection
against supply
chain risk

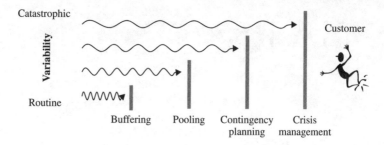

Figure 8.1 schematically illustrates four risk protection strategies:

Buffering: Maintaining excess resources (inventory, capacity, time) to cover for fluctuations in supply or demand.

Pooling: Sharing buffers to cover multiple sources of variability (e.g., demand from different markets or production from different processes).

Contingency planning: Establishing a preset course of action for an anticipated scenario. We can think of this as "virtual buffering," because it involves securing buffers only when needed, rather than holding them continuously in advance.

Crisis management: Generating responses to events for which buffers (individual or pooled) and contingency plans are inadequate. This is the last line of defense and so constitutes a default option; if the above proactive strategies are not used, reactive crisis management will be needed. The challenge is to do it well, rather than badly.

The characteristics of these four strategies for mitigating risk makes them appropriate for different situations, as illustrated graphically in Figure 8.2.

Buffering and pooling strategies hold resources in readiness for an event. Because this is costly, these strategies are economical only for events that have a comparatively high likelihood of occurring. For example, it may be appropriate to maintain safety stock of raw materials to cover against the possibility of yield loss due to quality problems. To protect against late deliveries, it may make sense to build in safety lead time. But it would almost certainly not make sense to hold safety stock to protect against a long-term disruption of supply due to a hundred-year flood because it would be likely to result in holding a large stock for a long time without use.

The one case where holding buffer resources as protection for a very unlikely event could make sense is where the consequences are

FIGURE 8.2

Matching risk
mitigation
strategies to
types of supply
chain risk

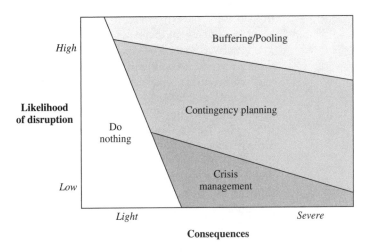

very severe. For example, the military holds supplies of weapons
and pharmaceutical companies hold supplies of drugs they are very
unlikely to use because the consequences of a shortage could be
devastating (i.e., measured in lives lost). This is why the buffer-
ing/pooling region in Figure 8.2 expands as the severity of the
consequences of an event increases.

When buffering and pooling are uneconomical because the
likelihood and severity of an event do not justify continually holding resources in readiness, we turn to contingency planning. Here
we do not hold resources, but instead develop a plan for obtain-
ing them when needed. While this will probably result in a slower
response than a buffering/pooling strategy, it is almost certainly
cheaper. For example, a contract with an alternate supplier to provide backup material in case of disruption of a primary supplier will
cost much less than holding a large supply of inventory, although
lead time will be increased.

While the resources involved in a contingency plan may be virtual, the time and effort required to create the plan are real. Hence,
it is not practical to create a contingency plan for every imagin-
able event that could present risk to a supply chain system. Like
buffering/pooling, contingency planning becomes more attractive
as the risk from an event becomes more severe. For example, a
dockworkers' strike that would impact all players in an industry
equally, and hence would not alter the competitive balance of the
market, might not warrant a detailed contingency plan on the part
of an individual firm. But a contingency plan probably does make
sense for a political disruption in a part of the world that would
interrupt a firm's supply but not that of its competition. Because of

this, the contingency planning region in Figure 8.2 expands as the severity of an event increases.

Finally, for cases where the likelihood and severity of an event do not warrant a contingency plan (or we were unable to imagine such an event to prepare one), we are left with crisis management as the only available response to a disruptive event. In essence, crisis management is like contingency planning without the planning. That is, we develop and execute a plan after an event has already occurred. For example, in 2000 Ford faced a serious crisis due to claims that its Explorer model was prone to rollover accidents. While Ford had in place organizational guidelines for handling product recalls (e.g., chain of command for decision making, guidelines for speaking to the press, etc.), it did not have a specific contingency plan for dealing with rollover accidents associated with tire problems. So, the company was forced to evolve its strategy (which included shutting down plants producing other vehicles to divert tires to Explorer customers needing replacements under the recall order) while the situation was evolving.

Clearly it is much more difficult to come up with an effective plan in the midst of a crisis than in advance under calmer conditions. But because it is not possible to have a plan for every contingency, crisis management is a necessary risk mitigation strategy. But crisis management need not imply chaos. As we describe below, many steps can be taken to prepare an organization to respond to a crisis, even when the nature of the crisis cannot be specified.

From an overall perspective, the key to managing risk in supply chain systems is making effective use of all four of the above mitigation approaches as part of a balanced preparation and response strategy. We have already discussed buffering in general terms in Chapter 5 and inventory buffering in detail in Chapter 7, so we will focus on the remaining three strategies—pooling, contingency planning, and crisis management—in this chapter.

8.2   Pooling

In Chapter 5 we noted that flexibility can improve the efficiency of buffering. For example, we will require less total safety stock if we hold inventory in a single centralized distribution center than if we hold separate supplies of safety stock at individual retail sites. The reason is that when stock is centralized (and therefore flexible with regard to destination), it can be shared among retail sites. Because it is unlikely that all sites will face abnormally high demand at the same time, less total stock will be required to provide the same level of protection in the shared stock case as in the separate stock case.

The core concept that underlies this approach of making buffers flexible so that they can be shared is **variability pooling**. In this section, we first give a brief mathematical description of variability pooling and then offer a range of applications.

8.2.1   Probability Basics

The mathematical idea behind variability pooling is simple but subtle. Essentially it has to do with the fact that the bad consequences of variability are due to extreme values. Unusually high (or low) demands, process times, delivery times, repair times, yield levels, and so forth, produce irregularities in an operations system that require some form of buffer. Pooling is the practice of combining multiple sources of variability to make extreme values less likely, which in turn reduces the total amount of buffering that is required.

To illustrate this concept, let us consider a nonoperations example. Suppose a cruise ship needs to provide lifeboats in case of an emergency. One option, albeit not a very practical one, would be to provide individual lifeboats for each passenger and crew member on board. Because people come in different sizes, these lifeboats would have to be designed to handle a range of loads. For the sake of this example, suppose that the weights of people who travel on the ship are known to be distributed normally with a mean of $\mu = 160$ pounds and a standard deviation of $\sigma = 30$ pounds. Furthermore, suppose that the authorities have designated that lifeboats must be sized to accommodate 99.99 percent of passengers. Because 99.997 percent of a normal population lies below four standard deviations above the mean, management of the cruise ship can meet the requirement by providing individual lifeboats that can carry

$$\mu + 4\sigma = 160 + 4(30) = 280 \text{ pounds}$$

Note that the average person weighs only 160 pounds, so the lifeboats are oversized by an average of $280 - 160 = 120$ pounds.

Another (more practical) alternative would be to provide multiperson lifeboats. For example, suppose the cruise ship decides to use 16-person lifeboats. Then, to accommodate the same fraction of people, they must size the boats at a level of four standard deviations above the mean weight of a group of 16 people. The mean weight of a randomly chosen set of 16 people is

$$\mu_{16} = 16\mu = 16(160) = 2,560 \text{ pounds}$$

But what about the standard deviation of the group weight? From basic probability we can find the *variance* of the group weight by adding the variances of individual weights.[1] Because the variance of the weight of an individual is the square of the standard deviation, the variance of the weight of 16 people is given by $16\sigma^2$ and the standard deviation of the group weight is

$$\sigma_{16} = \sqrt{16\sigma^2} = 4\sigma = 4(30) = 120 \text{ pounds}$$

Note that the mean weight increases proportionally in the number of people in the group, while the standard deviation of the weight only increases according to the square root of the number of people. Hence, the coefficient of variation, which we recall is the standard deviation divided by the mean, for the weight of a group of n people (CV_n) is

$$CV_n = \frac{\sigma_n}{\mu_n} = \frac{\sqrt{n}\sigma}{n\mu} = \frac{\sigma}{\sqrt{n}\mu} = \frac{1}{\sqrt{n}}CV_1$$

This result tells us that the larger the group of people, the smaller the relative variability in the total weight.

Now back to boat sizing. For a 16-person lifeboat to accommodate 99.997 percent of the groups it should be sized to hold

$$\mu_{16} + 4\sigma_{16} = 2{,}560 + 4(120) = 3{,}040 \text{ pounds}$$

If we compare this to the weight capacity of 16 single-person lifeboats, which would be $16(280) = 4{,}480$ pounds, we see that this represents a 32 percent reduction in capacity, which implies a corresponding reduction in materials, cost, and storage space. Presumably this is one reason we do not find single-person lifeboats on cruise ships.

What caused this reduction? By combining individuals in a single boat, we *pooled* their variability. Because weights vary both up and down, variations in individual weights tend to offset each other. For instance, a heavy person and a light person will tend to have an average weight close to the mean. Hence, while it is not unusual to find a single individual who weighs over 250 pounds (three standard deviations above the mean), it would be extremely unusual to find a group of 16 randomly chosen people with an

---

[1]Note that the variance of the group weight is only given by the sum of the individual weight variances if weights are independent. For this to be true, we must assume that people will enter lifeboats randomly, so that knowing the weight of one person in the boat does not tell us anything about the weights of the other people in the boat. If one lifeboat received all NFL linemen, while another received all ballerinas, then the independence assumption would be violated (and the NFL boat would probably sink).

FIGURE 8.3

Pooling of
weights for
lifeboat design

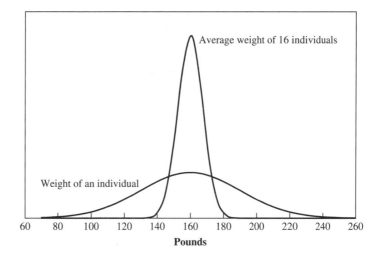

average weight over 250 pounds (we are talking about the general
population, not the National Football League). We illustrate this in
Figure 8.3 by comparing the distribution of weights of individuals
to the distribution of average weights of 16-person groups. Due to
pooling, providing the same level of protection against variability in
weights requires a smaller capacity buffer for a 16-person lifeboat
than for 16 single-person lifeboats.

This example made use of the normal distribution to provide
quantitative illustration of the concept of pooling. But the essence
of the idea does not depend on the assumption of normality. If
weights have a skewed distribution (e.g., there are more people with
a weight 100 pounds above the mean than 100 pounds below the
mean), then we can't use the same number of standard deviations
above the mean to get equal population coverage with single-person
boats and 16-person boats. But, while the math will be more difficult, the main qualitative result will be the same. The capacity of a
single 16-person lifeboat *will* be smaller than the total capacity of
16 single-person lifeboats capable of serving the same percent of
the passenger population.

We summarize the main pooling insight in the following principle:

Principle (Variability Pooling).   *Combining sources of
variability so that they can share a common buffer reduces the total
amount of buffering required to achieve a given level of performance.*

Although this principle implies that pooling will produce buffer
reduction benefits in a broad range of circumstances, the magnitude

of those benefits depends on the specifics. Most importantly, the effectiveness of pooling is affected by

- The magnitude of variability from the individual sources.
- The number of individual sources that can be combined.

To illustrate this, let us reconsider the lifeboat example. Suppose that individual weights still average $\mu = 160$ pounds but have a standard deviation of $\sigma = 50$ pounds (instead of 30). Therefore, the capacity of individual lifeboats needed to carry 99.997 percent of the population is now

$$\mu + 4\sigma = 160 + 4(50) = 360 \text{ pounds}$$

Because the standard deviation of the combined weight of a random group of 16 individuals is

$$\sigma_{16} = \sqrt{16\sigma^2} = 4\sigma = 4(50) = 200 \text{ pounds}$$

the capacity of a lifeboat to accommodate 99.997 percent of groups of 16 people is

$$\mu_{16} + 4\sigma_{16} = 2{,}560 + 4(200) = 3{,}360 \text{ pounds}$$

Hence, the difference between the capacity of a 16-person lifeboat and the capacity of 16 single-person lifeboats (i.e., $16(360) = 5{,}760$ pounds) represents a 42 percent reduction in capacity. This is larger than the 32 percent reduction when the standard deviation of individual weights was 30 pounds because the increased variability among individuals causes pooling to have a more dramatic effect.

If we return to our assumption that the standard deviation of individual weights is 30 pounds, but assume 36-person lifeboats, the lifeboats would need to be sized to hold

$$\mu_{36} + 4\sigma_{36} = 36\mu + 4\sqrt{36}\sigma = 36(160) + 4(6 \times 30) = 6{,}480 \text{ pounds}$$

The difference between the capacity of a 36-person lifeboat and the capacity of 36 single-person lifeboats (i.e., $36(360) = 12{,}960$ pounds) represents a 50 percent reduction in capacity (compared with the 32 percent reduction achieved by using 16-person lifeboats). Because more individuals are pooled in larger lifeboats, there is a greater reduction in variability and hence the need for excess capacity.

The variability buffering law is very general and fundamentally simple. It is basically the law of averages causing multiple sources of variability to cancel one another out. But because it is so general, applying it effectively requires some additional insights. Therefore, we now turn to some important examples of pooling in practice.

Insight by Analogy

Sports Championships

If you are a sports fan, you have probably noticed that the National Basketball Association (NBA) champion is rarely a surprise. In the not-too-distant past, the Lakers, Bulls, Pistons, and Celtics all put together strings of championship years in which they won when expected. In contrast, the National Football League (NFL) champion is quite often unexpected. In 2002, the Patriots won despite being a last-place team the year before. In 2003, the Buccaneers blew out the favored Raiders. In 2006, the Steelers won as a wild-card team.

Why does this happen? Is there something structural about basketball and football that inherently makes football less predictable?

It turns out there is a difference and it is related to pooling. To see this, note that both games involve a series of possessions in which first one team tries to score and then the other team tries to score. The team that has a higher average number of points scored per possession will have the higher score and therefore will win. But there is variability involved. A basketball team that scores 1.1 points per possession obviously doesn't score 1.1 points each time down the floor. Depending on the possession, it may score 0, 1, 2, 3, or possibly even 4 (by getting fouled on a 3-point shot) points. If games were infinitely long, the variability would average out and the team with the higher scoring average would prevail. But games are not infinitely long, so it is possible that the team whose true scoring average is higher might find itself behind at the end of the game.

A key difference between basketball and football is the number of possessions each team has. In the NBA, teams routinely average over 90 possessions per game, while in the NFL it is closer to 12 possessions per game. Because the variability in points per possession is pooled over more possessions in the NBA than in the NFL, it is much more likely that the team with the higher average will wind up with the higher score. Add to this the fact that the NFL playoffs are a single elimination competition, while NBA championships are decided by seven game series (which generates even more pooling), and it is no surprise that basketball dynasties emerge with regularity, while football champions are a never-ending source of surprise.

8.2.2   Applications of Pooling

In theory, pooling is an option wherever multiple sources of variability exist. However, for pooling to be feasible we must be able to share a common source of buffering across the variability sources. The most common form of pooling involves sharing inventory buffers to cover variability in multiple sources of demand. As we discuss below, there are a variety of ways this can be done. A less publicized, but equally important, application of pooling involves sharing capacity (equipment or labor) to meet different sets of processing requirements. The following examples illustrate some specific pooling practices.

Centralization

Pooling is a key motivation for using warehouses. For instance, consider a chain of grocery stores. Weekly demand for canned lima beans may vary considerably at the level of an individual grocery store. So, if the firm ships lima beans on a weekly basis to individual stores, each store will need to carry safety stock sufficient to keep stockouts to an acceptable level. But, in all likelihood, this will result in most stores having excess lima beans at the end of the week and a few stores stocking out. Without sharing of safety stock between stores, the excess in one store does not help make up a shortage in another.

To avoid this (and to reduce shipping costs by consolidating deliveries to stores), grocery store chains generally make use of regional distribution centers (warehouses). The supplier ships lima beans weekly to the distribution center, which in turn ships them daily (along with other products) to the stores that need them. This consolidates (pools) the safety stock in the distribution center and ensures that it is applied specifically to the stores that need it. The result is a smaller total safety stock of lima beans.

Although warehouses are almost as old as manufacturing itself, the concept of inventory centralization has taken on a fresh importance with the rise of e-commerce. For example, contrast the business operations of Amazon.com and Barnes & Noble (its traditional brick-and-mortar business, not its online business). Barnes & Noble sells books through stores and so must keep individual safety stocks in the stores themselves. Amazon has no physical outlets and can therefore maintain a single centralized stock. Thus, Amazon's system naturally pools safety stocks and therefore requires less total inventory to achieve a fill rate comparable (or superior) to that of Barnes & Noble. This enables Amazon to sell low-demand books that would be too expensive for Barnes & Noble to stock in its stores.

On the surface, this is just another illustration of warehousing; Amazon sells books out of a centralized warehouse, while Barnes & Noble sells them through individual retail outlets. But in reality the picture is more complex because inventory pooling can be virtual as well as physical. For example, if a customer fails to find a book at a Barnes & Noble store, the clerks can search their database to see if it is available in a nearby store. If it is, the customer can go and get it or have it shipped. As information and distribution systems become more efficient, it becomes increasingly attractive to layer this kind of virtual pooling system on top of a traditional distributed retail system to combine the benefits of both.

Centralization decisions need not be "all or nothing." For example, consider a firm that manufactures industrial equipment. Because the firm also services its equipment, it stocks spare parts to support repairs. But, because customers demand rapid repairs, the firm stores spare parts in regional facilities. Technicians can pick up parts in the morning for repairs to be completed that day. The firm also maintains a central distribution center, which supplies the facilities. But because shipping takes 24 hours, part shortages at the facilities can lead to costly delays in repairs.

This combination of a central distribution center and regional facilities is a fairly traditional multiechelon inventory system. Inventory at the distribution center is pooled, because it can be used by anyone in the system, and hence allows the firm to hold less inventory than if all safety stock were held at facilities. Inventory at facilities is not pooled, but is geographically close to customers and hence facilitates responsive delivery. A key to operating this system is determining how to split inventory between the distribution centers and the facilities. The inventory models of Chapter 7 can help in making this decision.

However, in some cases, it may be possible to achieve a desired level of responsiveness at a lower total cost by eliminating the distribution center entirely. For instance, suppose the distribution center is shipping parts to facilities via an overnight mail service. Then, presumably parts can be shipped between facilities just as quickly and cheaply. Furthermore, if the inventory in the distribution center were transferred to the facilities (so that inventory cost remained constant), the facilities would be more likely to have needed parts in stock (so customer service would improve). By replacing the physical pooling of the distribution center with virtual pooling facilitated by an information system, the inventory in the system would be both pooled and local.

Standardization

In most manufacturing systems, a great deal of the cost of producing and distributing products is fixed during the design process. Choices regarding materials, connectors, degree of customization, and many other design issues have a huge impact on the life cycle cost of a product.

A metric of particular importance is the number of components that go into a product. More components mean more fabrication and/or purchasing, more assembly, more inventories to maintain, and more complexity to manage. One way to address these costs is by working at the design stage to minimize the number of components needed to achieve a particular function. This practice, along with the process of simplifying the components themselves so as to make them easier to manufacture and assemble, is termed **design for manufacture**.

A powerful illustration of the importance of design is illustrated by the competition between Motorola and Nokia in the wireless phone market. Motorola invented mobile phone technology and held a dominant market share through the mid-1990s (33 percent as late as 1996). But by 1998, Nokia had come from almost nowhere to overtake Motorola and by 2002 had more than doubled (37 percent to 17 percent) Motorola's share of the worldwide mobile phone market. Moreover, while Motorola reported several consecutive quarters of significant losses in 2001–02 and saw its stock price collapse, Nokia reported a strong profit in the face of a weak economy in 2001. What happened?

The popular explanation that Motorola missed the transition from analog to digital phones has some validity, but does not explain Nokia's ongoing and increasing advantage. Indeed, no single explanation is sufficient; success in the marketplace is the result of a complex combination of strategy and execution. But it is telling that Nokia made use of simpler designs and fewer product platforms than did Motorola. Because its phones had fewer components and more shared components (e.g., chips, screens, batteries, etc.) across models, Nokia's product development and logistics processes were much easier to manage than Motorola's. From a supply chain science perspective, Nokia exploited the pooling principle better than Motorola. From a management perspective, Nokia created an advantage that persisted well beyond that obtained by its earlier move to digital technology.

Nokia's product design strategy was aimed at simplicity and commonality from the start. But it is also possible to remake a portfolio of products to obtain the same advantages. A classic example of this is the case of Black & Decker. Starting around 1970 with an uncoordinated set of consumer tools with many different motors, housings, and armatures, Black & Decker pursued a massive effort to standardize designs and share components. One component of this strategy was development of a universal motor (with a fixed axial diameter but a length that could be adjusted to change power output) for use across all tools. The heavy use of common parts both reduced development times for new products and (due to pooling) reduced inventory and supply chain costs. These benefits were so powerful that it precipitated a 5-year market shakeout that left only Black & Decker and Sears in the home hobbyist tool market.

Postponement

The Nokia and Black & Decker examples illustrate exploitation of the pooling principle through product design. But this principle also applies directly to supply chain decisions. A general strategy for using a single type of inventory to meet pooled demand for multiple products is called **postponement**. The basic idea is to hold partially completed goods in a generic state and customize them only when demand becomes known. For example, auto dealers do this when they install trim moulding, roof racks, floor mats, and other details so that they can provide a variety of choices to their customers without holding all combinations of options in their on-site inventory.

The benefits of postponement flow from the fact that product customization is delayed until the firm has accurate demand information. Such a delay is particularly important in the fashion industry, where initial estimates of demand are often very poor. An excellent illustration of the use of postponement in a fashion supply chain comes from Benetton, a global clothing manufacturer and retailer founded in 1965, on a line of traditional woolen sweaters.

To address the fashion concerns of its customers, Benetton offers knitwear products in several hundred style and color combinations. But, even if the company were able to estimate total demand for a particular style of sweater very precisely, it is highly unlikely that it could predict demand for every color. If Benetton estimated demand for green sweaters and underestimated demand for red sweaters, it would wind up with both lost sales (of red) and excess inventory (of green). Of course, if Benetton could produce sweaters with very short lead times, it could wait to see how demand is progressing during the season and then produce the colors needed. But capacity constraints and manufacturing times make this uneconomical.

So, instead, starting as far back as the 1970s, Benetton adopted a postponement strategy. It modified the traditional manufacturing process in which wool or cotton was first dyed and then knitted into a garment. By reversing this sequence, so that sweaters were first knitted from undyed gray stock and then dyed to color, Benetton was able to stock gray sweaters and use a dye-to-order policy to deliver the correct mix of colors to its retailers.

Note, however, that Benetton did not adopt this reverse process for all of its sweater production. Because dying finished products is more difficult than dying bulk wool or cotton, the cost of sweaters produced in this manner was higher. Moreover, it was not necessary to dye-to-order on all sweaters, because Benetton could estimate a base amount of each color that they would be almost certain to sell. By reserving a relatively small percentage of the total (say 10 or 15 percent) as gray stock, Benetton was able to add considerable flexibility in responding to deviations in demand from the forecast without creating excess finished goods inventory. This innovative production and supply chain strategy contributed to Benetton's rise to its current status as a highly recognizable $2 billion company.

In the Benetton case, the goal of postponement was reduction of cost due to obsolete inventory. But the practice of postponement is also a powerful method for delivering variety and short lead times to customers. For example, in the 1980s and early 1990s, IBM manufactured printed circuit boards for its products in Austin, Texas. One particular line produced hundreds of different end items. However, all of these were made from a set of about eight "core blanks" (laminates of copper and fiberglass onto which the circuitry for a specific board would be etched). Because there were so many different circuit boards, holding finished goods inventory would have been prohibitively expensive; each end item would require separate safety stock. So, IBM produced them in a make-to-order fashion, starting production from the lamination process that made the core blanks. However, in the search for ways to reduce customer lead times, IBM noted that it could make core blanks to stock and thereby remove that portion of the cycle time from the lead time seen by the customers. The product had a natural postponement property—customization happened only after core blanks were machined, etched, and finished into circuit boards. Because core blanks were generic, safety stock would be pooled and therefore much smaller than the amount that would be required at the finished goods level. Hence, by splitting the line into a make-to-stock portion (up to core blanks) and a make-to-order portion (the rest of the line), IBM was able to continue to offer high levels of variety with shorter customer lead times and very little increase in inventory costs.

Worksharing

Although pooling is frequently invoked with respect to inventory, the pooling principle can be applied in many other contexts. We introduced this section with a lifeboat example that did not involve inventory at all. The generic wording of the pooling principle was deliberate; the concept potentially applies anywhere there are multiple sources of variability that could be addressed with a common buffer.

A common application of pooling, which is almost never referred to as pooling, is the use of cross-trained labor to staff multiple tasks. In unromantic technical terms, an operator is a source of capacity. Unless a particular worker is a sharp system bottleneck, he/she will occasionally be idled due to blocking/starving, machine outages, material shortages, or other sources of variability. This idle time represents excess capacity. Because the excess is the result of variability, it is a variability buffer. (Remember that the buffering principle says that variability *will* be buffered. Whether the worker idle time was deliberate does not affect the fact that it is indeed a variability buffer.)

If a particular worker can do only one thing (e.g., staff a specific machine), then he/she may be idled fairly often (e.g., whenever that machine is down or out of work). But, if the worker can do multiple things (e.g., float between several machines), then he/she is much less likely to be idled. In scientific terms, the buffer capacity provided by a cross-trained worker is pooled between multiple task types. Just as pooling inventory reduces the amount of inventory buffering required, pooling worker capacity via cross-training reduces the amount of buffer capacity (idle time) for a given level of variability. The practical result is that systems that make use of cross-training can achieve higher worker utilization (productivity) than systems with specialized workers. Of course, other factors such as the ability of workers to perform new tasks efficiently, motivational effects, impacts on long-term problem-solving, and so forth, will affect the success of a cross-training strategy in practice.

A division of R.R. Donnelley, which performed premedia print production of catalogs and other documents, made good use of the pooling principle in its cross-training strategy. Initially, the system was configured as a series of operations (color console editing, page-building, RIP, sheet proofing, etc.) staffed by specialists who handed jobs from one to another. But, because of high variability in task times, it was common for workers at stations to be idled. So, Donnelley restructured its workforce into cross-trained teams that would follow jobs (almost) all the way through the system (a couple of tricky operations still required specialists). Pooling the variability in the individual operations for a job nearly eliminated the inefficient idling of workers. Also, because workers stayed with a job through the entire process, customers had a clear contact person and overall quality was improved due to better communication about job requirements.

Chaining

Worksharing is a mechanism for pooling capacity, with labor serving as the source of capacity. We can also pool capacity in the form of physical equipment.

For example, an automobile assembly plant might be tooled to produce more than one model of car. Then, if demand turns out to be high for one model, but low for the other model, the plant will be able to meet total demand efficiently. But if demand for both models is high (or low) this strategy won't help much. So it may make sense to extend the pooling strategy across multiple plants.

Figure 8.4 illustrates a system in which six assembly plants must fill demand for six different models of automobile. Figure 8.4(a) depicts a "full flexibility" system in which every plant can produce every model. This means that as long as total capacity exceeds total demand, we will be able to meet it. Full flexibility on the part of the plants means that capacity is completely pooled. However, making the plants flexible enough to produce every type of car will require a significant investment in tooling, so this solution is apt to be very expensive, if it is even feasible.

A more practical solution would be to equip each plant to produce only a few models. Fortunately, Jordan and Graves (1995) showed that it is possible for such partial-flexibility strategies to work well. Specifically, they demonstrated that a "chained" system,

FIGURE 8.4

Full flexibility and chained flexibility

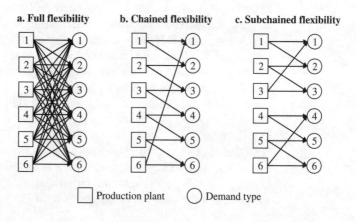

a. Full flexibility   b. Chained flexibility   c. Subchained flexibility

☐ Production plant   ○ Demand type

in which overlapping assignments fully connect the plants in a loop or chain, as shown in Figure 8.4(b), provides almost as much protection against demand fluctuation as the full-flexibility system using the same total capacity. The reason is that in a chained system, capacity from any plant can be used to offset demand for any model, although possibly indirectly.

For instance, suppose that demand for model 2 is low, but demand for model 4 is high. Because plant 2 is not equipped to produce model 4, we cannot take direct advantage of the excess capacity at plant 2 to satisfy excess demand for model 4. But we can use capacity from plant 3 to satisfy demand for model 4 and then use the excess capacity at plant 2 to satisfy the newly uncovered demand for model 3. In this way, we can indirectly use capacity at plant 2 to fill demand for model 4. Indeed, there is a path from every plant to every model in the chained system, so we can channel capacity from any plant to any demand type.

This example considers chaining as protection against routine demand variability. But it can also provide protection against more severe production outages. For instance, suppose that plant 2 in Figure 8.4(b) experiences a serious fire that takes it off-line for several weeks. During this time, at least some of the demand for model 2 could be supplied by plant 1, while plant 6 provides supply of model 1, plant 5 provides supply of model 6, and so on. As long as only one plant goes down, the system can shift production to meet demand for all products, up to the total capacity of the remaining plants.

In theory, chaining is an elegant and efficient way to pool capacity with minimal investment in flexibility. However, for the system to shift capacity from any plant to any model, it requires that the chain be fully connected. If, for instance, we were to eliminate the ability of plant 6 to produce model 1, then the chain would be broken. Hence it would no longer be possible to shift capacity from anywhere to cover demand for model 1. This in turn means that the only capacity available as backup for model 2 comes from plant 1. Similarly, the only capacity available as backup for model 3 comes from plants 1 and 2. And so on. The elimination of just one link in the chain severely limits the overall flexibility of the system and thus significantly reduces its ability to respond to fluctuations in demand or disruptions in production.

Unfortunately, it is not always practical to establish a complete chain. For instance, suppose that the six models in Figure 8.4(b) represent vehicles of increasing size, ranging from a subcompact to a giant SUV. While it may be reasonable to produce models 1 and 2 (a subcompact and a compact) in the same plant, the tooling required to produce models 1 and 6 (a subcompact and a giant

SUV) in the same plant is probably excessively expensive. So, we might be better off chaining subsets of the product line, as shown in Figure 8.4(c), where the top chain includes the smaller vehicles, while the bottom chain includes the larger vehicles. While this subchained system would not be as robust as the full chain, it might be considerably cheaper to achieve and hence be a more practical pooling strategy for buffering demand and production disruptions.

Hedging

Finally, we note that an extremely straightforward application of pooling is diversifying operations across multiple markets to reduce overall risk. Because the performance of businesses in separate economies is unlikely to be perfectly correlated, gains in one market tend to offset losses in another market. For example, in recent years most major companies in the automotive industry have pursued a strategy of increasing the fraction of vehicles produced outside their home market. This makes them less reliant on demand in any one region and helps dampen the impact of currency fluctuations and regional economic downturns.

An even simpler hedging strategy than multinational diversification is business disruption insurance. Such policies are explicitly written to pay out when events result in costly supply chain disruptions. But major disasters in recent years, ranging from the 9/11 attacks to Hurricane Katrina, have pushed up insurance premiums. So, while small businesses may have no choice but to rely on insurance for a major portion of their risk protection, larger firms with more opportunities for diversification are increasingly using other mitigation strategies to supplement insurance.

8.3   Contingency Planning

As pointed out in Figure 8.2, buffering and pooling strategies only make economic sense as protection against an uncertain risk if either the likelihood or the consequences are high. Routine demand fluctuations occur all the time and so warrant safety stock. Rare but highly consequential events may also be appropriately mitigated by using safety stock. For example, having a plant destroyed by a tornado is unlikely, but if the plant produces an essential drug (e.g., insulin, without which customers face life-threatening symptoms), the consequences of an outage may be severe enough to warrant holding a supply of finished goods just in case.

But there are far too many types of disruptions to maintain extra resources for protection against all of them, even if these resources are used as efficiently as possible via pooling strategies.

FIGURE 8.5

Contingency
planning
process

For example, while a firm might be able to keep some temporary workers on retainer to fill in for people who call in sick, it would be far too expensive to maintain an entire backup labor force just in case the regular workforce went on strike. So, to be prepared for cases like these, firms prepare contingency plans.

In the terminology of this book, a contingency plan is a strategy for securing buffer resources if and when they are needed. For instance, a firm might decide that if a labor strike occurs they will (a) take specified steps to keep the duration of the strike to a minimum and (b), failing that, hire replacement workers. Because they are not yet hired, the replacement workers represent a "virtual" or "contingent" buffer resource, rather than an actual one.

But developing a contingency plan involves more than simply specifying virtual resources. We must also decide which events warrant such resources, determine how they will be secured, and make the organization ready to bring the contingent resources on-line quickly. Thinking of contingency planning in this way enables us to break the process into the following steps, which are illustrated schematically in Figure 8.5.

1. *Anticipate an event or class of events for which a contingency plan is needed.* This involves identifying scenarios that are both dangerous enough and likely enough to justify devoting resources to develop a protection plan.

2. *Design the plan to be implemented if the anticipated event occurs.* This may involve establishing roles for people, defining a communication plan, locating contingency resources (e.g., a backup supplier for a critical part), prioritizing the steps to be taken (e.g., in a staged response in which "Plan B" will be adopted if "Plan A" fails to produce the desired results), and anything else relevant to making an effective response to a disruptive scenario.

3. *Prepare the organization to implement the plan.* Depending on the nature of the plan, this could involve establishing monitoring mechanisms to identify a disruptive event quickly, training people in their respective roles, establishing formal contracts or informal relationships with parties outside the organization, and many other steps.

4. *Execute the plan if and when the event occurs.*

5. *Update the plan over time.* An update can occur as part of a routine review process in which scenarios, plans, and preparation

strategies are reconsidered in light of changing conditions. It can also be the result of a formal learning process in the wake of an event. Carefully evaluating the success and/or failure of a plan that was executed almost always suggests ways to improve plans for the future.

The range of issues to be addressed in these steps means that contingency planning is a broad management challenge, involving forecasting, training, resource allocation, incentives, communication, and many other dimensions. As such, it has been addressed by various management scholars from a case study and best practices standpoint.

For example, Bazerman and Watkins (2004) define events that an organization should have anticipated, prioritized, and responded to, but did not, as *predictable surprises*. In the terms of this chapter, these are events for which a contingency plan should have been prepared and executed. But, because this was not done, the events were handled in a reactive crisis management mode, rather than a proactive contingency planning mode. They classify the September 11 attacks, the Enron collapse, and the 2003 blackout of the northeastern U.S. as predictable surprises because, they argue, sufficient information existed to anticipate these events and the consequences were important enough to warrant developing a plan.

They go on to describe the types of organizational failures that can prevent proper detection of and response to predictable surprises:

- *Scanning failures*—a threat or event is not detected due to inadequate resources or lack of organizational attention.
- *Information failures*—data are available to identify a threat and formulate a response, but the organization fails to assemble the various pieces of data into a useful body of information.
- *Incentive failures*—the organization fails to act on available insight due to a lack of incentive.
- *Learning failures*—lessons from previous events are not adequately distilled and disseminated to the right people in the organization.

Dissecting previous crises to develop lists of insights can certainly shed light on how to improve the contingency planning process. Indeed, we can view this approach as systematically addressing the "Update" phase of Figure 8.5. But the scientific approach can also contribute to contingency planning by providing principles with which to systematically organize practice insights and preparation strategies.

In particular, as we have already noted, the variability buffering principle of Chapter 5 is central to contingency planning in any environment where business continuity is a concern. Disruption of an operation—whether due to execution failure, a natural disaster, political turmoil, terrorism, or whatever—is a form of variability. If not buffered by inventory or capacity, this variability will be buffered by time, which means delays will occur.

However, because capacity and inventory buffers are expensive, an even more important principle is the buffer flexibility principle. The pooling approaches discussed previously are one way to exploit this principle to make buffer resources more efficient by sharing them across multiple uses. But pooling is not the only way to make use of flexibility. Another generic strategy is the use of **contingent resources**, which represent resources that become available to the organization on an as-needed basis during an event. Examples include:

- *Flexible supply contracts:* Sheffi (2005) reports that a typical Hewlett-Packard supply contract specifies that suppliers should be able to ramp up production by 50 percent within 2 weeks and 100 percent within 4 weeks. This gives the company the ability to respond to demand spikes.
- *Multisourcing:* Using more than one supplier for a given component can provide even more ability to ramp up production. In addition, if one of them is disrupted, the others can ramp up to cover the lost supply. The risk mitigation benefits of multisourcing need to be balanced with the benefits of a deep relationship with a sole supplier. We will discuss the implications of the supplier network on organizational flexibility in the next section.
- *Reserve shipping capacity:* Pepsi keeps shippers on retainer to act as a "popup fleet" that can be brought online when extra delivery capacity is needed (e.g., when hot weather leads to a sudden increase in demand for soft drinks).
- *Temporary workers:* Many firms make use of "temps" whose hours can be adjusted up or down to vary production capacity.

Beyond contingent resource strategies, an organization can increase its flexibility in a variety of structural ways. These can help prepare it to execute a preset contingency plan or to manage a crisis in an adaptive manner. We discuss these in the following section on crisis management.

8.4   Crisis Management

The key difference between contingency planning and crisis management is that the former develops a plan of action in advance of the event, while the latter develops a plan in real time while the event is unfolding. In reality, no amount of advance planning can anticipate every detail of a response. Some amount of dynamic response (crisis management) is likely to be needed even in the most carefully planned situations. At the same time (we hope), few events are so completely unexpected that no advance planning whatever is possible. Hence, real-world responses to disruptive events are almost always a combination of contingency planning and crisis management. The challenge is to attain the right mix.

Using a predominantly crisis management approach to address events for which a contingency plan was warranted generally leads to undesirable outcomes. For example, in his classic book on crisis management, Fink (1986) describes a scenario in which a firm's accounts receivable are running late, causing a cash-flow shortage right before payday. The treasurer, who is well aware of the possibility and consequences of such an event, monitors cash flow to spot any problems and is prepared with a plan. He takes out a short-term loan and covers payroll expenses without incident. No one would even refer to the event as a crisis.

But, suppose the treasurer happens to be away on a family emergency and the CEO, who assumes that all is well, signs the checks as usual. Of course they bounce. Recognizing the situation, the bank immediately begins to cover the checks. But rumors about the ability of the company to meet payroll get started. The CEO responds to inquiries from the press that there is no truth to the rumors that the firm is going out of business. But suppliers who see the story get nervous and demand payment on the balance owed them and refuse to extend additional credit. This really does hurt cash flow, which causes the firm's debt ratio to grow and the bank to also restrict credit. Eventually, employees who are demoralized by the situation begin to leave. Unable to stop the downward spiral, the firm winds up going out of business.

While Fink's story is hardly a likely scenario, it is certainly possible. Triggered by an event that should have been handled as a routine contingency, the crisis was fueled by the organization's inability to respond effectively along the way. Without effective contingency planning or crisis management capabilities, even a

FIGURE 8.6

Crisis
management
process

relatively minor event can lead to major consequences. Moreover, even if a contingency plan is in place, a lack of knowledge on the part of individuals (e.g., the CEO or whoever was covering for the treasurer in the above case) can undermine its execution.[2]

Building crisis management capabilities is a very similar task to building contingency planning capabilities. From an operations perspective, the steps involved in crisis management are very much the same as those in contingency planning. But they have a slightly different sequence, as illustrated in Figure 8.6, and a somewhat different emphasis.

1. *Anticipate the needs of the organization during an event.* In contrast to contingency planning, in which specific events or types of events are identified, anticipation is a broader, less precise function in crisis management. For instance, even if we do not specify the type of event for which we are planning, we can anticipate the need for a decision hierarchy, designated media spokesperson, clear communication channels, and so forth.

2. *Prepare the organization to act in the event of a crisis.* As we noted above, many of the measures that would be used to prepare an organization to execute a contingency plan (e.g., establishing monitoring mechanisms to identify a disruptive event quickly, training people in their respective roles, establishing formal contracts or

---

[2]Perhaps the most famous example of a key individual not knowing his role in a crisis is that of Alexander "I'm in control here" Haig. On March 30, 1981, President Ronald Reagan was shot and hospitalized. As every schoolchild in America is taught, the line of succession to the presidency is the vice president, speaker of the house, president pro tem of the Senate, and then the secretary of state. So the nation was surprised when Secretary of State Alexander Haig, in a press conference immediately after the assassination attempt, announced, "I'm in control here, in the White House" pending the return of the Vice President George Bush from a speaking engagement in Dallas. He also stated "you have the President, the Vice President and the Secretary of State, in that order."

The event of the president being shot was certainly not a remote possibility. At the time Reagan was shot, four previous presidents had been killed in office and two others had been victims of assassination attempts. The framers of the Constitution anticipated this and spelled out the line of succession to the presidency. Moreover, in the wake of the Kennedy assassination, the Twenty-Fifth Amendment, which explicitly calls for the vice president to assume the powers and duties of the office if the president is temporarily incapacitated, was ratified. But when the crisis occurred, our secretary of state did not know his proper role.

informal relationships with parties outside the organization, etc.) are also appropriate for crisis management preparation.

3. *Design the response to the crisis.* Unlike contingency planning, a crisis management plan must be designed while the event is already underway. This means that time pressure is generally much more intense. Consequently, organizational shifts (e.g., use of task forces) are often used to facilitate rapid plan development and responsive adjustment as conditions change.

4. *Execute the response.* In both contingency planning and crisis management, ultimate success depends heavily on the quality of execution. All the planning in the world cannot resolve a disruptive event if the plan is not carried out effectively. Hence, it is toward execution that all planning must ultimately be directed.

5. *Update capabilities over time.* As with contingency planning, updating can occur routinely as capabilities are reviewed in the context of evolving risks. It can also be the result of a retroactive analysis of the response to a crisis.

In both contingency planning and crisis management, supply chain science principles are of the greatest value in preparation. Cultivating an organization that is nimble and responsive in the face of a disruptive event is not too dissimilar from cultivating a supply chain that is efficient and responsive to fluctuations in supply and demand. The details may be more complex, but the underlying principles are similar.

Figure 8.7 illustrates four main dimensions of organizational preparedness. The elements on the horizontal axis (flexibility and empowerment) represent structural features that support an organization's ability to respond to an event, while the elements on the vertical axis (awareness and communication) represent dynamic behaviors that support a response.

Flexibility refers to the ability of an organization to adapt to changing, possibly unfamiliar, conditions. In Chapter 5, we discussed flexibility in the context of variability buffers (i.e., capacity, inventory, and time) and noted that flexibility is enhanced by the ability of resources to serve multiple purposes. For example, inventories of generic parts are more flexible than inventories of highly customized parts because generic parts can be used to build multiple finished products. Organizations can also be made more flexible by enabling resources to be used for multiple purposes. But because organizations are large and complex systems, there are many ways to enhance flexibility. The challenge is to find suitable policies for a given organization.

A common strategy for making human resources more flexible is work standardization. For example, UPS makes use of highly

FIGURE 8.7

Dimensions of
organizational
preparedness

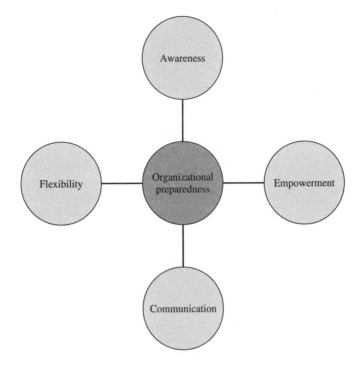

standardized equipment and procedures in its facilities. So it is a simple matter for an employee to move from one facility to another. This workforce flexibility paid dividends in 1994 when an unusual storm, which combined 16 inches of sleet and snow with subzero temperatures, paralyzed transportation in the Louisville area and resulted in a 5-day ban on nonessential road travel (Gerth 2004). But, because the airports were opened within a day, UPS had package shipping capability before its local Louisville employees could drive to work. So the company flew in employees from other locations to process packages stuck at the Louisville hub. The familiar standardized processes allowed the imported employees to feel right at home and to work efficiently.

Many firms make use of similar standardization policies. For instance, Intel uses a method called Copy EXACTLY! to transfer technology from one facility to another (McDonald 1998). The main objective is to bring new semiconductor facilities online quickly with equivalent yields and quality metrics as existing facilities. But the uniformity also means that capacity is flexible. So, when faced with possible disruption by SARS in 2003, Intel spokesman Chuck Mulloy said, "If there's a problem, we can move the capacity around. We have designed the system so we don't have chokepoints" (Ristelhueber 2003).

Another characteristic of flexible organizations is *speed*. Shorter lead times mean that commitments can be delayed, which enhances flexibility. For instance, in the early 1990s IBM manufactured raw circuit boards in Austin, Texas. On one of its lines, cycle times were in excess of 30 days. But its frozen zone (i.e., the window in front of the due date in which customers can no longer change their orders) was 20 days. This meant that circuit boards had to be started before customer orders were firm. Hence the inevitable quantity changes, mix changes, and cancelations resulted in large quantities of half-finished product sitting on the production floor with no associated customer order. After a concerted cycle time reduction effort, the plant managed to reduce cycle times to under 10 days. As a result, orders did not have to be released to the plant floor until they were firm. Changes and cancelations affected only the work backlog, which was trivial to change. The plant hence became much more robust to demand-side disruptions.

Speed can also improve flexibility with regard to supply-side disruptions. For example, Sheffi (2005, p. 226) compared the experiences of Dell and Apple in the wake of the Taiwan earthquake of September 21, 1999. Although both companies typically made use of build-to-order systems, Apple had booked 160,000 advance orders for its new iBook. So its customers were exposed to component lead times, which were inflated by several weeks when many Taiwan wafer fabs were taken off-line by the earthquake. The result was a loss of market share for Apple.

In contrast, Dell, which was also affected by the component shortages, carried a minimal order backlog. Without a commitment to specific configurations, it was able to sell products for which it had components. Consequently, despite the disruption, Dell was able to increase earnings in the third quarter by 41 percent over the previous year (Lee and Wolfe 2003).

In addition to taking steps, such as standardization and cycle time reduction, to enhance structural flexibility, an organization can proactively encourage its personnel to remain flexible. For example, a Wal-Mart supply chain executive suddenly asked his staff to pretend that a particular distribution facility had burned to the ground and that they had until the end of the day to figure out how to service Wal-Mart's stores without the disrupted facility (Bednarz 2006). Exercises like these help people think beyond the confines of their normal routines and can lead to new ideas for making the organization more flexible in the face of a crisis.

Empowerment is the authorization of employees at all levels to make independent decisions. One of the most famous examples of empowerment under normal conditions is the Toyota andon system. Under it, line-level employees are allowed to stop the entire production line if they spot a problem. This both facilitates a rapid response to quality issues and promotes an overall culture of quality.

Responsive decision making is even more important under crisis conditions. Possibly the most dramatic example occurred on September 11, 2001, when Ben Sliney, the FAA National Operations Manager, ordered the entire nationwide air traffic system shut down and approximately 3,950 flights in the air to land immediately. Convinced of the need for speed, he made this decision without consulting FAA head Jane Garvey, Transportation Secretary Norman Mineta, or any of his other superiors. Remarkably, it was Sliney's first day on the job. The 9/11 Commission subsequently concluded that this was an unprecedented order that the "air traffic control system handled . . . with great skill" (9/11 Commission 2004).

To be prepared to make quick independent decisions in emergencies, an organization must cultivate a culture of empowerment. For example, Southwest Airlines places great emphasis on the freedom employees have to act in the best interests of the company. So, when CEO Herb Kelleher instructed his staff to develop an electronic ticketing system because competitor airlines had substantially increased the price of using their travel agents' reservation systems, he was pleasantly surprised to find that they had already begun development (Kelleher 1997). Employees with that much foresight and courage of conviction are well prepared to act as needed in a crisis situation.

Awareness is critical for an organization to detect and respond to an emerging crisis. In military and intelligence organizations this dimension can be of staggering importance. Imagine the impact on world history if the U.S. military had absorbed the available warning signals and had acted to deter the attack on Pearl Harbor. Similarly, had U.S. intelligence been able to detect and thwart the 9/11 attacks, recent history would have been dramatically different.

But the importance of awareness is not limited to defense organizations. For example, in August 2001, Baxter International faced a crisis when elderly patients died shortly after dialysis treatment in Madrid (Young 2001). Because of standard procedures, the hospital notified Baxter as the maker of the filters used in the process. Despite the fact that deaths of elderly kidney-dialysis patients is not unusual, the firm responded by investigating the situation. When six more dialysis patients died in Valencia after receiving treatment using the same lot of filters, Baxter knew something was wrong (Hammonds 2002). Ultimately, the problem was traced to perfluorocarbon liquid left in the filters, which resulted in over 50 deaths. Baxter discontinued the deadly filters, at a substantial loss. But failure to detect the problem as quickly as they had would have made a tragic situation even worse.

Organizational awareness can be the result of management sensitivity to an emerging situation, such as that at Baxter. But it can also be facilitated by simple technology. An illustration of this occurred in 1995 when Texas Instruments (TI) was made aware of the Kobe earthquake several hours before the Japanese Prime Minister (Sheffi 2005, p. 161). TI had alarms in place that were set off when the earthquake interrupted a trans-Pacific data link. Alerted by the alarms, managers contacted the Kobe facilities and found out immediately what was going on. In contrast, the Japanese government had to communicate through a formal hierarchy, which took more than 4 hours as officials debated whether the news was important enough to warrant bothering their superiors.

Awareness in an organization can be learned. For example, some firms run tests in which they place an unfamiliar person or object in a facility. Observing how long it takes people to act and what they do gives them a sense of the alertness of the organization. Once people hear that they may be tested also provides incentives for them to pay attention to potentially dangerous situations.

Communication is almost always central to crisis management. Most texts on the subject stress the public relations aspect of crisis communications. For example, Fink (1986) devotes two chapters to crisis communication, one on "controlling the message" and one on "handling a hostile press." Advice in this arena includes practical suggestions such as

1. *Make sure the internal communicator (e.g., vice president of public relations) is someone with authority and credibility.* For example, Lawrence G. Foster, a main spokesperson for Johnson & Johnson during the 1982 Tylenol cyanide poisoning crisis, was a member of the executive committee and reported directly to J&J chairman, James Burke. This gave him the power to act quickly and decisively in dealing with the press and presented a believable face to the public.

2. *Prepare for crisis communication by gathering relevant information.* For example, a firm that carefully tracks safety records will be ready to respond to an accident with statements like "Today's incident was the first accident that caused a loss of work time in 5 years" and "The equipment involved in the accident was serviced and certified only 3 weeks ago." By responding rapidly with factual information, an organization can head off speculation and potentially damaging rumors in the media.

3. *Avoid responding to inquiries with "no comment" and never assume that statements can be made "off the record."*[3] The former makes the speaker seem to be hiding something, while the latter is simply naive in this era of aggressive journalism.

While public relations can be an important element of crisis management, any principles that can be invoked to guide it must come from fields like psychology or communications studies. Supply chain science has little to offer. But PR is not the only place where effective communication can facilitate a response to a crisis situation. Both internal communication between individuals in an organization and external communication with people and groups outside the organization can be critical to finding solutions and implementing them in a timely fashion. The science of networks, of which supply chain science is part, can offer insight.

While mathematical models have been used to analyze supply chain networks for many years, such tools have only recently been applied to social networks (see Barabasi 2002, Cross and Parker 2004, and Watts 2003 for overviews). The basic idea is to represent an organization as a network where nodes represent people and links represent communication between them.[4] By examining the structure of the social networks within an organization we can gain insight into its ability to perform various functions.

For example, Figure 8.8 gives a social network illustration of a classical hierarchical organization with a central leader who communicates with an inner circle of managers, who in turn communicate with group (department) leaders. Tightly connected departments (or teams) with centralized management supervision are well suited to executing routine tasks. But communication is seldom limited to connections defined in a formal organization chart. Rotation through job assignments, committee work, and social interaction generally leads to informal links, as shown in Figure 8.9. These extra links make the organization more densely connected and more capable of creative problem solving and knowledge transfer.

In crisis conditions, a formal hierarchy, even supplemented by informal links, may be too slow to cope with a rapidly evolving situation. Just getting on a busy manager's calendar may be a time-consuming task in normal conditions. When a crisis erupts,

---

[3]Pat Buchanan, Ronald Reagan's communication director, once told a reporter, "No comment—and that's off the record" (Fink 1986, p. 114).

[4]The simplest social networks represent all links as the same strength. For example, a link exists between two people if they talk on a regular basis, if one of them seeks advice from the other, or some other type of communication occurs. More sophisticated networks have links of varying strength to represent the extent of communication. Even more sophisticated networks evolve over time by adding and deleting nodes and/or altering links over time.

FIGURE 8.8

Structure of a
hierarchical
organization

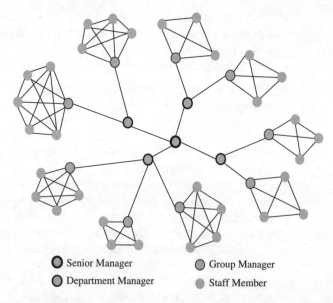

O   Senior Manager   ◉   Group Manager

◉   Department Manager   ◦   Staff Member

communication delays can be extremely damaging. So, firms often
appoint a task force to manage the response. Figure 8.10 illustrates
the organization of Figure 8.9 with selected (light colored) nodes
designated as a task force. The tight face-to-face communication
between these individuals greatly speeds the problem solving process and promotes broad dissemination of information during the
crisis.

FIGURE 8.9

Hierarchical
organization
with informal
links

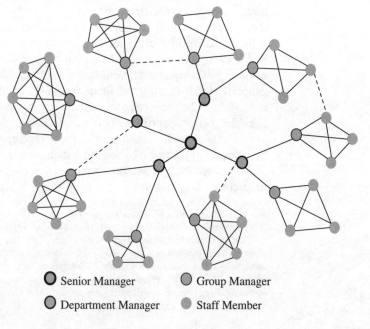

O   Senior Manager   ◉   Group Manager

O   Department Manager   ◦   Staff Member

FIGURE 8.10

Hierarchical
organization
with task force
in operation

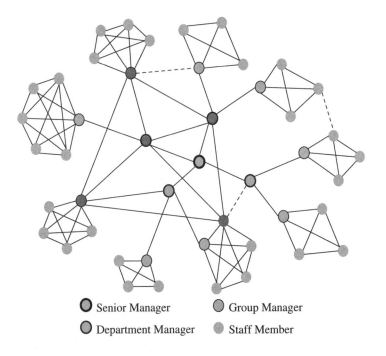

○ Senior Manager   ○ Group Manager

○ Department Manager   • Staff Member

In modern interconnected supply chains, communication networks extend well beyond the organization. The importance of effective communication across a large-scale supply chain was illustrated when a 1997 fire badly damaged the Aisin Seiki factory in Kariya, Japan. At the time, this plant supplied 99 percent of the P-valves used in the brake systems of Toyota cars. Toyota's second supplier, Nisshin Kogyo, could not possibly increase production by enough to make up for the shortfall (Nishiguchi and Beaudet 1998). With only hours of supply of P-valves on hand (due to its vaunted just-in-time system) Toyota faced a shutdown of plants all over the world.

To formulate a response, Toyota and Aisin called suppliers in their respective keiretsus.[5] Because of the close relationships among these firms, it was simply assumed that each would do its part to resolve the crisis. Working together closely in a warroom conference (i.e., task force) mode, Toyota and Aisin, along with dozens of keiretsu members, divided up blueprints and valvemaking assignments (Sheffi 2005, p. 212). The suppliers began to deliver P-valves within 2 days and all Toyota plants were running within 5 days of the fire. In total, Toyota lost only 4.5 days of

---

[5]A "keiretsu" is a uniquely Japanese alliance of firms with interlocking business relationships.

production, even though Aisin lost at least 5 weeks of production (Nishiguchi and Beaudet 1998). The tight communication and collaboration afforded by the keiretsu system facilitated a remarkably nimble response to what could have been a disastrous disruption.

Like awareness, communication can be learned by organizations. The keiretsu system, and related alliance structures, is certainly one way to promote deep communication among firms. But individual organizations can also take steps to improve internal communication. For example, Southwest encourages communication across job functions through their "Walk a Mile" program, which permits any employee to do any other employee's job for a day (within reason, of course; flight attendants cannot swap jobs with pilots). Southwest reports that 75 percent of its employees have participated in the program (Kelleher 1997).

Principles in Practice

Nokia

On March 17, 2000, a Royal Philips Electronics semiconductor plant in Albuquerque, New Mexico, was struck by lightning. The resulting fire was minor—it was out before firefighters even arrived. But the damage to the clean room environment effectively shut down the plant for weeks and dramatically changed the landscape of the global cellular telecommunications industry.

Both Nokia and Ericsson had been sourcing microchips from the Philips plant. But, while Nokia was able to quickly shift production to other Philips plants and some Japanese and American suppliers, Ericsson was trapped by its single-source strategy and thus had no way to make a rapid adjustment in response to the disruption. As a result, by the end of the first disruption-impacted quarter, Ericsson's losses totaled $400 million in sales (Eglin 2003). Even more importantly, 6 months after the fire, Ericsson's market share of the global handset market had fallen from 12 percent to 9 percent, while Nokia's had continued its rising trend unabated to more from 27 percent to 30 percent. Ericsson never recovered the ground it lost during this crisis and ultimately withdrew from the cell phone market in 2001.

The reason the Philips fire had such a dramatically unbalanced impact on the two firms was that Nokia, much more than Ericsson, addressed all of the dimensions of organizational preparedness:

Flexibility: Nokia had redesigned its products to allow use of a broader range of chips, and hence a wider set of suppliers. In contrast, Ericsson's products were more exclusively dependent on the chips supplied by Philips.

Empowerment: Nokia appointed an internal troubleshooter who had authority to act decisively. As a result, Nokia was able to start the process of procuring alternate supplies much more quickly than the comparatively bureaucratic Ericsson.

Awareness: Nokia had installed a sensitive monitoring system that enabled it to detect delays in shipments, even before being notified of the fire by Philips.

Communication: Nokia transferred information within its organization more quickly than did Ericsson. Nokia also had more effective communication links to organizations outside its own company.

The net effect of these preparatory steps was that by the time Ericsson began to look for alternate sources of chips, Nokia had already located them and locked up the available supplies. In the end, the Philips fire was a relatively minor event for Nokia but an unmitigated disaster for Ericsson.

Questions for Thought

1. A common property of forecasting systems is that they tend to be effective in predicting demand at the aggregate level, but highly inaccurate at predicting demand at the end-item level. For example, an apparel manufacturer may be able to project total demand for a given style of sweater, but not demand for individual colors or sizes. An auto manufacturer may be able to predict total demand for a given model of vehicle, but not demand for specific option packages. Explain this phenomenon using the concept of variability pooling.

2. Suppose that Boundaries Bookstore sells books in traditional bricks-and-mortar outlets, while Jungle.com sells books over the Internet. Hence, Boundaries holds separate stocks of a given book in each store, while Jungle.com holds all its inventory in a central warehouse. Both firms use a classic base stock model (see Chapter 7) in which the reorder point (ROP) is given by

$$\text{ROP} = \mu + z\sigma$$

where μ and σ are the mean and standard deviation of monthly demand and z is a safety factor. In such a system, the $z\sigma$ term represents the safety stock (i.e., inventory held to provide good customer service despite variability in demand).

a. Suppose that Boundaries has 100 outlets and uses a safety factor of $z = 2$ to control safety stocks. If a particular book sells an average of 10 copies per month at each store, with a standard deviation of 3, how much safety stock will the firm carry across all its outlets?

b. Suppose that Jungle.com sells the same number of books (i.e., 1,000 copies) as Boundaries. Furthermore, suppose that its demand process behaves like the sum of the demand at the 100 Boundaries stores. That is, each Boundaries store has monthly demand with a standard deviation of 3, or a variance of $3^2 = 9$. If we assume that demand at each Boundaries store is independent, the variance of total demand is the sum of the individual demand variances or $100 \times 9 = 900$. Hence, the standard deviation of total demand at Boundaries is $\sqrt{900} = 30$. If Jungle.com has demand with these parameters (mean = 1,000, standard deviation = 30), and its uses the same safety factor ($z = 2$) so that its service level is the same as Boundaries', how much safety stock will the firm carry?

c. Which firm carries less safety stock? Explain why one store can provide the same level of service with so much less safety stock.

3. Firms typically carry some safety stock of raw materials as a buffer against a delivery delay from a supplier. Why is safety stock not generally an attractive buffer against a catastrophic disruption of a supplier?

4. Since the 1990s there has been a trend toward using fewer suppliers. But some have argued that a sole-sourcing strategy can make a firm more vulnerable to supply disruptions. Their reasoning is that having multiple suppliers for a component provides an automatic backup if one of them is disrupted.

   However, as discussed in this chapter, Toyota was almost completely reliant on Aisin for P-valves. Do you think that this was a dangerous strategy, or can you think of reasons why a sole-sourcing strategy may be consistent with a sound risk management program? Explain why.

5. Many firms form task forces to respond to a crisis (e.g., the war room conference held by Toyota and Aisin). Appealing to the framework of this chapter, explain why such an approach makes sense as a crisis management tool.

9   COORDINATION

In interfirm supply chains, individual decision makers optimizing their local objectives generally suboptimize the overall system because risk falls disproportionally on one party.

9.1   Introduction

Most supply chains involve multiple levels and multiple organizations. For example, a producer may supply a distributor, which in turn supplies retailers. A manufacturer may receive components from (tier one) suppliers, which in turn receive components from (tier two) suppliers. A firm that repairs industrial equipment may stock spare parts at a central warehouse, in regional distribution centers, and on-site at machine locations. In each of these situations, inventory, possibly in different stages of completion, is held at multiple levels. Moreover, in the first two cases, these levels correspond to separate organizations, while in the third case the levels are controlled by a single organization. Coordinating the stocks and flows of inventory in such multilevel systems is a central challenge of supply chain management.

Multilevel supply chains can be structured in a variety of ways. Figure 9.1 illustrates a few possibilities. The structure of a given supply chain depends on product design, market geography, customer expectations, and, of course, management decisions. Within a structure, many variations are possible in stocking strategies, shipping policies, information and communication procedures, and other parameters. Because of this, multilevel systems represent a complex but vital management problem.

FIGURE 9.1

Example configurations of multilevel supply chains

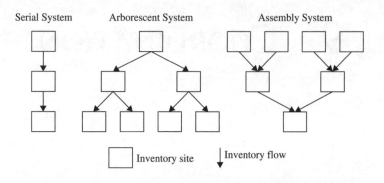

To a large extent, understanding and managing a multilevel supply chain is a matter of applying the science of previous chapters. Principles of capacity, variability, batching, flows, buffering, pull, inventory, and pooling are essential building blocks of a science of supply chain management. But bringing them together in a coordinated manner is not trivial. Besides being complex, supply chains generally involve many decision makers, often with conflicting priorities and asymmetric information. Providing systems, information, and incentives to help the various parties to work together is vital to the overall effectiveness of a supply chain.

As we have stressed throughout this book, a supply chain consists of a network of flows, like those discussed in Chapter 4. As long as inventory is moving between and through levels of a supply chain, all of the insights of Part II are relevant. In particular:

• *Bottlenecks cause congestion.* Highly utilized resources (manufacturing processes, transportation equipment, support services, etc.) cause queueing and delay. For example, a warehouse that is operating very close to capacity is likely to have orders queue up and get filled after their due dates. A heavily utilized port is likely to cause delay in inbound and outbound shipments. An overworked purchasing clerk will not be able to order materials responsively and will therefore inflate replenishment lead times.

• *Variability degrades performance.* Variability in demand rates, processing times, delivery times, and other factors affecting flows requires buffering (in the form of inventory, capacity, or time) and therefore reduces performance. For example, a retail outlet that is supplied by an unreliable vendor requires more shelf stock, and hence is less cost-efficient, than an identical outlet supplied by a reliable vendor. An OEM whose customers have volatile demand patterns but insist on responsive delivery has to maintain excess capacity, which inflates unit costs. A manufacturing firm with an inconsistent supplier has to build in safety lead times on its purchase orders, which in turn results in increased raw materials inventory and holding cost.

  • *Variability is worst at high utilization resources.* A highly utilized process has little excess capacity to act as a buffer against variability. Hence, such variability must be buffered almost entirely by inventory and time. For example, subjecting a high-utilization plant to an extremely variable demand process results in more WIP and cycle time than subjecting a low-utilization plant to the same demand process. Increasing the variability of customer service times in a call center (e.g., by giving agents a broader range of call types to deal with) has a modest effect on average wait times in a low-utilization system, but causes a dramatic increase in average wait times in a high-utilization system.

  • *Batching causes delay.* Processing or moving items in batches inflates the amount of inventory in a supply chain. By Little's law, this implies that it also increases the cycle time. For example, a plant that delivers an item to a warehouse only in full truckloads will carry finished goods inventory (FGI) at the plant as the trucks are waiting to be filled. Likewise, average inventory levels at the warehouse will be high due to the bulk shipments. If, however, the plant shares trucks between products, so that individual products are delivered to the warehouse in partial truckloads, then stock levels at both the plant and the warehouse will be reduced. By Little's law, this will also reduce the total amount of time an item spends in both locations.

  • *Pull is more efficient than push.* Any routing within a network can achieve a given throughput with a smaller WIP level under a pull protocol than under a push protocol. The reason is that a pull system only releases work into the routing when there is capacity to handle it. For example, a warehouse could implement a CONWIP-style stocking system by generating replenishment orders only when downstream demands create "inventory voids" in the target stock levels. In contrast, a warehouse that generates replenishment orders according to forecasts of future orders will run the risk of "inventory explosions" if demand declines relative to the forecast.

The analogy between an intraplant production network and an interplant supply chain network is apt for working stock, cycle stock, and congestion stock (see Section 7.2 for definitions). But when we consider safety stock, an important difference arises. Because of the geographic dispersion of a supply chain, the location (as well as the amount and type) of inventory is important. Conceptually, this means that while flow and inventory principles are fundamental to both production and supply chain networks, the pooling principle is also key in supply chain networks. High-efficiency supply chains make effective use of all of these principles.

9.2   Hierarchical Inventory Management

If we focus on the movement of material, a supply chain can be viewed as a flow network. If, instead, we focus on the stocks of material, a supply chain can be viewed as a hierarchical inventory system. While various architectures are possible (see Figure 9.1), the basic mechanics involve each level receiving a supply of inventory from the level above it and servicing demand from the level below it.

If we zero in on a single stock point of a supply chain (e.g., a warehouse, FGI at a plant, retail stock at a store, etc.) we can apply the insights and models of Chapter 7 to manage inventory at this location. But, of course, the data we use to describe a single stock point will depend on the rest of the supply chain. Specifically, as we illustrate in Figure 9.2, we need to know how long it takes to receive a replenishment order, how much variation there is in replenishment deliveries, and whether these deliveries are made in batches (e.g., full trucks). These parameters will be influenced by policies used for the levels above the stock point. We also need to know how much demand to expect, how variable the demand is likely to be, and whether the demand will occur in batches. These parameters will be influenced by the policies used for the levels below the stock point.

For example, consider a supply chain configured like the arborescent structure in Figure 9.1 that distributes spare parts for machine tools. The top level represents the main distribution center, the middle level represents regional facilities, and the bottom level represents customer sites.

Inventory can be held at all three levels. Spare parts held at the customer sites facilitate quick repairs, because they are already

FIGURE 9.2

Decomposing a
supply chain

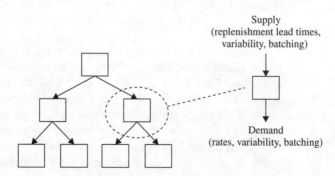

Supply
(replenishment lead times,
variability, batching)

Demand
(rates, variability, batching)

located at their point of use. Parts held at the distribution center facilitate pooling efficiency, because they can be shipped to any customer site. Parts held at regional facilities offer intermediate response (they are geographically closer to the customer sites than is the distribution center) and intermediate pooling efficiency (they can be shipped to any customer site in their region). The decision of what inventory to hold where involves a **pooling-versus-proximity** trade-off. Such trade-offs are extremely common in supply chains.

We can analyze this spare parts supply chain by decomposing it in the manner depicted in Figure 9.2. At the top (distribution center) level it makes sense to use the continuous review reorder point approach policy discussed in Chapter 7. The demand rate for a given part is the aggregate demand for that part for the entire system. The replenishment lead time is the lead time of the supplier or manufacturer. Hence, it is straightforward to compute the mean and standard deviation of demand during replenishment lead time. This enables us to use the formulas of Chapter 7 to compute the order quantity (OQ) and reorder point (ROP) for each part.

We could use a similar approach to analyze the middle (facility) level. Here, the demand rate is still easily computed as the aggregate demand for sites in the facility's geographic region. But the replenishment lead time is more subtle. If the part is in stock at the distribution center when the facility needs it, then lead time is just the shipping time from the distribution center to the facility. But if the distribution center stocks out, then the lead time will be the time it takes to get the part from the supplier, which could be considerably longer. Therefore, both the mean and the standard deviation of the replenishment lead time to a facility depend on the likelihood of a stockout at the distribution center. This in turn depends on the stocking policy used at the distribution center.

In general, more inventory at the distribution center means less chance of a stockout and hence shorter and more reliable deliveries to the facility. So, holding more stock at the distribution center permits the facilities to hold less stock to achieve the same level of service to the customers.

To determine the cost-minimizing balance of inventory at the two levels, we can try a range of service targets for the distribution center. For a given service target (e.g., the fraction of orders the distribution fills from stock), we first compute the stocking policy (OQ and ROP values), along with the amount of inventory we will have on hand, at the distribution center. Then, using the stockout probabilities, we estimate the mean and standard deviation of the lead time to the facilities and compute stocking policies and average on-hand inventory levels for them. We can do the same thing to compute policies and inventory levels for the customer sites.

FIGURE 9.3

Two-echelon
spare parts
supply chain

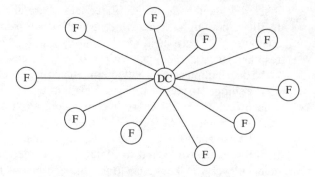

Finally, we see which distribution center service target yields the lowest total inventory required to achieve a given level of service at the customer level.

While the mathematical details of carrying out this search are beyond the scope of this book (see Hopp and Spearman 2000, Chapter 17, for the necessary formulas), we can illustrate the general concepts by considering the simple two-echelon example shown in Figure 9.3. In this system, repair parts for servicing customer equipment are stocked in a central distribution center (DC) and 10 regional facilities. When a customer needs a part, he/she is serviced by the nearest facility, provided it has the necessary part in stock. If it does not, the facility orders the part from the DC, and then the part is shipped via overnight delivery. If the DC is also out of stock, the facility must wait until the part arrives from the supplier. Hence, the lead time for a part depends on the stocking policies at both the DC and the facility.

To generate numbers, we suppose the system stocks five different parts (A, B, C, D, and E) with cost, average annual demand, and lead times given in Table 9.1. For simplicity we assume that the demand rates are identical for all 10 facilities (i.e., on average each experiences one-tenth of the total annual demand, but there is randomness in the demand, which necessitates safety stock). We assume that the DC orders parts on average 12 times per

TABLE 9.1   Data for two-echelon inventory example

Item	Unit Cost ($)	Total Average Demand (units/year)	Lead Time (days)
A	$100	100	60
B	1000	10	30
C	20	50	100
D	10	100	15
E	100	1000	30

year (once a month), but uses an EOQ-type analysis to set order quantities that balance the frequency of ordering among parts. The result will be that expensive parts will be ordered more frequently than once per month, while inexpensive parts will be ordered less frequently. We also assume that facilities receive regular shipments from the DC and so have no incentive to order in batches; hence they use a base stock policy in which a replenishment part is ordered each time a demand causes the stock level to fall below the base stock level.

Using the reorder model from Chapter 7, we can find the optimal OQ and ROP for each part at the DC to achieve any target service (fill rate) level. Then, using the stockout probabilities to adjust lead times to the facilities, we can apply the reorder point model again to optimize the reorder points at the facilities to achieve a target backorder level. Note that, by Little's law, the average time customers wait to get parts is proportional to the number of outstanding backorders. Hence, by holding the backorder level constant, we ensure that customers get the same responsiveness of delivery, regardless of the fill rate at the DC. What is changed as we vary the fill rate at the DC is the allocation of inventory among the DC and the facilities.

Figure 9.4 shows the resulting inventories (in units of dollars) for various DC fill rates when the backorder level (i.e., average number of customers waiting for parts at any given time) is held at a constant 0.1 per facility (i.e., since the average number of customers waiting at each of the 10 facilities is 0.1, on average one customer is waiting for a part somewhere in the system at any given time). Note that when the DC fill rate is low, the facilities need to hold more inventory to keep backorders low. The reason is that low service from the DC means occasional long waits for parts

FIGURE 9.4

Allocation of inventory in two-echelon spare parts supply chain

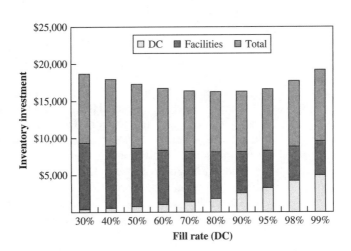

from the supplier. So the facilities must hold their own inventory so that they do not rely on the DC too often. As more inventory is held at the DC to increase its fill rate, the facilities can rely more on the DC and can therefore reduce their own inventories. But as the fill rate at the DC gets closer and closer to 100 percent, the benefit to the facilities diminishes. The reason is that, because there is a 1-day lead time to get parts from the DC, the facilities need to hold a fair amount of inventory to meet the target of 0.1 outstanding backorder per facility, even if the DC never has any stockouts. So, as stockouts at the DC become rarer, the necessary stock level at the facilities approaches this limit.

In our simple example, Figure 9.4 shows that total inventory at the DC and facilities is minimized when the fill rate at the DC is 80 percent. But total inventory is quite insensitive to the DC fill rate. As long as the stocking policy at the facilities is optimized for the fill rate at the DC, we can use any DC fill rate between 70 percent and 90 percent and achieve almost the same result. When the DC fill rate is 70 percent, the system holds 83 percent of total inventory at the facilities; when it is 90 percent, the system holds only 68 percent of total inventory at the facilities. Hence, we can conclude that there is considerable flexibility in the proportion of inventory to allocate across levels of a supply chain. However, it is important to note that this is only true if inventory control policies are coordinated across levels. Using ad hoc methods, such as the days-of-supply method discussed in Chapter 7, can lead to very large inefficiencies.

Finally, we note that the above optimization procedure not only allocates inventory between the facilities and the DC but it also allocates the investment among the various parts. As we discussed in Chapter 7, the optimal solution will tend to carry more overall inventory for parts that are inexpensive, have long lead times, or have high demand variability. But this multi-echelon model also leads to some additional insights into which types of parts to stock at each level in the supply chain. The following three parameters are the main determinants of the pooling-versus-proximity trade-off:

1. *Volume.* The higher the demand for a part, the lower in the supply chain it should be stocked. Holding a high-volume part close to customer usage points has a larger effect on customer service than holding the same amount of a low-volume part, simply because the high-volume part is used more frequently. Low-volume parts are better held at a (high-level) centralized location to take advantage of pooling efficiencies.

2. *Variability.* The more variable the demand for a part, the higher in the supply chain it should be stocked. Higher variability

enhances the effect of pooling. If, for example, demand at the customer sites were perfectly predictable, then we could simply deliver the inventory to these sites as needed. But if demand is highly unpredictable, then local inventories will need to include high levels of safety stock to ensure good customer service. Pooling these inventories at a centralized site reduces the amount of safety stock required.

3. *Cost.* The more expensive a part, the higher in the supply chain it should be stocked. All things being equal, pooling produces more savings for an expensive part than for a cheap one. Conversely, a dollar spent on holding local inventory buys more customer service if spent on a cheap part than an expensive one.

We summarize these parameters in the following principle:

Principle (Multi-Echelon Inventory Location). *In a multiproduct, multi-echelon supply chain with an objective to achieve high customer service with minimal inventory investment, a low-volume, high-demand variability, and/or high-cost part should be stocked at a central (high) level, while a high-volume, low-demand variability, and/or low-cost part should be stocked at a local (low) level.*

This concise statement offers useful intuition on allocating inventory in a supply chain. However, it cannot provide precise quantitative guidance on stocking levels. In an optimized system, it may well make sense to hold inventory of certain parts at more than one level. In our spare parts example, it is appropriate to hold a small stock of a part at a customer site, to facilitate quick emergency repairs, plus inventory of the part at the distribution center to be used for replenishment of the sites. The optimal amounts depend on the factors listed in the above principle, as well as system parameters, such as lead times from suppliers, shipping times betweeen inventory levels, and customer expectations. Because these subtleties become more pronounced as the number of parts and the number of levels in the supply chain increase, supply chains can be very complex to control. It is this complexity that makes supply chain management such an interesting challenge, as well as a potential source of significant competitive advantage.

9.3   The Inventory/Order Interface

The pooling versus proximity trade-off is fundamental to the design, control, and management of supply chains. As we have already noted, inventory that is held physically close to the end user (e.g., shelf stock in supermarkets, on-site spare parts, in-plant raw material supplies) can be delivered quickly when needed. But it tends to be inflexible because an item located at one site is not easily available to fill demand at another site. In contrast, centralized inventory (e.g., warehouse stock, FGI at the factory) is very flexible but may not be physically close to the demand site.

Hierarchical inventory management is one lever for exploiting the pooling-versus-proximity trade-off. Another is changing the mechanisms that govern the product flows by means of the inventory/order (I/O) interface, which we define as follows:

Definition (Inventory/Order Interface).   *The inventory/order (I/O) interface is the point in a flow where entities switch from make-to-stock to make-to-order.*

Figure 9.5 illustrates the I/O interface and how its position can be shifted to serve different strategic goals. In this figure, the stylized McDonald's system makes use of a warming table. Production upstream of the warming table is make-to-stock (i.e., it maintains specified levels of each product on the warming table), while production downstream from it is make-to-order (i.e., it is triggered directly by customer orders). In contrast, the stylized Burger King

FIGURE 9.5 Illustrations of the inventory/order interface

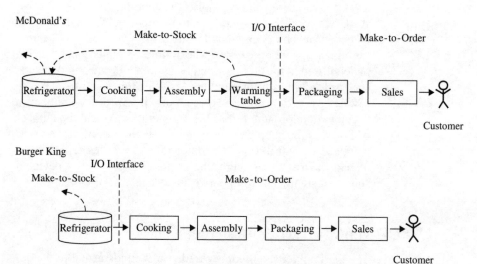

system does not have a warming table and hence cooks hamburgers to order. Hence, the entire production system beyond the refrigerator (raw materials) is make-to-order.

The McDonald's and Burger King systems generate different mixes of performance measures. The McDonald's system achieves speed via proximity (hamburgers are closer to customers and so are delivered more quickly). However, it achieves this speed at the expense of variety. If a customer orders a standard hamburger from the warming table, it will be delivered quickly. But if the customer makes a special request for extra pickles, the hamburger will have to be made from scratch and hence will be delayed. To function efficiently, the McDonald's system must encourage most customers to order standard products.

In contrast, the Burger King system can provide variety because all inventory is held in the form of generic (pooled) raw materials and hence can be used to produce any final product. Custom orders for "no ketchup" are no problem, because all hamburgers are made from scratch. But, this customization comes at the expense of speed. Customers must wait for the entire production cycle (as opposed to only the packaging and sales steps at McDonald's), so the delivery speed is slower.

The location of the I/O interface should be chosen to strike an appropriate balance among cost, customization, and speed. By moving the I/O interface closer to the customer, we eliminate a portion of the cycle time from the lead time seen by the customer. The cost of holding this inventory depends on the diversity of the products. In a system that produces a single product (e.g., a styrene plant), the cost of holding inventory at the raw material or finished goods levels is almost the same (the difference is only due to the costs of production—energy, yield loss, etc.). So, moving the I/O interface from raw materials to finished goods is inexpensive and therefore probably makes sense as a means for improving customer responsiveness. But in a system with many products (e.g., a custom furniture shop), it would be prohibitively expensive to hold inventory at the finished goods level.

The McDonald's and Burger King systems represent environments where the number of products is extremely large. The reason is that the products are meals, of which there are millions of possibilities. If a restaurant were to try to stock bags of all potential combinations of hamburgers, cheeseburgers, fries, desserts, drinks, and so forth, it would quickly run out of space and would experience tremendous spoilage costs. Thus, placing the I/O interface after the packaging operation would be ludicrous. But, by stocking product at the item level rather than the meal level (i.e., locating the

I/O interface in front of packaging), McDonald's is able to vastly reduce the number of stock types that must be held. The customer must still wait for the items to be combined into meals, but this is a quick process. The slight delay is a small price to pay for the vast reduction in cost. The Burger King system reduces the number of stock types even more by holding inventory further upstream at the component level (meat patties, cheese, lettuce, etc.). Inventory costs will be lower and flexibility will be higher, but because the customer must wait for the cooking and assembly stages, lead times will be longer.

The inventory versus speed trade-off is influenced not only by the location of the I/O interface, but also by the underlying production process. For example, to achieve fast-food lead times with an I/O interface in front of cooking, Burger King had to design rapid cooking and assembly operations. In other instances, where the objective is to move the I/O interface closer to the customer to improve delivery speed, products must often be redesigned to delay customization, a practice known as **postponement**, which we discussed in Chapter 8.

We can summarize our insights about the position of the I/O interface in the following principle:

Principle (Inventory/Order Interface Position). *Long production lead times require the I/O interface to be located close to the customer for responsiveness, while high product proliferation requires it to be located close to raw materials for pooling efficiency.*

Note that the I/O interface can be varied by product or time. For example, at McDonald's, popular Big Macs are held on the warming table, while less-popular Filet-o-Fishes are not. So, the I/O interface is located after assembly for Big Macs, but after raw materials for Filet-o-Fishes. Furthermore, whether a particular item is stored on the warming table depends on the time of day. During the lunch-hour rush, many items are stocked on the warming table, while during low-demand periods, the warming table is empty. The reason, of course, is that holding stock is more effective when usage rates are high, because it will turn over quickly, provide fast service to many customers, and be less prone to obsolescence. The shift in the I/O interface can also take place over longer time cycles. For example, a manufacturer of residential windows might build up stocks of standard sizes during the summer construction season, but only build to order during the winter slow season.

Principles in Practice

Hewlett-Packard

A well-publicized example of using clever product design to facilitate locating the I/O interface close to the customer was that of the
HP Deskjet printer in the 1980s (see Lee, Billington, and Carter 1993
for a more detailed description). Originally, European models of this
printer were manufactured in the United States and shipped to individual countries. Because of different electrical standards, printers had
to be customized by country. HP could have located the I/O interface
on the American side of the Atlantic by building printers to order for
the individual countries. But, because production and shipping times
were long, this would have resulted in uncompetitive lead times. So,
to improve responsiveness, HP located the I/O interface in Europe and
tried to match production to future demand via forecasting. However,
inevitable forecasting errors caused overages and shortages in the various markets and, because printers were different, a shortage in one
country could not be canceled out by an overage in another. Changing
technology rapidly made models obsolete, causing excess inventory to
be marked down or written off.

To reduce the inventory cost of having the I/O interface close to
customers in Europe, HP adopted a postponement strategy. They manufactured generic European printers in the United States without power
supplies. Then, after shipping them to Europe, they installed the appropriate power supplies in the distribution center. This "customize to
order" policy allowed HP to pool the European inventory and thereby
avoid the problem of simultaneous shortages and overages. Forecasting
now had to be accurate at the aggregate level only, so HP was able to
greatly reduce losses due to obsolescence.

9.4   The Bullwhip Effect

An interesting phenomenon that occurs in multi-echelon supply
chains is the tendency for demand fluctuations to increase from
the bottom of the supply chain to the top. Known as the **bullwhip
effect**, this behavior is illustrated in Figure 9.6. Note that even
though demand at the bottom of the supply chain (retail level) is
quite stable, the demand seen at the top level (by the manufacturer)

FIGURE 9.6

Demand at
different levels
of the supply
chain

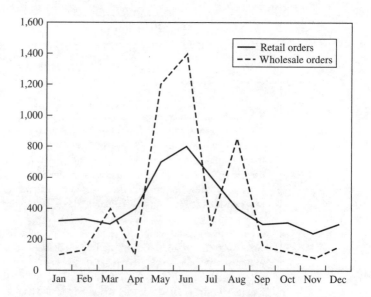

is highly variable.[1] Because all variability must be buffered, this has important consequences for the overall efficiency of the supply chain. Therefore, it is important to understand why this effect occurs and what can be done about it.

Lee, Padmanabhan, and Whang (1997) identified the following as the most common factors that lead to the bullwhip effect:

1. *Batching.* At the lowest level, which is closest to the customer, demand tends to be fairly steady and predictable because many customers buy the product in small quantities. But retailers buy from distributors in lots to facilitate efficient delivery. The distributors order from the manufacturer in even larger lots, because their volumes are higher. As a result, relatively smooth customer demand is transformed into very lumpy demand at the manufacturer level.

2. *Forecasting.* In interfirm supply chains where levels correspond to different companies, demand forecasting can amplify order variability. The reason is that each firm observes demand and independently adds buffers. For example, suppose a retailer sees

---

[1]Cachon, Randall, and Schmidt (2006) examined aggregate industry data and concluded that the bullwhip effect is most pronounced at the wholesale level, but is not large at the manufacturer or retail level. However, because they only analyze data aggregated across industries, their results do not rule out a strong bullwhip effect within individual firms at any level. Indeed, the author has observed statistics from private companies that show a large amplification of demand variability at the manufacturer level.

a small spike in demand. To make sure the order quantity covers both anticipated demand and safety stock, the retailer places an order that shows a slightly larger spike than the one in demand. The distributor then makes a forecast on the basis of retailer orders. Again, because stock must cover both anticipated demand and safety stock, the distributor places an order that represents an even larger spike than that in the retailer order. So, the manufacturer sees an amplified spike in demand. The reverse happens when the retailer sees a dip in demand, which causes the manufacturer to see an amplified dip. The result is that demand volatility increases as we progress up the supply chain.

3. *Pricing.* Promotional pricing, or the anticipation of it, can cause demand to be aggregated into spikes. Whenever a product is priced low, customers tend to "buy forward" by purchasing more than needed. When prices are high, customers hold off buying. Depending on how the manufacturer, distributor, and retailer make use of promotional pricing, this effect can greatly increase the volatility of demand.

4. *Gaming behavior.* In a perfect world, customers order what they actually want to buy. However, in the real world, where orders may not be filled, there is incentive for customers to play games with their orders. For example, suppose that when a product is in short supply the supplier allocates it to customers in proportion to the quantities they have on order. If customers know this, then they have an incentive to exaggerate their orders to increase their share of the rationed product. When the shortage disappears, customers cancel the excess orders and the supplier is stuck with them. This behavior tends to increase orders when actual demand is high (because that is when shortages occur), but not when actual demand is low. The result is an amplification in the swings in demand.

We can summarize these factors in the following principle:

Principle (Bullwhip Effect).   *Demand at the top (manufacturing) level of a supply chain tends to exhibit more variability than demand at the bottom (retail) level due to batch ordering, forecasting errors, promotional pricing, and gaming behavior by customers.*

Identifying these as the main causes of the bullwhip effect suggests that the following are options for mitigating it:

1. *Reduce batching incentives.* Because batch orders amplify demand variability, policies that facilitate replenishment of stock in smaller quantities reduce this effect.
   a. *Reduce cost of replenishment order.* If it costs less to place an order (e.g., because the participants in the

supply chain make use of **electronic data interchange (EDI)**, smaller orders will become economical.

   b. *Consolidate orders to fill trucks.* If a wholesaler or distributor orders a product in full truckloads, this is good for transportation cost, but bad for batch size. So, if instead multiple products share the same truck, transportation costs can be kept low with smaller batch sizes. Third-party logistics companies can facilitate this.

2. *Improve forecasting.* Because forecasts made on the basis of local demand (e.g., that seen by the distributor or manufacturer) instead of actual customer demand aggravate the bullwhip effect, policies that improve visibility to demand reduce demand volatility.

   a. *Share demand data.* A straightforward solution is to use a common set of demand data at all levels in the supply chain. In intrafirm supply chains (i.e., owned by a single firm) this is fairly simple (although *not* automatic). In interfirm supply chains, it requires explicit cooperation. For example, IBM, HP, and Apple all require sell-through data from their resellers as part of their contracts.

   b. *Vendor-managed inventory.* Manufacturers control resupply of the entire supply chain in **vendor-managed inventory (VMI)** systems. For example, Procter & Gamble controls inventories of Pampers all the way from its supplier (3M) to its customer (Wal-Mart). Hence, demand data is automatically shared and inventory can be pooled more effectively across the levels of the supply chain.

   c. *Lead time reduction.* Because safety stocks increase with replenishment lead time, shorter lead times cause less amplification of demand spikes. Variability reduction, postponement strategies, and waste elimination policies can achieve shorter lead times.

3. *Increase price stability.* Because price fluctuations cause customers to accelerate or delay buying, policies that stablize prices reduce demand volatility.

   a. *Everyday low pricing.* Eliminating or reducing reliance on promotional pricing and shifting to "everyday low prices" or "value prices" is a straightforward way to reduce price swings. Such schemes can also be part of effective marketing campaigns.

   b. *Activity-based costing.* By accounting for inventory, shipping, and handling, activity-based costing (ABC) systems can show costs of promotional pricing that do not show up under traditional accounting systems. Hence, they can help justify and implement an everyday low-pricing strategy.

4. *Remove gaming incentives*. Because gaming behavior distorts customer orders, policies that remove incentive for this kind of behavior can reduce the distortion and the resulting effect on demand variability.

   a. *Allocate shortages according to past sales*. By allocating supply of a scarce product on the basis of historical demand, rather than current orders, the supplier can remove incentive for customers to exaggerate orders.

   b. *Restrict order cancelation*. Many firms make use of frozen zones and/or time fences that limit customers' freedom to cancel orders. (Generally, the options for changing an order diminish as time draws closer to the order due date.) This makes gaming strategies more costly. How far a supplier can go with such policies depends, however, on the importance of flexibility for competitiveness in the marketplace.

   c. *Lead-time reduction*. Long lead-time components tend to aggravate gaming behavior because customers know that manufacturers must order components well in advance, often before receiving firm orders for the products that will use them. Therefore, to be sure that the manufacturer won't run short of these components, customers have incentive to inflate demand projections for distant future periods and then reduce these when it comes time to convert them into firm orders. Of course, if the frozen zone or time fence policy prohibits such changes in customer orders, this cannot occur. But lead times on components are frequently longer than a frozen zone that customers would tolerate. Hence, working with suppliers of such components to reduce lead times may be the most practical alternative.

9.5 Supply Chain Contracts

If a firm controls all levels of a supply chain, then it can make use of an optimization approach, such as that suggested in Section 9.2, to coordinate the stock levels and flows. However, most modern supply chains involve multiple decision makers. Retailers purchase products from manufacturers who purchase materials from suppliers. If the various firms involved in a supply chain act independently to maximize their individual profits they may very well produce an uncoordinated system that does not optimize overall profit.

To see this, consider a single seasonal product, say winter parkas, sold through a retail outlet. For simplicity, we assume that the retailer makes use of a periodic review policy in which it places one order per year and that excess inventory is scrapped.

We start by considering an **intrafirm supply chain**, where the retailer and the manufacturer are owned by the same firm. We let c represent the unit manufacturing (wholesale) cost and p_r represent the retail price. Because there is only a single organization involved, the objective is to maximize total profit. We can do this by noting that the cost of being one unit short of meeting demand is $k = p_r - c$ and the cost of having one unit of extra inventory is $h = c$ (we scrap any additional inventory and lose the wholesale cost). Then we can apply the periodic review model of Chapter 7 to compute the optimal order-up-to level (OUTL) as the value of x that satisfies

$$P(D \leq x) = \frac{k}{k+h} = \frac{p_r - c}{p_r - c + c} = \frac{p_r - c}{p_r}$$

That is, the firm should order enough parkas to ensure that the likelihood of being able to satisfy demand is equal to $(p_r - c)/p_r$.

As a concrete example, suppose the unit manufacturing cost of a parka is $c = \$25$ and the retail price is $p_r = \$100$. In the intrafirm supply chain the retailer should order enough parkas to ensure that the probability of being able to meet demand is

$$P(D \leq x) = \frac{p_r - c}{p_r} = \frac{100 - 25}{100} = 0.75$$

If demand is normally distributed with mean $\mu = 10{,}000$ and a standard deviation $\sigma = 2{,}000$, then we can compute the amount of parkas to order as

$$\text{OUTL} = \mu + z_{0.75}\sigma = 10{,}000 + (0.675)2{,}000 = 11{,}349$$

where $z_{0.75} = 0.675$ is the 75th percentile of the standard normal distribution.[2] Because lost sales are more costly than excess inventory, it is optimal to order more parkas than the firm expects to sell. But this value strikes the optimal balance between the risk of too much inventory and too little.

---

[2]This value can be looked up in a standard normal table, or computed as NORMSINV(0.75) in Excel.

Now consider the **interfirm supply chain** in which the manufacturer and retailer are two separate firms. In this case the manufacturer first sets a wholesale price, which we denote by p_w, where $c < p_w < p_r$ (so that both manufacturer and retailer can make a profit). Then the retailer decides how many parkas to purchase. The unit cost to the retailer is p_w so our model suggests that the retailer should order enough parkas to make the likelihood of being able to satisfy demand equal to

$$P(D \leq x) = \frac{k}{k+h} = \frac{p_r - p_w}{p_r}$$

We know from our discussion of the periodic review inventory model in Chapter 7 that decreasing the ratio $k/(k+h)$ causes the order-up-to level to decrease. The reason is that the retailer must increase the amount of inventory to increase the likelihood of being able to meet demand. Because of our assumption that $p_w > c$, it follows that $(p_r - p_w)/p_r < (p_r - c)/p_r$. Hence, the order-up-to level will be smaller in the sequential supply chain than in the integrated supply chain.

We illustrate this in Figure 9.7, where $OUTL_{intra}$ represents the optimal order-up-to level in the intrafirm supply chain and $OUTL_{inter}$ denotes the order-up-to level for the interfirm supply chain. The graph in Figure 9.7 plots the distribution of demand for parkas, so the area under the curve to the left of a value of OUTL represents the probability that demand is less than or equal to OUTL. This shows that raising the effective cost to the retailer from k to p_w causes the order-up-to level to decrease.

FIGURE 9.7

Impact of buybacks on optimal order-up-to level

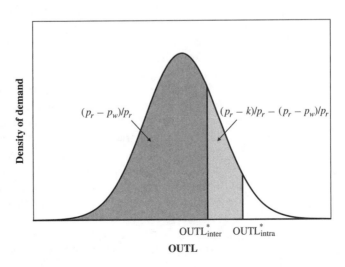

Returning to our numerical example, suppose that the manufacturer and retailer are separate firms and the manufacturer charges a wholesale price of $p_w = \$50$ for the parkas. In the interfirm supply chain, without any contract, the retailer will purchase enough parkas to ensure the probability of meeting demand is

$$P(D \leq x) = \frac{p_r - p_w}{p_r} = \frac{100 - 50}{100} = 0.5$$

Hence, if we again assume that demand is normally distributed with mean 10,000 and standard deviation 2,000, this optimization will lead the retailer to purchase

$$\text{OUTL} = \mu + z_{0.5}\sigma = 10{,}000 + (0)2{,}000 = 10{,}000$$

parkas. That is, instead of buying extra parkas to cover demand above the expected level, as we observed in the integrated supply chain, the retailer will only stock enough parkas to meet expected demand.

Because we know that the solution to the integrated supply chain maximizes total profits, the solution to the sequential supply chain must be suboptimal. The underlying cause of this inefficiency is known as **double marginalization** (i.e., separate markups by both the manufacturer and the retailer). By appropriating some of the profit the manufacturer raises the price to the retailer. But the manufacturer does not take on any of the risk of having too much inventory. So the retailer balances the full risk against the partial profit and logically orders fewer parkas. The result is lower sales (due to more stockouts) and reduced total supply chain profit.

Correcting the inefficiency caused by double marginalization by aligning the policies at the various levels of a supply chain is often referred to as **channel coordination**. The objective is to achieve performance at or near the overall optimum. Of course, one obvious option is vertical integration; if a single firm owns the entire supply chain then it can (in theory, at least) optimize it. But this is not realistic in most industries. In general, firms have limited core competencies. A retailer may not be an effective manufacturer and a final assembly manufacturer may not be an effective parts producer. As a result, most supply chains involve more than one firm.

Coordinating decisions in an interfirm supply chain requires cooperation among the various decision makers. This is usually achieved by using some form of contract. Many variants are possible, but all coordination contracts work by sharing risk among firms and giving them an incentive to optimize total profits. We can state this general observation as a principle:

Principle (Risk-Sharing Contracts).   *In interfirm supply chains, individual decision makers optimizing their local objectives generally suboptimize the overall system because risk falls disproportionally on one party. Contracts that share risk can incentivize individual decision makers to make globally optimal choices.*

We can illustrate how supply contracts work to align incentives by considering a simple **buyback contract**, in which the manufacturer agrees to purchase unsold goods from the retailer at a prespecified price. In the context of our model, this contract does not change the cost of being one unit short of demand, which remains $k = p_r - p_w$. However, it reduces the cost to the retailer of having one unit of excess supply to $h = p_w - p_b$, where p_b represents the buyback price. Hence, acting to optimize local profits, the retailer should set its order-up-to level (OUTL) to the value of x that satisfies

$$P(D \leq x) = \frac{k}{k + h} = \frac{p_r - p_w}{p_r - p_b}$$

Because the negative p_b term in the denominator serves to increase the ratio $k/(k + h)$ (i.e., the probability of being able to meet demand), this serves to increase the optimal order-up-to level. Therefore, by sharing risk between the manufacturer and retailer, a buyback policy can offset the distortion caused by the manufacturer charging a wholesale price that is higher than the manufacturing cost.

Notice that if $p_b = p_w$ (i.e., the manufacturer will buy back all excess at the original wholesale price), then $P(D \leq x) = 1$, which means that the retailer will order enough parkas to meet any possible level of demand (i.e., $x = \infty$). This is perfectly logical, because $p_b = p_w$ means that the manufacturer assumes all of the risk of an oversupply. But it is not very practical from the manufacturer's perspective. Hence, in practice, we expect $p_b < p_w$, so that the risk is shared between the manufacturer and the retailer. When this is the case, the retailer will order more than it would without a contract, but not an unlimited amount.

In our numerical example, if the manufacturer were to offer the retailer a buyback contract with a buyback price of $p_b = 37.50$, then the retailer will purchase enough parkas to ensure the probability of meeting demand is

$$P(D \leq x) = \frac{p_r - p_w}{p_r - p_b} = \frac{100 - 50}{100 - 37.50} = 0.75$$

Hence, the resulting order-up-to level in the interfirm supply chain with the buyback contract will be the same as it would be in the intrafirm supply chain (i.e., the retailer will purchase 11,349 parkas). Therefore, total profits will be maximized. Notice that in this case, a buyback price of $37.50 is exactly what is needed to achieve the optimal order-up-to level. Setting the price higher than this will cause the retailer to stock too much; setting it lower will cause it to stock too little.

Finally, we note that the buyback contract will result in a specific distribution of total profits between the manufacturer and the retailer. If this distribution is inappropriate (what is appropriate will depend on the relative power of the two firms), then it can be adjusted by means of a fixed payment from one party to the other. As long as the payment is fixed it will not have any impact on the inventory policy.

A variant on the buyback contract is the **quantity flexibility contract**, in which the manufacturer allows the retailer to return, at full wholesale price, excess inventory up to some limited amount. Because the retailer can purchase stock up to the limit without risk, it may as well do so. Hence, the manufacturer can induce the retailer to purchase the quantity that maximizes total profits. Again, distribution of these profits can be adjusted by means of a fixed payment.

The buyback and quantity flexibility contracts serve to motivate the retailer to increase inventory (and hence sales) by reducing the cost of liquidating excess inventory. Another approach for achieving the same thing is to reduce the cost of purchasing the inventory in the first place. In a **revenue-sharing contract**, the manufacturer sells the item to the retailer at a discounted price in return for a share of the sales revenue from each unit sold by the retailer. This reduces the upfront risk on the part of the retailer, so a revenue-sharing contract can also induce a retailer to increase its stock purchases up to the profit-optimizing amount.

Yet another approach for inducing the retailer to increase stock levels is to increase the profit margin on sales. In a **sales rebate contract** the manufacturer offers a rebate on sales above a specified level. In our model, this has the effect of increasing the cost of having too little inventory because more revenue is foregone in a lost sale.

Many other specific contracts can be used to increase the overall efficiency of interfirm supply chains (see Cachon 2003 for an overview of supply chain contracts). Which is best will depend on details of the situation, such as the relationship between the two firms, the marketing strategy for the product, and many other issues. The point of our discussion here is that there is a range of alternatives for constructing effective supply contracts.

Principles in Practice

Blockbuster

The traditional arrangement between movie studios and the video rental industry was to have the stores purchase tapes (for about $65 per movie) and keep all of the rental income (about $3 per rental). This meant that a tape had to be rented 22 times to be profitable. Not surprisingly, video stores were reluctant to purchase too many copies of any given title, for fear of being stuck with tapes that never paid back their purchase price. Of course, this also meant that customers were quite likely to find titles out of stock, which meant that the video stores lost potential rental revenue. Customers were also unhappy at frequently being unable to rent new-release videos.

In 1998, Blockbuster entered into revenue-sharing agreements with the major studios, under which the studio reduced the purchase price to about $8 per tape in return for a portion (about 40 percent) of the rental revenue (see Cachon and Lariviere 2001 for a discussion). The rental company kept about $1.80 of the $3 rental fee, so roughly five rentals made a tape profitable. As a result, Blockbuster could afford to stock more copies of titles, customers were more likely to find them in stock, and more rental income was generated. The income from the greater number of tapes purchased plus their share of the rental income made the studios better off. And the reduced tape cost and larger number of rentals made the rental stores better off.

With the new revenue-sharing contract in place, Blockbuster introduced marketing campaigns with slogans like "Go Away Happy" and "Guaranteed to be There." Test markets showed as much as a 75 percent increase in rental revenue. A year later the company had increased its overall market share from 25 percent to 31 percent and its cash flow by 61 percent. The incremental gain in market share was equal to the entire share of its number-two rival, Hollywood Entertainment.

9.6 Information Management

In much of this book, we have viewed supply chains as networks of material flows. But to an increasing degree, supply chains are also networks of information flows. Hence, supply chain management is as much about managing information as it is about managing material. Advances in information technology (IT) have made vast amounts of data available to decision makers. The challenge is to convert these data into information that can be used to make better decisions.

IT is much too vast a topic to cover comprehensively here, so we provide only a brief overview of key issues involved in collection, sharing, and use of information in the context of supply chain coordination.

9.6.1   Collection

Before we can use data in a model or analysis we must first collect them. Despite significant advances in IT, which automate certain aspects of data acquisition, collecting the right data in the right form still requires decisions and effort on the part of people. As such, it remains a very significant task.

Data Accuracy

The old computer science adage—garbage in, garbage out—applies with a vengeance in supply chains. No amount of sophistication in hardware or software can make up for poor data. For example, while the inventory models discussed in Chapter 7 are vastly superior to ad hoc methods (e.g., days-of-supply stocking rules) found in practice, they cannot be effective if inventory data are inaccurate. Unfortunately, research suggests that inventory records in supply chains are often very poor.

For example, Raman, DeHoratius, and Ton (2001) studied a very large publicly traded retailer with billions of dollars of annual sales and the latest in scanning and database technology. They found that over 65 percent of the items stocked in the store had discrepancies between the physical inventory and the quantity shown in the system. Moreover, these discrepancies were not small; the average difference between physical and system inventory was 35 percent of the target inventory level for the item.

Information problems extend beyond inaccuracies in inventory totals. Raman et al. (2001) also studied 242 stores of another large sophisticated retailer and found that customers could not find 16 percent of items in a store because the items were in the wrong place—either in an incorrect aisle or misplaced in a backroom or storage area. They also plotted a histogram of the percent of items that were not found on the sales floor at the time of an annual audit even though inventory was available in the store (i.e., the entire stock was in the backroom). The mode of this histogram occurred at 3.4 percent of the items, but had occurences as high as

10 percent. That is, some stores had 10 percent of their entire catalog of offerings not available to customers despite having inventory of these items on site.

The immediate impact of not having stock available on the floor is obvious—lost sales. Raman et al. estimate that loss of sales, coupled with increased carrying costs, reduced profits by roughly 10 percent at the first retailer and 25 percent at the second retailer. To put these in perspective, they point out that these losses are equivalent to the entire profit at 100 stores for the first retailer and 50 stores for the second retailer.

But the impact of inaccurate data goes beyond the immediate impact on sales. To illustrate this, suppose the retailer makes use of a reorder point model to control inventory for an item. That is, whenever the stock level in the system falls below a specified level (the reorder point), a replenishment order is placed. Suppose, however, that the replenishment quantity is larger than the amount of inventory that can be displayed on the floor (shelf space is a very precious commodity in retail stores). This means that the excess stock will be stored in the backroom and, judging from the findings of Raman et al. (2001), probably lost. If the lost quantity in the backroom exceeds the reorder point, then even when stock on the floor falls to zero, a replenishment order will not be generated by the system. As a result, until a manual intervention is made, the store will continue to hold stock but will make no sales.

A similar dynamic can result from shoplifting. Stolen items leave the shelf, but are not scanned through a register and hence do not get subtracted from inventory levels in the database. So, again, the store could find itself with no inventory on the shelf but no replenishment orders being generated by the system.

Another scenario that can lead to discrepancies between physical inventories and system records occurs when cashiers combine items for scanning purposes. For example, suppose a customer buys 25 cans of soup, consisting of a mix of chicken, beef, and vegetable. Knowing that all of them are the same price, the cashier scans one can (say chicken) and then uses the keypad to multiply by 25. While this speeds service and results in a correct bill, it subtracts 25 cans from the chicken soup stock in the system and none from beef or vegetable soup. A few such incidents at the cash register and the inventory data could be seriously out of sync with reality.

The findings of Raman et al. (2001) suggest that scenarios like these are playing out every day in retail outlets, and presumably elsewhere in supply chains, all over the world. The implication for management is that purchasing a sophisticated database and barcode scanning system is not sufficient to manage a complex supply chain. Policies and technologies that facilitate more accurate tracking of the quantity and location of items throughout the supply chain are also essential.

One approach to collecting better inventory data is the good old-fashioned audit. Periodically performing a manual count of the number of items for each SKU (stock keeping unit) and correcting system records certainly helps reduce the impact of the above-cited scenarios. Unfortunately, in most retail settings, the emphasis of audits is on measuring "shrinkage" (missing items due to theft or damage). Hence, if a manual count of cans of soup matches the total amount in the system closely, a shrinkage audit is a success, even if the counts of individual SKUs (e.g., chicken, beef, and vegetable) are not accurate. To be effective in improving performance of supply chain management systems, such audits must focus on the accuracy of both the total and the mix of inventory at each point in the supply chain.

RFID

Because audits are slow and expensive, they are used infrequently (e.g., anually). So inventory records can get seriously inaccurate between audits. Recognizing this, firms are looking to technology for help. The most promising technical solution on the near-term horizon is RFID (radio frequency identification).[3]

RFID works by embedding tiny chips (called *tags*) in items, pallets, or even people. The tag generates a radio signal that is captured by a receiver and decoded to provide information (e.g., an identifier within a database). Unlike barcode readers, RFID tags do not need a direct line of site to be read. With current technology, "passive" tags (i.e., tags without an internal power source) can be read from a distance of a few meters, while "active" tags (i.e., tags with an internal power source) can be read from a distance of 100 meters. Active tags can also store more information than passive tags.

The supply chain benefits of RFID are easy to envision. For instance, suppose that cases received by a retail store contain an RFID label. By installing readers at receiving doors, backroom storage areas, a sales floor door, and a box crusher area, the store will be able to infer the latest inventory levels in the backroom. If individual items contain RFID tags, then floor stocks could be similarly monitored in real time. This information could be used to generate pick

---

[3]The potential applications of RFID extend well beyond inventory tracking in supply chains. For example, some countries are embedding tags in passports that store personal information, including a digital picture. Tags are also being used in cars for electronic toll collection (e.g., Illinois' I-Pass system) and for smart key access (i.e., keys that unlock and permit starting a car while still in the driver's pocket or purse).

lists for the warehouse, as well as stocking priorities for the sales floor. Needless to say, RFID tags in individual items could be integrated with security systems to provide a significant barrier to theft. Elsewhere in the supply chain, RFID would facilitate continuous tracking of the amount and type of inventory. By making inventory data more accurate, this technology would eliminate wasteful stock in the supply chain and reduce unnecessary stockouts.

At the time of this writing, the major barrier to widespread adoption of RFID technology in supply chain settings is cost. A simple passive tag currently costs 20 cents or more, with active tags and tags embedded in labels or plastic can cost considerably more. Many writers speculate that the technology will not take off until the price falls to 5 cents per tag, although even this may be too expensive for use in individual items with low margins (e.g., adding a 5-cent tag to the wrapper of a 50-cent candy bar is probably not economical).

Because the cost issue involves a chicken and egg dilemma (i.e., cost will not fall until volumes increase to allow economies of scale, and vice versa), Wal-Mart chose to leverage its size to stimulate RFID. In 2004, Wal-Mart required its top 100 suppliers to tag cases and pallets with RFID tags by January 2005, its next 200 suppliers by January 2006, and the next 300 by January 2007. Over 1,000 Wal-Mart stores were using the technology by the end of 2006. Presumably, Wal-Mart is beginning to reap the benefits of more accurate inventory data. But when we will cross the tipping point beyond which RFID will become ubiquitous in supply chains is still an open question.

Forecasting

The problem of data collection goes beyond sensing items and storing records about them. Data and information often come from multiple sources (models, people, firms, etc.), which poses a problem of aggregating the information into a useful whole. This is particularly important when the data concern forecasts about the future.

For example, Fisher et al. (1994) described the process used by Sport Obermeyer to forecast demand for winter parkas. Initially, a buying committee discussed each parka and arrived at a consensus forecast (i.e., a single number prediction of sales). But the authors recognized that this process did not collect data about the uncertainty of the forecast. So they recommended, and Sport Obermeyer adopted, a new system in which each buyer produced an individual forecast without a group discussion. With these forecasts, Sport Obermeyer could compute a mean *and* a standard deviation of forecasted sales, which could be used in the periodic review model (with only one period, corresponding to a season) of Chapter 7.

As an illustration, consider two parkas named the Tundra and the Blizzard. Ignoring the problem of forecasting specific sizes and colors, suppose the firm's buyers are charged with forecasting total sales during the season for each parka. Further suppose that the average of the buyers' forecasts is 1,200 parkas for each model. However, the standard deviation of the forecasts for the Tundra is only 30, while the standard deviation for the Blizzard is 150. Finally, suppose that the unit margin for both Parkas is $60, while the cost of a markdown is $20 (i.e., a parka will be sold at $20 below wholesale cost if inventory exceeds demand). In the notation of Chapter 7, $s = 60$ is the unit shortage cost, while $h = 20$ is the unit overage cost.

By the logic of the periodic review model, enough parkas should be ordered so that the probability of meeting demand is

$$\frac{s}{s+h} = \frac{60}{60+20} = 0.75$$

Because the 75th percentile of the standard normal distribution is $z = 0.675$, we can compute the optimal order quantities of each parka as

$$OQ^*_{Tundra} = 1,200 + 0.675(30) = 1,220$$

$$OQ^*_{Blizzard} = 1,200 + 0.675(150) = 1,301$$

Figure 9.8 illustrates these order quantities graphically. Intuitively, the fact that it is more costly to have too few parkas than too many leads to the conclusion that we should order more Blizzards than Tundras to hedge against the greater uncertainty in demand for Blizzards. If it were more costly to be short than over, the

FIGURE 9.8 Impact of forecast variability on optimal order quantity

a. Blizzard: Mean = 1,200, Std Dev = 30

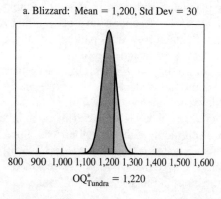

800   900 1,000 1,100 1,200 1,300 1,400 1,500 1,600

$OQ^*_{Tundra} = 1,220$

b. Tundra: Mean = 1,200, Std Dev = 150

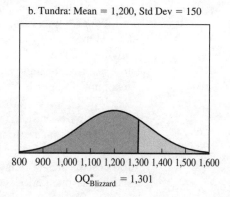

800   900 1,000 1,100 1,200 1,300 1,400 1,500 1,600

$OQ^*_{Blizzard} = 1,301$

conclusion would reverse; it would become optimal to order fewer Blizzards than Tundras.

From a principles perspective, the conclusion from this forecasting discussion is that uncertainty implies variability in the forecasting process. To account for this variability in the planning process, we must collect data to characterize it. Using individual forecasts to compute a standard deviation of future demand is one way to quantify forecast uncertainty.

9.6.2   Sharing

To be useful, data must be accessible to those who need it. Unfortunately, in complex supply chains, this is often not the case. The reason is that many different parties play a role in both collecting and using information. Hence, managing the flow of information is every bit as important as managing the flow of material in a supply chain.

Sharing information is not a trivial problem, even within a single organization. Firms often employ different information systems for different functions. For example, customer service may use one system, accounting another, manufacturing and distribution still another. Even if data are transferred between these systems, they can become unsynchronized when the transfer is not made in real time. For this reason, the ideal information system would have a single source of data that is updated and used by all parties in an organization. Software firms, such as SAP, have made billions using exactly this pitch to sell software with the heading of *enterprise solutions*.

But, while large enterprise systems can provide a common platform for sharing information within an organization, they are by no means turnkey solutions. An integrated software system is so big and so complex that implementation is always a substantial challenge. Even the largest enterprise system cannot handle every type of transaction in an organization; new software must be integrated with existing systems. But even more daunting is the fact that processes and people must also adapt to the new system. As such, system implementations are really exercises in change management. So it is not surprising that most firms have stories of struggles, if not outright failures, with IT system implementations. Indeed, Cliffe (1999) reported that 65 percent of executives surveyed believed that new enterprise resources planning (ERP) systems could be harmful to their businesses. Nevertheless, as the supply chains become larger, leaner, and more complex, the need for timely and accurate information continues to increase. Hence, despite their reservations, managers are continuing their efforts to make centralized IT systems live up to their potential.

While integrating information within an organization is difficult, integrating information across a multiparty supply chain is even more daunting. Most supply chains are inherently competitive—reducing the price of an item benefits the buyer at the expense of the seller. Hence, there will always be a measure of distrust between supply chain parties. Nevertheless, there are powerful benefits to information sharing across firm boundaries that provide motivation to overcome this underlying distrust.

For instance, we know from the bullwhip effect principle that demand variability is amplified as we move upward in the supply chain. Information visibility plays an important part in this behavior. Simchi-Levi, Kaminski, and Simchi-Levi (2003, Chapter 4) show that variance of demand increases additively in the number of supply chain levels if each level of the supply chain shares both its orders and forecasts of future demand with the next level in the supply chain. However, if each level only shares orders, without sharing forecasts, variance of demand increases multiplicatively in the number of levels. The point is that sharing information, in this case demand forecasts, can significantly reduce the bullwhip effect. Because increased demand variability forces each party to build in expensive inventory or capacity buffers, everyone in the supply chain can in theory be made better off by sharing information.

The ideal for information sharing within a supply chain is to enable everyone to directly view **point of sales (POS)** data on transactions with the customers. Indeed, many retailers (e.g., Wal-Mart) have begun sharing POS data with their suppliers, and firms (e.g., WWRE—WorldWide Retail Exchange) have begun offering services to facilitate the exchange. Of course, there are limits on the information firms are willing to share, so security is a significant concern in POS data-sharing arrangements.[4] But this concern is being addressed, at least in situations with large retailers who deal with many suppliers and so reveal relatively little of their overall business to any single supplier. Indeed, Wal-Mart is so confident in the value of information sharing that it has begun sharing RFID data on the location of stock throughout its supply chain with its suppliers.

Finally, while sharing POS and real-time inventory location data across the entire supply chain is something of an end point for information sharing, it is only the beginning of partnering opportunities. Stronger collaborative practices and even full strategic partnering (Lewis 1990) are often used in conjunction with data sharing. One collaborative practice is **vendor-managed inventory (VMI)**, under which the supplier of an item actually owns the inventory

---

[4]WWRE partnered with VeriSign, a provider of secure infrastructure systems, to protect the security of transactions between supply chain partners.

until it is scanned at a register as a customer sale. This turns full responsibility for controlling stock to the supplier, who presumably has incentive to avoid stockouts without excess inventory. P&G has such an arrangement for supplying products to Wal-Mart, while Motorola has a similar arrangement for supplying handsets to cellular service providers. Another collaborative practice is **collaborative planning, forecasting, and replenishment (CPFR)**, which is a voluntary standard that enables manufacturers and retailers to share data, forecasts, and plans in a collaborative environment.

Finally, in strategic partnerships, firms go well beyond information sharing and collaborative planning to fully joint initiatives that take advantage of each party's individual strengths. For example, in the 1990s Hewlett-Packard and Cisco recognized that their products were highly complementary. To build a networking solution, a firm needed both computers and printers (HP) as well as routers and network infrastructure (Cisco). As a result the two firms already had many customers in common. To increase their joint sales, HP and Cisco entered into a joint marketing agreement in 1997. Over time, the partnership grew to include co-branded support services, joint technology development, and coordinated product development. By working together, the two firms have been able to offer integrated solutions that neither would have been able to provide on its own.

9.6.3 Use

Collecting and sharing data does not by itself improve management. Most managers already have more data than they use now. So, while new collection, storage, and display technologies are appealing, they will only make a real difference if the data become information used in the management process.

One area where firms habitually fail to make use of data is in characterizing variability. The above-cited Sport Obermeyer example is typical. Seeking simplicity, Sport Obermeyer collapsed forecasts to single number projections of sales. While simple, this approach completely failed to characterize the risk of variable demand. So, the shift to individual forecasts, which permitted calculation of a standard deviation of future demand, enabled Sport Obermeyer to use its forcasting data in a much more powerful way. Variability data are similarly important in many other planning and evaluation situations, but are rarely used.

Some examples of data that are typically available in a supply chain system and usually ignored include

• *MTTF and MTTR.* Almost all firms collect MTTF (mean time to failure) and MTTR (mean time to repair) data to compute resource availabilities.[5] But availability only captures part of the story. As we discussed in Chapter 2, process time variability increases waiting time. For a given availability level, increasing MTTR increases variability and hence waiting time. This implies that long, infrequent outages of any resource are more disruptive than short, frequent outages.[6] To make appropriate diagnostic decisions about where variability in process times is most disruptive, managers need to evaluate MTTR, as well as availability, of their operations.

 • *Variability in vendor lead times.* While procurement departments are always concerned about price and usually concerned about on-time delivery, they often do not characterize delivery performance by suppliers in an appropriate manner. For instance, simply tracking the percentage of orders that arrive by their due date does not tell us how late the late deliveries were. Similarly, tracking the average lateness (i.e., where earliness represents negative lateness, so early deliveries cancel out late ones) does not capture the disruptiveness of the variability in delivery times.

Even worse, some firms adjust due dates in the system whenever an order is late. For instance, if a shipment is scheduled for delivery on the 15th of the month, but the supplier calls to say it will be delayed until the 22nd, the customer firm changes the due date in its database to the 22nd. So when performance statistics are tracked, the actual delivery date will be compared to the adjusted due date, rather than the original. Obviously this practice covers up supplier problems. So, while it may be appropriate to change due dates for short-term planning, it is essential to retain original due dates for long-term vendor tracking and management.

But using original due dates does not by itself capture information about supplier variability. One way to do this is to compute the **lateness**, which is given by the difference between the actual delivery date and the original due date, for each order from a given supplier. Then compute two summary statistics for these lateness values: (1) **average tardiness**, which is the average of the lateness values with any negative values (i.e., early deliveries) replaced by zeros, and (2) **standard deviation of lateness**. Looking

---

[5]Recall that availability is computed as $AVAIL = \dfrac{MTTF}{MTTF + MTTR}$.

[6]Note that we are talking about *unplanned* outages here. Preventive maintenance operations, which schedule outages in advance and take steps to prepare (e.g., building up downstream inventories to prevent starvation of other operations), may well be more efficient as relatively long, infrequent events. But when outages are unplanned, as is the case with emergency failures, short is always better. The reason is that less buffering, in the form of inventory, capacity, or time, is required to compensate for a short outage than for a long one.

at these two statistics for all suppliers will indicate which suppliers tend to be late (high average tardiness) and which suppliers have unpredictable performance (high standard deviation of lateness). Hopp and Spearman (1993) showed that both of these quantities are important in setting optimal safety lead times. Conceptually, a supplier that tends to be late, unpredictable, or both needs to be buffered with longer safety lead times than a supplier that is on time and predictable. Monitoring supplier performance in terms of both mean and standard deviation provides a basis for setting more effective safety lead times, and for highlighting suppliers who may need help (or replacement) to improve performance.

Consider Figure 9.9, which shows the distribution of lateness for two suppliers. While mean lateness (but not mean tardiness) for the two suppliers is the same, the standard deviation of lateness is 2.5 days for supplier 1 and 6 days for supplier 2. In qualitative terms, supplier 2 delivers early more often than supplier 1, but also delivers much later from time to time. As a result, if we want to be 95 percent confident of having a delivery when we need it, we must build in 4 days of safety lead time for supplier 1 and 11 days of safety lead time for supplier 2. This means that components from supplier 1 will have to wait an extra 4 days in raw materials inventory, while components from supplier 2 will have to wait an extra 11 days. If we do not build in the extra 7 days of safety lead time for supplier 2, then we will stock out more often (i.e., we will buffer the extra variability with time instead of inventory). Either way, we will pay for supplier variability. Hence, it makes sense to use available data to track suppliers and take appropriate actions to help them reduce delivery time variability.

FIGURE 9.9

Effect of supplier variability on safety lead time and inventory

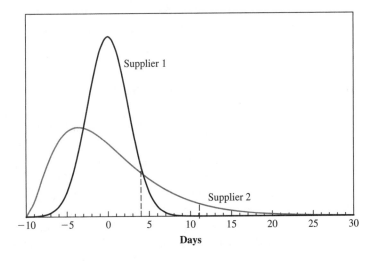

Days

• *Part cost and criticality.* Finally, we should observe that not all underutilized data involve variability. For example, we noted in Chapter 7 that many firms make use of days-of-supply policies for governing inventories in supply chains. While such policies are simple, they can be very ineffective. The reason is that they do not strike any kind of balance between the costs and benefits of holding inventory. The cost of holding inventory depends on the cost of the items being held—a 30-day supply of 15-cent washers costs almost nothing to hold, while a 30-day supply of luxury automobiles may represent a significant investment. So it is astounding that many supply chain managers use policies that do not take into account part cost.

On the benefits side, the value of holding stock somewhere in the supply chain depends on how critical the parts are to the system. For example, an automobile dealer who cannot get quick access to repair parts is going to have very unhappy customers. But this same dealership might be able to tolerate delays in getting nonessential add-ons (e.g., deluxe wheels or a roof rack), because customers would schedule installation of such items. Hence, critical parts needed for emergency repairs should be stocked locally at the dealer or at least at a nearby distribution center, while noncritical accessories might reasonably be stored at a central warehouse. While it seems obvious that different policies should be used to handle critical and noncritical parts, many supply chains do not take this distinction into account.

The point of these examples is to remind the reader that the principles laid out in this book, along with the models based on them, provide a vehicle for making effective use of a range of data. Even before RFID and other sensing and IT tools become ubiquitous and cost-effective, most supply chains can improve efficiency and reliability by making better use of data already available.

9.7   Restructuring Supply Chains

The above discussions illustrate a number of ways in which performance can be improved for a given supply chain configuration. But, it is important to remember that the configuration is not set in stone. Sometimes the biggest gains can be made by radically restructuring the supply chain itself. Suggestions on what types of changes might be most effective can be derived from the basic principles we have reviewed above.

For example, we have observed that increasing the number of levels in a supply chain makes it more difficult to coordinate. So,

FIGURE 9.10

Actual and
virtual
distribution
centers

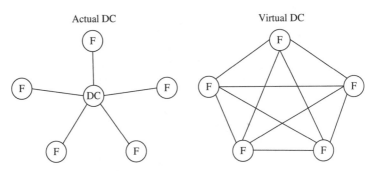

one potential path for dramatically improving a supply chain is
to eliminate levels. In the spare parts supply system depicted in
Figure 9.3 it might be possible to eliminate the distribution center
altogether, as illustrated in Figure 9.10. By storing all inventory at
the facilities and customer sites, the system would be more likely
to be able to deliver a needed part to a customer quickly. If the
facilities could efficiently cross-ship parts the system would act like
a "virtual distribution center" and achieve the benefits of pooling
without physical centralization of inventory. Of course, achieving
this would require an effective IT system (to track inventory) and
an efficient distribution system (to support cross-shipping). But if
these could be developed, the virtual pooling system could achieve
levels of efficiency that are impossible with the hierarchical system.

A compelling example of the power of reducing supply chain
levels is the case of Dell Computer. Dell's direct marketing model
eliminated the distributor and retailer of traditional PC supply
chains. This enabled Dell to pool inventory at the component level,
rather than at the finished goods level, which is vastly more efficient. It also shortened lead times (from manufacturing to customer
delivery), which enabled Dell to introduce technological innova-
tions into the market more quickly. The extraordinary success of
the Dell system is a matter of public record.[7]

A second observation we can exploit to find ways to restructure
a supply chain is that increasing the number of parts in a system
increases cost. For a given level of demand, more parts means
less pooling and therefore more safety stock. Having more parts
also increases purchasing costs, obsolescence costs, product design
costs, and quality control costs. However, if having more parts
enables the firm to offer more variety to customers, then it may also
offer revenue enhancement benefits. Finding ways to support high

---

[7]Dell has recently begun selling PC's at Wal-Mart, to reach customers who will
not buy online. But, because this retain model is much less efficient than their core
direct marketing model, for the reasons we discussed in Section 8.2.2, Dell can only
offer a much more limited array of models in the stores than they offer online.

variety without stocking excessive numbers of parts is a potential path for radical restructuring.

A well-known case of a firm using product redesign to dramatically reshape its supply chain is that of Black & Decker in the early 1970s (see Meyer and Lehnerd 1997 for a discussion). Prior to this time, the company had introduced consumer power tools a few at a time, with little consideration of the costs of complexity. As a result, its supply chain involved a huge number of parts (e.g., 30 different motors, more than 100 armatures, and dozens of switches). So, Black & Decker embarked on a major effort to redesign its products to make over 100 basic tools (drills, saws, grinders, sanders, etc.) from a small set of standardized components. For example, it designed a universal motor that could be used across a wide variety of tools. This dramatically reduced the number of parts in the supply chain, which enabled inventory cost savings via pooling and manufacturing cost reductions via use of standard processes, even though variety at the customer level was increased. The impact of this strategy was so powerful that within a few years most of Black & Decker's domestic competitors, including Stanley, Skil, Sunbeam, General Electric, Porter Cable, and Rockwell, abandoned the consumer power tool business.

Finally, a third observation that offers possibilities for supply chain restructuring is that increasing the number of decision makers makes a system more difficult to coordinate. As we noted above, decision makers who see only part of the supply chain will suboptimize because of misaligned economic incentives and lack of information. A way to avoid this suboptimization is to concentrate decision making in the hands of a single decision maker or a closely cooperative partnership of the involved firms.

An example of a firm that has pioneered several innovative ways to improve supply chain coordination via the sharing of decision making and information is Wal-Mart. Since the 1980s, Wal-Mart has made use of VMI, in which vendors (e.g., Procter & Gamble) determine, within agreed upon limits, the amount of retail inventory to stock (Buzzell and Ortmeyer 1995). Wal-Mart has also made use of consignment inventory, in which the vendor actually owns the retail inventory until it is sold. More recently, in the 1990s, Wal-Mart has been making use of CPFR, allowing its vendors to access point-of-sale data through a Web-enabled retaillink® system (Stank, Daugherty, and Autry 1999). Each of these systems provides suppliers with significant amounts of information and authority for controlling inventory throughout the supply chain. The phenomenal success Wal-Mart has achieved over the past two decades is not entirely due to these policies, but there is no doubt that they have played a substantial role.

We can draw two important lessons from these observations and examples:

1. *Leaders think big.* Evolutionary improvements in management practice are vital to survival. Improvements in forecasting methods, stocking policies, tracking techniques, and so forth, can certainly improve performance of a supply chain and help a firm remain cost-competitive. But firms that truly distinguish themselves from the competition are often those that revolutionize the business paradigm in their industry. The above examples illustrate cases where firms pursued ambitious efforts to radically remake the structure of their supply chains, and translated these into market leadership.

2. *Practices progress, but principles persist.* For example, a basic principle is that pooling inventory improves efficiency. But pooling can be achieved through direct marketing, product standardization, supply contracts, and many other methods. Hence, it is natural to expect specific practices to evolve over time as firms find new ways to exploit basic concepts. Firms that understand the key principles underlying supply chain performance will be in the best position to lead (and profit from) revolutionary change, while everyone else will be forced to copy in a struggle to keep up.

Questions for Thought

1. In Chapter 4 we observed that reducing variability increases the efficiency of a flow, in the sense of being able to convert a given amount of WIP into a greater level of throughput. In Chapter 5 we noted that all variability must be buffered by inventory, capacity, or time. This means that a high variability flow will require a large amount of WIP to operate close to capacity, which implies an inventory buffer and, because cycle times will also be longer, a time buffer as well. If WIP is kept low, the flow will run well below the bottleneck rate, which implies a capacity buffer. These same basic principles apply to flows within a production system and across facilities in a supply chain network.

   With this in mind, identify the possible buffers that could arise from each of the sources of variability in a supply chain flow:

   a. Customer preferences shift, altering the demand mix for products generated by the flow.

   b. Materials from a supplier are found to be defective when they arrive at the final assembly operation.

   c. Products outsourced to an overseas contract manufacturer are received only in large lots, due to production and shipping economies of scale.

   d. A supply plant goes off-line for an extended period due to a hurricane or fire.

2. Consider a two-level supply chain like that shown in Figure 9.3 in which customers obtain spare parts from regional facilities, which are supplied by a central distribution center that obtains stock from various suppliers. Suppose that both the distribution center and facilities make use of reorder point policies (with different parameters, of course) to control inventory of each part.

Describe the impact on the average waiting time experienced by customers at the facility level if we make each of the following changes:

   a. Reduce the lead time required to replensh stock at the distribution center.

   b. Increase the reorder points of all items stocked at the distribution center (so that the overall inventory level at the DC is increased).

   c. Leave the reorder points for items unchanged but purchase replenishments from suppliers in larger order quantities.

   d. Increase the reorder points for all items at the facilities.

   e. Allow shipment of parts between facilities (i.e., if a facility needs a part that is out of stock at the DC, it can get it from another facility).

3. In the mid-1990s, Cadillac introduced a new vehicle delivery system in which popular configurations were stocked at regional distribution centers. The goal was to enable a customer to go to any Cadillac dealership, purchase one of these "pop cons" and have it delivered within 24 hours. Customers who bought models not on the "pop con" list would have a traditional lead time of several weeks.

   a. Describe how Cadillac's strategy addresses the inventory/order interface.

   b. Why might owners of larger dealerships object to this strategy? What could General Motors do to encourage them to support it?

4. We noted that the bullwhip effect is caused by a variety of factors. For each case below, identify the causes you think are most likely to be significant in producing the bullwhip effect and suggest options for mitigating it.

   a. A supply chain, consisting of a manufacturer, distributor, and retailer, sells several models of ballpoint pens whose prices and demand are very stable.

   b. A supply chain, consisting of a producer, distributor, and retailer, sells video games, which have highly unpredictable demand.

   c. A supply chain, consisting of a food processing plant, wholesaler, and retailer, sells a variety of canned soups that occasionally go on sale as part of promotions to attract customers into the store.

5. In this chapter, we showed that risk-sharing contracts can induce a retailer to set stock levels so as to maximize systemwide profits. However, an assumption implicit in our argument was that both the manufacturer and retailer have the same forecast (i.e., distribution) of demand. What will happen to the effectiveness of such a contract if the manufacturer's forecast of demand is higher than the retailer's forecast? (You may use the buyback contract to illustrate your reasoning.)

6. Traditionally, Coke and Powerade were bottled by local bottlers who delivered them directly to stores. But in 2006, Wal-Mart asked that Coke be delivered directly from bottlers to stores but that Powerade be

delivered to warehouses, from which Wal-Mart personnel would move it into stores. Why do you think Wal-Mart wanted to structure its supply chain differently for the two beverages? (Hint: Coke sells at a much faster pace than Powerade.)

Note: This new delivery policy was perceived by the local bottlers as a threat to their role, which prompted them to file a lawsuit claiming it violated their agreement with Coca-Cola.

7. Identify how the principles of variability buffering, batching, pull efficiency, variability pooling, inventory/order position, bullwhip effect, and risk-sharing contracts apply to each of the following supply chain restructuring situations. (Note that not all principles are relevant to each case; just identify the ones that are most important.)

   a. Zara, a Spanish clothing manufacturer and retailer, holds inventory of uncut fabric in front of its production process and excess capacity in the sewing operation to respond quickly to surges in demand.

   b. In its celebrated direct marketing system, Dell eliminated the retailer level of the supply chain and shipped computers directly from manufacturing facilities to customers.

   c. To support the manufacturing side of its system, Dell reduced the number of suppliers from which it purchased parts by over 75 percent.

   d. Motorola implemented a VMI program with cellular service providers, under which Motorola owns and manages inventories in both distribution centers and retail stores.

   e. U.K.-based grocer Tesco transformed its distribtion centers into cross-docking operations where products from different suppliers are consolidated to be sent to individual stores. This pushed the inventory holding and order-picking activities back onto the suppliers and allowed Tesco to reduce its inventory significantly.

   f. BMW overhauled its production sequence to allow customers to alter their custom orders (e.g., change engine, color, and equipment options) for 7 Series cars up to 1 week before vehicle assembly begins. They did this by storing key components (e.g., painted bodies) in warehouses and moving them to the assembly plant right before the start of assembly.

   g. Using a process widely studied in the lean literature, Johnson Controls, Inc. (JCI) delivered seats to a Toyota assembly plant in Georgetown, Kentucky. Under this system, Toyota sent a broadcast signal to JCI each time an auto body left the paint operation. JCI used these signals to pull materials and components and assemble the seats (which varied from vehicle to vehicle) and ship them to Toyota in the specified sequence. A seat was matched up with its vehicle 4 hours and 20 minutes after the car left the paint department. As a result, neither Toyota nor JCI held a significant amount of finished seat inventory.

   h. Pepsi equipped its sales representatives with wireless PDAs, which provided them with detailed data on past sales for each customer. This helped them better plan their customers' orders and avoid last-minute rush orders to make up for shortages. It also enabled salespeople to immediately transmit orders back to headquarters, rather than storing them up and entering them at the end of the day.

A SUMMARY OF NOTATION

AVAIL availability; the fraction of uptime at a station.

ARATE arrival rate; the rate at which entities enter a station, line, or system.

b backordering cost; usually measured as the cost to carry one customer order on backlog for one period (usually a year, but sometimes a week or some other interval, depending on the problem context). Note that *b* is not generally a measurable quantity, because it depends on customer goodwill and other intangibles. But we can use it to control the trade-off between inventory cost and customer service and help us find a reasonable compromise.

BNR bottleneck rate; the capacity of the station with the highest utilization in a flow.

BSIZE batch size; number of entities processed sequentially between setups or simultaneously in a batch operation.

BSL base stock level; the target level of on-hand plus on-order inventory in a base stock system.

c unit cost; the cost to produce (or purchase) one unit of a product.

CT cycle time; the total amount of time an entity spends in a flow, including both (value-added) processing time and (non-value-added) waiting time.

CV coefficient of variation of a random variable; the standard deviation divided by the mean.

CWIP critical WIP; the minimum amount of WIP needed to achieve full capacity of a line operating under the best case and computed as $\text{BNR} \times \text{RPT}$.

D demand; usually measured as the average number of product units (or dollar value of the units) required by customers in a year. Sometimes *D* is measured over a shorter time period, such as a week.

FGI finished goods inventory; entities that have completed processing but have not yet been delivered to customers.

h holding cost; the total cost to hold one unit of inventory in stock for one period (usually a year, but sometimes a week or some other interval, depending on the problem context).

k shortage cost; the lost revenue for each unit by which inventory is insufficient to meet demand.

LT lead time; the interval between an order and the promised delivery. Note that lead time can refer to replenishment orders from a firm to a supplier or customer orders from a customer to the firm.

μ mu, the Greek letter that is standard statistics notation for the mean. In this book, the mean we are concerned with is the mean demand. Specifically, we are interested in the mean demand that occurs while we are waiting for a replenishment order. In a periodic review system this translates into the mean demand during the period (e.g., week), while in a continuous review system this translates into the mean demand during the replenishment lead time.

MTTF   mean time to failure; the average time between outages (breakdowns) of a server.

MTTR   mean time to repair; the average repair time of a server.

OUTL   order-up-to level; the target inventory level for the beginning of each period in a periodic review system.

PRATE   process rate; the capacity (i.e., maximum number of entities per unit time) of a station.

o   ordering cost; the fixed cost associated with placing a replenishment order.

OQ   order quantity; the number of units ordered simultaneously in a replenishment order.

p_r retail price for an item.

p_w wholesale price for an item.

p_b buyback price for an item; the price a manufacturer will pay a retailer for excess inventory that is returned in a system using a buyback contract.

PT   process time; the time a server spends performing a required task on an entity.

r   unit revenue; the net revenue associated with selling one unit of a product.

RMI   raw material inventory; stock that has not yet been released into a flow.

RPT   raw process time; the average time an entity (moving in standard move batches) takes to go through an empty line.

σ sigma, the Greek letter that is standard statistics notation for the standard deviation. In this book, the standard deviation we are concerned with is the standard deviation of demand. Specifically, we are interested in the standard deviation of the demand that occurs while we are waiting for a replenishment order. In a periodic review system this translates into the standard deviation of demand during the period (e.g., week), while in a continuous review system this translates into the standard deviation of demand during the replenishment lead time.

S   service. For make-to-stock systems, service is typically measured by "fill rate," which represents the fraction of customer orders that are filled from stock. For make-to-order systems, service is usually characterized by the fraction of customer orders that are filled within the quoted lead time.

SS   safety stock; the expected amount of inventory that will be in stock when a replenishment order arrives.

ST   setup time; the time required for a server to switch from processing one type of entity to another.

TH   throughput; the *rate* of nondefective entities processed per unit time.

UTIL   utilization; the fraction of time a server is busy and is computed as rate divided by capacity (ARATE/PRATE).

WIP   work in process; entities that have been released into a specified flow or routing but have not yet exited.

WT   waiting time (also known as queueing time); the time an entity waits for processing by a server because it is behind other entities.

B SUPPLY CHAIN SCIENCE PRINCIPLES

Principle (Capacity). *The output of a system cannot equal or exceed its capacity.*

Principle (Utilization). *Cycle time increases with utilization and does so sharply as utilization approaches 100 percent.*

Principle (Little's law). *Over the long-term, average work-in-process (WIP), throughput (TH), and cycle time (CT) for any stable process are related as follows:*

$$\text{WIP} = \text{TH} \times \text{CT}$$

Principle (Queueing). *At a single station with no limit on the number of entities that can queue up, the waiting time (WT) due to queuing is given by*

$$\text{WT} = V \times U \times T$$

where

> V = *a variability factor*
>
> U = *a utilization factor*
>
> T = *average effective process time for an entity at the station*

Principle (Batching). *In a simultaneous or sequential batching environment:*

1. *The smallest batch size that yields a stable system may be greater than one.*

2. *Delay due to batching (eventually) increases proportionally in the batch size.*

Principle (Best-Case Performance). *Any process flow with bottleneck rate BNR, raw process time RPT, and work-in-process level WIP will have*

$$\text{TH} \leq \min \left\{ \frac{\text{WIP}}{\text{RPT}}, \ \text{BNR} \right\}$$

$$\text{CT} \geq \max \left\{ \text{RPT}, \ \frac{\text{WIP}}{\text{BNR}} \right\}$$

Principle (Worst-Case Performance). *Any process flow with bottleneck rate* BNR, *raw process time* RPT, *and work-in-process level* WIP *will have*

$$TH \geq \frac{1}{RPT}$$

$$CT \leq WIP \times RPT$$

Principle (Variability Buffering). *Variability in a production or supply chain system will be buffered by some combination of inventory, capacity, and time.*

Principle (Buffer Flexibility). *Flexibility reduces the amount of buffering required in a production or supply chain system.*

Principle (Buffer Position). *For a flow with a fixed arrival rate, identical nonbottleneck processes, and equal-sized* WIP *buffers in front of all processes,*

- *The maximum decrease in* WIP *and cycle time from a unit increase in nonbottleneck capacity will come from adding capacity to the process directly before or after the bottleneck.*

- *The maximum decrease in* WIP *and cycle time from a unit increase in* WIP *buffer space will come from adding buffer space to the process directly before or after the bottleneck.*

Principle (Pull Efficiency). *A pull system achieves higher throughput for the same average* WIP *level than an equivalent push system.*

Principle (Pull Robustness). *A pull system is less sensitive to errors in* WIP *level than a push system is to errors in release rate.*

Principle (Safety Stock). *In a base stock system, safety stock increases with both the target fill rate and (for a sufficiently high target fill rate) the standard deviation of demand during replenishment lead time.*

Principle (Variability Pooling). *Combining sources of variability so that they can share a common buffer reduces the total amount of buffering required to achieve a given level of performance.*

Principle (Multi-Echelon Inventory Location). *In a multiproduct, multi-echelon supply chain with an objective to achieve high customer service with minimal inventory investment, a low-volume, high-demand variability, and/or high-cost part should be stocked at a central (high) level, while a low-volume, low-demand variability, and/or low-cost part should be stocked at a local (low) level.*

Principle (Inventory/Order Interface Position). *Long production lead times require the I/O interface to be located close to the customer for responsiveness, while high product proliferation requires it to be located close to raw materials for pooling efficiency.*

Principle (Bullwhip Effect). *Demand at the top (manufacturing) level of a supply chain tends to exhibit more variability than demand at the bottom (retail) level due to batch ordering, forecasting errors, promotional pricing, and gaming behavior by customers.*

Principle (Risk-Sharing Contracts). *In interfirm supply chains, individual decision makers optimizing their local objectives generally suboptimize the overall system because risk falls disproportionally on one party. Contracts that share risk can incentivize individual decision makers to make globally optimal choices.*

The 9/11 Commission Report. 2004. *Final Report of the National Commission on Terrorist Attacks Upon the United States*. Washington: U.S. Government Printing Office.

Askin, R., and J. Goldberg. 2001. *Design and Analysis of Lean Production Systems*. New York: Wiley.

Barabasi, A-L. 2002. *Linked: How Everything Is Connected to Everything Else and What It Means*. Cambridge, MA: Perseus Books Group.

Bazerman, M. H., and M. Watkins. 2004. *Predictable Surprises*. Boston, MA: Harvard Business School Press.

Bednarz, A. 2006. "Supply Chain Execs Share Disaster-Planning Techniques: Lessons of New Orleans Continue to Resonate." (n.d.) http://www.networkworld.com/news/2006/053006-supply-chain.html?prl (October 18).

BusinessWeek. 2002. "Cisco: Behind the Hype." January 21.

Buzacott, J. A., and J. G. Shanthikumar. 1993. *Stochastic Models of Manufacturing Systems*. Englewood Cliffs, NJ: Prentice-Hall.

Buzzell, R. D., and G. Ortmeyer. 1995. "Channel Partnerships Streamline Distribution." *Sloan Management Review* **36**(3):8596.

Cachon, G. 2003. "Supply Chain Coordination with Contracts." In S. Graves and T. de Kok (eds.), *Handbooks in Operations Research and Management Science: Supply Chain Management*. Amsterdam: North-Holland.

Cachon, G., and M. Lariviere. 2001. "Turning the Supply Chain into a Revenue Chain." *Harvard Business Review* **79**(3):20–21.

Cachon, G., T. Randall, and G. Schmidt. 2006. "In Search of the Bullwhip Effect." Working paper, Wharton School, University of Pennsylvania, Philadelphia.

Cliffe, S. 1999. "ERP Implementation," *Harvard Business Review* **77**(1): 16–17.

Conner, G. 2001. *Lean Manufacturing for the Small Shop*. Dearborn, MI: Society of Manufacturing Engineers.

Cooper, R. 1990. *Introduction to Queueing Theory*, 4th ed. Washington: Ceep Press.

Cross, R. L. and A. Parker. 2004. *The Hidden Power of Social Networks: Understanding How Work Really Gets Done in Organizations*. Boston, MA: Harvard Business School Publishing.

Eglin, R. 2003. "Can Suppliers Bring Down Your Firm?" *Sunday Times (London)*, p. 6 (Appointments section).

Fink, S. 1986. *Crisis Management: Planning for the Inevitable*. Lincoln, NE: Backinprint.com.

Fisher, M., J. Hammond, W. Obermeyer, and A. Raman. 1994. "Making Supply Meet Demand in an Uncertain World." *Harvard Business Review* **72**(3):83–93.

Gerth, J. 2004. "Epic Storm Taught Area a Chilling Lesson." *Courier-Journal* (Louisville, KY), January 16.

Goldratt, E. and J. Cox. 2004. *The Goal*, 3rd ed. Great Barrington, MA: North River Press.

Gross, D. and C. Harris. 1998. *Fundamentals of Queueing Theory*, 3rd ed. New York: Wiley-InterScience.

Hall, R. 1991. *Queueing Methods for Services and Manufacturing.* Englewood Cliffs, NJ: Prentice-Hall.

Hall, R. W. 1983. *Zero Inventories*. Homewood, IL: Dow Jones-Irwin.

Hammonds, K. H. 2002. "Harry Kraemer's Moment of Truth." *Fast Company* **64**:93.

Heyman, D., and M. Sobel. 2003. *Stochastic Models in Operations Research, Volume 1: Stochastic Processes and Operating Characteristics*. Mineola, NY: Dover.

Hopp, W., and M. Spearman. 1993. "Setting Safety Leadtimes for Purchased Components in Assembly Systems." *IIE Transactions* **25**(2):2–11.

Hopp, W., and M. Spearman. 2000. *Factory Physics: Foundations of Manufacturing Management*, 2nd ed. New York: McGraw-Hill.

Jordan, J., and F. Michel. 2001. *The Lean Company: Making the Right Choices*. Dearborn, MI: Society of Manufacturing Engineers.

Jordan, W. C., and S. C. Graves. 1995, "Principles on the Benefits of Manufacturing Process Flexibility." *Management Science* **41**(4):577–594.

Kelleher, H. 1997. "A Culture of Commitment," *Leader to Leader* **4**, (n.d.) leadertoleader.org/leaderbooks/l2l/spring97/ kelleher.html (October 16).

Lee, H. L., C. Billington, and B. Carter. 1993. "Hewlett-Packard Gains Control of Inventory and Service through Design for Localization." *Interfaces* **23**(4):1–11.

Lee, H. L., V. Padmanabhan, and S. Whang. 1997. "The Bullwhip Effect in Supply Chains." *Sloan Management Review* **38**(3):93–102.

Lee, H. L., and M. Wolfe. 2003. "Supply Chain Security without Tears." *Supply Chain Management Review* **7**(1):12.

Lewis, J. 1990. *Partnerships for Profit*. New York: Free Press.

McDonald, C. J. 1998. "The Evolution of Intel's Copy Exactly! Technology Transfer Method." *Intel Technology Journal*, November.

Meyer, M. H., and A. P. Lehnerd. 1997. *The Power of Product Platforms: Building Value and Cost Leadership*. New York: The Free Press.

Nishiguchi, T., and A. Beaudet. 1998. "The Toyota Group and the Aisin Fire." *Sloan Management Review* **40**(1):49–59.

Nahmias, S. 1997. *Production and Operations Analysis,* 3rd ed. Burr Ridge, IL: Irwin.

Ohno, T. 1988. *Toyota Production System: Beyond Large-Scale Production.* Cambridge, MA: Productivity Press (translation of *Toyota seisan hoshiki,* Tokyo: Diamond, 1978).

Raman, A., N. DeHoratius, and Z. Ton. 2001. "Execution: The Missing Link in Retail Operations. *California Management Review* **43**(3):36.

Ristelhueber, R. 2003. "SARS Virus Casts Pall over Electronics Supply Chain." *Electronic Supply & Manufacturing*, April 4.

Ross, S. 2002. *Introduction to Probability Models*, 8th ed. San Diego, CA: Academic Press.

Schonberger, R. 1982. *Japanese Manufacturing Techniques: Nine Hidden Lessons in Simplicity*. New York: The Free Press.

Sheffi, Y. 2005. *The Resilient Enterprise: Overcoming Vulnerability for Competitive Advantage*. Cambridge, MA: MIT Press.

Silver, E., D. Pyke, and R. Peterson. 1998. *Inventory Management and Production Planning and Scheduling,* 3rd ed. New York: Wiley.

Simchi-Levi, D., P. Kaminski, and E. Simchi-Levi. 2003. *Designing and Managing the Supply Chain,* 2nd ed. New York: McGraw-Hill.

Stank T. P., P. J. Daugherty, and C. W. Autry. 1999. "Collaborative Planning: Supporting Automatic Replenishment Programs." *Supply Chain Management* 4(2):75–85.

Watts, D. J. 2003. *Six Degrees: The Science of a Connected Age*. New York: W.W. Norton.

Womack, J., D. Jones, and D. Roos. 1991. *The Machine that Changed the World*. New York: HarperPerennial.

Young, E. 2001. "Dozens of Dialysis Deaths across Europe." *New Scientist,* October 16.

Zipkin, P. 2000. *Foundations of Inventory Management*. New York: Irwin/McGraw-Hill.

Page numbers followed by n indicate material found in notes.